From Topic Boundaries to Omission

Studies in
Interpretation

VOLUME I

From
Topic Boundaries
to
Omission

New Research on

Interpretation

Melanie Metzger, Steven Collins,
Valerie Dively, and Risa Shaw,
Editors

GALLAUDET UNIVERSITY PRESS

Washington, D.C.

Studies in Interpretation

A Series Edited by Melanie Metzger and Earl Fleetwood

Gallaudet University Press

Washington, D.C. 20002

http://gupress.gallaudet.edu

ISBN 1-56368-148-X

ISSN 1545-7613

Cover design by David Alcorn

Interior design by Richard Hendel

Composition by Alcorn Publication Design

∞ The paper used in this publication meets the minimum requirements of American National Standard for Information Sciences—Permanence of Paper for Printed Library Materials, ANSI Z39.48–1984.

Contents

Foreword

It is an honor and a privilege to write a foreword for this volume. This work is the first volume in the *Studies in Interpretation* series, a much-needed series that will fill a significant gap in the field of interpretation. The volumes in this series will offer a consistent source of current information on the theory and practice of interpretation as it pertains to signed and spoken languages, a source that captures the information between two covers as opposed to random, unrelated papers and workshop handouts. It provides a crucial refereed outlet and forum for research being done on interpretation. And at a time when all issues pertaining to signed language interpretation and spoken language interpretation are being examined and discussed on a global level, it will provide an international perspective on these issues.

The papers in this first volume get the series off to an excellent start with a focus on both interactive and monologic issues. This volume and, indeed, all the volumes in the series will serve as valuable resources for working interpreters, interpreter trainers, student interpreters, and consumers of interpreting, both hearing and deaf.

Ceil Lucas
Series Editor,
Sociolinguistics in Deaf Communities

Introduction

Interpreters and translators can be found working wherever individuals from diverse language communities come together. We interpret and translate interviews so basic in nature that outcomes might determine whether or not a family will have food on the table. We interpret and translate at conferences that are so technically and ethically far-reaching that even the nature of nature itself, the human genome, might be the subject of our efforts. A seemingly infinite number of unique linguistic grammars and situated sociocultural behaviors make up the threads with which we weave our daily work. In our work, we create tapestries of meaning so others might more readily interact with one another as they move through their lives.

The weaving of tapestries serves as a common backdrop for our efforts. Still, idiosyncrasies of particular languages and cultures differentiate the textures that result from our cognitive craft. Even the linguistic modes that we confront can significantly shape the very nature of our efforts. For example, Nida (1976), Wilss (1982), Cokely (1992) and others have noted that interpreting between written texts (i.e., translation) offers the luxury of time, continuous access to a source text, opportunity to review and correct, and the benefit of seeking feedback in a manner that is rarely (if ever) possible in the formulation of face-to-face, simultaneous interpretations. Thus, interpretation and translation, though certainly related tasks, are distinct in their demands.

Issues related to mode and to the interpreting process carry particular significance for those concerned with signed language interpreting. Although much of the cognitive work managed by interpreters is similar regardless of mode, a noteworthy observation is that spoken language interpreters usually interpret between monolinguals whereas signed language interpreters might interpret for bilinguals who simply do not have direct or equal access to both linguistic modes and, subsequently, to both of the languages of a given encounter (Davis, 1989; Roberts, 1987; Wilss, 1982). This reality serves to define some of the processes and products of our work.

For example, where deaf bilingual consumers and the issue of language access come together, implications certainly exist for the interlocutors in a particular interaction. Moreover, situations of this kind weave broad patterns and textures into the age-old discussion of interpretations as being form-based or meaning-based. Form-based products, which prioritize preserving the form of the source message over the meaning of that message, might not make sense to a monolingual person. Nevertheless, products such as these might actually be preferable to a bilingual consumer in at least some circumstances.

An example of an issue related to interpreting processes can be found where translation is contrasted with interpretation. Translation, by its very nature, is less restricted by time than is interpretation. The translator is able to tailor the fabric of meaning that, relatively speaking, consecutive and simultaneous interpreters might barely have time to stitch. Nevertheless, as Hatim and Mason (1990) point out, both written and face-to-face conveyance of messages from one language to another provide "evidence of a communicative transaction taking place within a social framework" (p. 2). This transaction is true regardless of any modality, linguistic, or cultural distinctions in our work.

Anthropologists and sociologists come together to seek underlying patterns in human behavior. Psychologists examine recognizable and recurring behaviors within individuals to better understand the workings of the human mind. Science teaches that pursuing the study of recurring patterns that are based on actual events can offer an ever expanding view of the world, leading to advancement and improvements beyond expectation. In a similar way, this series of studies on interpretation and translation, and this volume in particular, endeavors to gather empirical research that addresses theoretical issues related to translation and interpretation of spoken, written, and signed languages. Our hope is that this series will serve as a source of research findings that help us better understand and improve our work as signed and spoken language interpreters and translators.

The six chapters of this volume focus on interpretation, including monologic situations and multiparty contexts. These chapters highlight interpreted encounters that incorporate spoken languages (i.e., English and Spanish) and signed languages (i.e., American Sign Language, Australian Sign Language). They include studies of interpreted medical, religious, and educational encounters. Both live (recorded) interpreted interactions and analyses of videotaped source texts are included within.

The first section of this volume concentrates on issues that arise in interpreted interaction. In the first chapter, Angelelli builds on a growing body of research in which sociolinguistic analysis suggests that interpreters are not the uninvolved conduits they were once thought to be (compare Metzger, 1995, 1999; Roy, 1989, 2000; Wadensjö, 1992, 1998). Angelelli finds evidence of visibility on the part of interpreters working in medical settings. She finds a variety of behaviors, including explanations, expansions, and summaries, that demonstrate ways in which medical interpreters produce more than simple form- or meaning-based translations.

The next chapter adds to recent studies of interpreter involvement in discourse. Sanheim replicates a study of turn exchanges in an interpreted encounter (Roy, 1989, 2000), applying the results of Roy's study of an interpreted student-professor conference to interpreted medical discourse, with data taken from a study of interpreters' linguistic strategies (Metzger 1995, 1999). In support of the findings of Roy (1989, 2000), Sanheim finds that turns are grouped into three general categories: regular, overlapping, and those with lag. In addition and in keeping with Metzger (1995, 1999), an examination of the dyadic nature of the interpreted interaction shows that the interpreted discourse is not a simple triadic encounter but one in which the interpreter has an influence on the interactive discourse in a manner that differs with previous thought about interpretation.

The third chapter in the section on interaction is a case study of a videotaped Caucasian Deaf Protestant worship service that occurred during an annual church revival worship service. In Chapter 3, Richey examines speaker-initiated interactions that occurred between a visiting Deaf preacher and a Deaf congregation as well as the linguistic decisions faced by the interpreters as a result of these interactions. Through an examination of pastor-initiated adjacency pairs, Richey finds that church worship services, which are typically monologic events in similar hearing church settings, can be interactive in a Deaf church.

The second section of this volume focuses on the interpretation of monologic discourse. In her chapter, Napier analyzes the types of omissions that occur in the interpretation of a university lecture from spoken English into Australian Sign Language. By providing interpreters with a lexically dense source text and exploring the interpreters' metalinguistic awareness of the omissions in the target text, Napier develops a taxonomy of omission types that includes both intentional and unintentional omissions on the part of the interpreter. Her analysis re-formats what was once considered to be a type of error in the work that interpreters do, indicating that some types of omissions may even be desirable in a good interpretation.

The final two chapters in this section focus on the issue of meaning versus form.

In the fifth chapter, Sofinski focuses solely on the signing of interpreters who transliterate (i.e., move messages between spoken English and English-like signing) primarily for deaf children in public schools. Sofinski provides an analysis of the nonmanual elements used in the signed transliteration products of five full-time educational interpreters. He finds both syntactic and pragmatic nonmanual features in the target that vary from the source text form. Notably, he finds that, even when the target text is English-like in form, few of the English sentences from the source were replicated by the interpreters. This finding supports a growing body of research that suggests form-based transliteration produces a target text that is not a verbatim rendition of the source, though it may capture the intended meaning of the source.

In the final chapter, Winston and Monikowski present some preliminary findings from a comparison of interpreted texts, three of which attempt to interpret from spoken English into American Sign Language and three of which attempt to transliterate from spoken English into English-like signing. The analysis focuses primarily on the prosodic features used for indicating major topic segments in a source spoken English text with a discussion of the similarities and differences between the segment boundaries as they are produced by the three interpreters in their target interpretations and transliterations of the same source text. Pausing is found to play an interesting role in the analysis.

This volume examines some of the threads with which interpreters and translators weave their work and, in so doing, offers new insights into the processes and products of interpretation. The individuals who have contributed to this first volume and to the establishment of this new series are too numerous to mention. However, we would be remiss if we did not extend our sincerest gratitude to the contributors who took the time to gather the data and turn them into useful findings and to the myriad of language users, deaf and hearing, who not only allowed themselves to be recorded in addition to being subjected to the ministrations of interpreters as a part of their daily lives but also were willing to allow these results to be shared in a public forum. We would also like to thank all those who took the time to review the manuscripts and comment on them as well as those who engaged in the copyediting process. To Deirdre Mullervy and Ivey Wallace, this volume and this series would not exist without your much-appreciated support. To Robert E. Johnson, Carol J. Patrie, Cynthia Roy, Jeffrey Davis, and Elizabeth Winston as well as Clayton Valli, who is sorely missed, we thank you each for your part in creating and maintaining the graduate program in interpretation at Gallaudet University. To Ceil Lucas, whose tireless work on the *Sociolinguistics in Deaf Communities* series provides evidence of the effect of a series of data-based research on a growing field and whose vision and courage in setting the precedent for a series at the press are most certainly what made this volume and this new series a possibility; thank you for all that you do. Thank you, also, to the students and graduates of the Master of Arts in Interpretation program at Gallaudet University who have contributed not only to the desire for this series but also to its content. Special thanks to Earl Fleetwood, Karen Malcolm, Jayne McKenzie, and to Eric, Jill, Dawson, and all our friends and loved ones whose sacrifices and contributions helped to make this volume a reality.

REFERENCES

Cokely, D. (1992). *Interpretation: A sociolinguistic model.* Burtonsville, MD: Linstok Press.

Davis, J. (1989). Distinguishing language contact phenomena in ASL interpretation. In C. Lucas (Ed.), *The sociolinguistics of the deaf community* (pp. 85–102). San Diego: Academic Press.

Hatim, B., & Mason, I. (1990). *Discourse and the translator.* London: Longman.

Metzger, M. (1995). *The paradox of neutrality: A comparison of interpreters' goals with the realities of interactive discourse.* Unpublished doctoral dissertation, Georgetown University, Washington, DC.

Metzger, M. (1999). *Sign language interpreting: Deconstructing the myth of neutrality.* Washington, DC: Gallaudet University Press.

Nida, E. (1976). A framework for the analysis and evaluation of theories of translation. In R. Brislin (Ed.), *Translation: Applications and research* (pp. 47–91). New York: Gardner.

Roberts, R. (1987). Spoken language interpreting vs. sign language interpreting. In G. K. Kummer, *Proceedings of the 28th Annual Conference of the American Translators Association* (pp. 293–306).Medford, NJ: Learned Information.

Roy, C. (1989). *A sociolinguistic analysis of the interpreter's role in the turn exchanges of an interpreted event.* Unpublished doctoral dissertation, Georgetown University, Washington, DC.

Roy, C. (2000). *Interpreting as a discourse process.* New York: Oxford University Press.

Wadensjö, C. (1992). *Interpreting as interaction: On dialogue-interpreting in immigration hearings and medical encounters.* Linköping, Sweden: Linköping University, Linköping Studies in Arts and Science.

Wadensjö, C. (1998). *Interpreting as interaction.* London: Longman.

Wilss, W. (1982). *The science of translation: Problems and methods.* Tübigen: Gunter Narr Verlag.

Part I Interactive Discourse

The Visible Co-Participant:

The Interpreter's Role in

Doctor-Patient Encounters

Claudia Angelelli

Speakers of the more dominant and less dominant cultures come into contact through interpreters. The ways in which interpreters play their roles may vary significantly according to the different settings in which interpretation takes place (e.g., court, community, or conference interpreting) or according to the rules that the various professional associations prescribe. The role of the interpreter is complex and multifaceted. Understanding this role will lead to a deeper understanding of how communication happens between minority and majority speakers when it is brokered by an interpreter. Understanding the complexities that are associated with the role of the interpreter is crucial to studying intercultural communication in its broadest sense (Angelelli, 2000). This chapter explores an example of medical interpreting and demonstrates the complexities underlying this kind of interaction.

Interpreters have traditionally been portrayed as invisible language "conduits" (Reddy, 1979) whose role is defined as decoders and encoders of two languages (Seleskovitch & Lederer, 1989; Weber, 1984). This notion of invisibility has various underlying assumptions. One assumption is that meaning is monolithic rather than co-constructed. Another assumption is that the interpreter can temporarily block the self and all the behaviors that may result (automatically or voluntarily) as a consequence of being a social person who interacts with the other two parties (Berk-Seligson, 1990; Metzger, 1999; Roy, 1989; Wadensjö, 1998b). This extreme view is still prevalent in professional organizations and schools that train translators and interpreters.

The next section briefly discusses how new trends in the literature portray the role of the interpreter in various settings and specifically looks at the medical setting where the interpreted communicative event (ICE) discussed in this chapter occurs.

NEW TRENDS IN THE INTERPRETING LITERATURE

In the last two decades, research that has crossed over from socio-linguistics has begun to emphasize crucial differences among different types of interpretation, specifically among conference, court, medical, and community interpreting. The differences that have been the focus of the dialogic research (Wadensjö, 1995, after Bakhtin, 1981) lie along the nature of the communicative event (Hymes, 1974). Interpretation is no longer seen as a two-party conversation with what I call an "invisible" interpreter assisting communication (Michael & Cocchini, 1995) but, rather, as a three-party conversation in which the interpreter plays an active or, in my term, "visible" role (Angelelli, 2001).

Well-documented ethnographies of interpreters in the courtroom (Berk-Seligson, 1990) or studies at the police station (Wadensjö, 1995) show evidence of the visibility of interpreters. In the courtroom, as at the police station, interpreters become visible simply by making use of different linguistic devices. The use of (a) either a more or a less polite way of addressing one of the parties or (b) the restatement of an utterance in different forms (by adding or omitting jargonistic remarks or by switching from formal to informal register) are examples of those devices.

In the court setting, this active role was explored by Berk-Seligson (1990) in her ethnography of the courtroom. By the manipulation of the use of polite forms, interpreters in the bilingual courtroom become more or less visible. When rules that relate to the work of an interpreter in a court of law are established, however, the complexity of the job as laid down by Berk-Seligson is reduced to a controllable and automatic neutral position.

Focusing on community interpreting, Wadensjö (1995) provides evidence of social and interactive skills in her study of community interpreting at a Swedish police station. Her work addresses distribution of responsibility and looks mainly at how responsibility "for the progression and the substance of interaction is distributed in and through talk" (p. 112).

She presents a piece of authentic discourse: a fragment of a dialogue at a Swedish police station between an immigration officer and a recent Russian immigrant during which the officer asked the immigrant about her future plans. From the discourse analysis performed, Wadensjö concludes that the interpreter's role during the interaction goes beyond a traditional channel that simply expresses information. She argues that interpreters co-construct meaning together with the interlocutors, and all parties to the conversation share that responsibility during interpretation. In this sense, the co-construction of meaning and the responsibility that interlocutors and the interpreter have as team players within a conversation point to other skills that interpreters demonstrate beyond those of linguistic codeswitching and information processing. Her work points out social skills that do not seem to be addressed by the literature on interpretation.

Interpreting in the community has also been studied extensively (Metzger, 1999; Roy, 1989, 2000; Wadensjö 1995, 1998a, 1998b), although the issue of interpersonal role is not at the core of the studies. For example, Roy (2000) discusses interpreting as a discourse process. She presents one conference, mediated by an ASL-English interpreter, that occurs between a professor and a deaf student to show the active participation of the interpreter in the interaction. Like Wadensjö and Metzger, Roy uses Goffman's (1981) framework of roles to address "the shifts interpreters make from relaying messages to managing and coordinating talk" (Roy, 2000, p. 111). Roy's analysis specifically looks at two instances where a participant addresses the interpreter directly and the interpreter speaks back to this participant. The role is analyzed in terms of "responsibility for the flow and maintenance of communication" by focusing on turn taking (2000, p. 121).

Metzger (1999), Roy (2000), and Wadensjö (1998b) are calling for a systematic study of the role of the interpreter that expands on the present notion limiting the interpreter's role to interpreting what is said. These researchers state the need for describing the social role of the interpreter. This chapter begins to address this call by investigating the interpersonal role as it materializes in a medical setting.

INTERPRETING IN A MEDICAL SETTING

The medical setting has been the target of various studies on communication (Davidson, 1998; Kaufert & Putsch, 1997; Prince, 1986; Shuy,

1976). Some of these studies were done in bilingual settings. For example, Davidson (1998) focused on cross-linguistic communication in a study that investigated medical discourse mediated by an interpreter. He examined the construction of reciprocity and meaning in interpreted conversations and developed a model of turn taking that he applied to 10 interpreted and 10 same-language medical interviews. He concluded (a) that the difficulties in interpreted conversations lie not only in the construction of reciprocal understanding but also in the accurate transformation of semantic and pragmatic content and (b) that the role of the interpreter as linguistic facilitator varies toward the parties involved in the interaction. For the physicians, the interpreter is an instrument to keep the patient on track; for the patients, the interpreter is a co-conversationalist. The study, however, did not investigate the different aspects of the interpersonal role of the interpreter.

Also in a cross-linguistic environment, Prince (1986) investigated conversations between doctors and patients and focused on questions as the unit of analysis. She found asymmetric distribution in the number of questions asked and answered during a doctor-patient interview. Doctors asked the vast majority of information-seeking questions. Interpreters initiated only 1% of the questions. Three interpreter-related distortions identified in the discourse were (1) instances in which the interpreter answered instead of translated questions (generally occurring in the Patient-Substitute Model); (2) incomplete translations (generally occurring in multiple-part questions); and (3) incorrect translations (sometimes related to the level of technicality of the term used, to the lower language proficiency of either the doctor or the interpreter, to the mishearing of information, or to a failure to check information). Prince's work did not analyze the role of the interpreter, but her work had important pedagogical implications at the time.

Kaufert and Putsch (1997) looked at the dilemmas faced by medical personnel when two cultural systems clash at emergency situations. Their studies consider day-to-day workplace pressures and ethical dilemmas, and they focus on informed consent and end-of-life decisions mediated by interpreters. The cases used are part of a larger ethnographic study on the role of health interpreters for an aboriginal population in Winnipeg, Canada. Observations from health care providers in Seattle are also included. The discussion centers on issues of power and dominance in clinical communication, the challenge of monolingualism in multicultural medical practice, and the role of language intermediaries (interpreters). The authors, Kaufert and Putsch, object to the role of neutrality prescribed for interpreters by the code of ethics of certain interpreter organizations (e.g., the Washington State Supreme Court's Code of Conduct for Court Interpreters) and argue for ethics that would address instances when interpreters "act as advocates for patients" (1997, p. 77). The authors state that "health care interpretation often occurs across major gulfs of culture, class and language; and therefore it is unlike interpretation in the courts or in business or international negotiation. Attempts to encourage mutually shared understanding require the health care interpreter to engage in explanation, cultural brokerage and mediation when these actions are necessary" (p. 75). The study, however, did not explore the nature of the explanation or the brokerage that would constitute the interpersonal role for which they were advocating.

Even though any argument for an inaccurate interpretation would be senseless, an argument to prescribe and to promote the belief that the interpreter could be invisible would also be senseless. The next section presents examples of interpreter's visibility during a doctor-patient interview. These segments are part of a larger study that concluded with three propositions relevant to explaining the powerful role of interpreters, propositions that have so far been overlooked (Angelelli, 2001). First, interpreters perceive their role as visible in all the settings where they work. Thus, to a greater or lesser degree, interpreters perceive themselves as aligning with one of the parties, expressing affect and information, controlling the flow of the communication traffic, establishing trust and fostering mutual respect, and interpreting culture as well as language.

Second, interpreters perceive their role as visible, but visibility is also evident when they enact their role. In the communicative events studied at a hospital in northern California, interpreters were visible. Visibility was evident by interpreters claiming text ownership. Text ownership was consequential to both the personal and medical information that was expressed during the interpreted interview.

Third, interpreters not only perceive their role as visible and enact it visibly but also talk about their visible role in their own words. They use different metaphors to describe their role. For example, they speak of themselves as mine diggers who have to explore and dig for information when patients do not volunteer it. They also compare themselves to a diamond connoisseur who needs to be able to sort the diamonds from the dirt and still keep the dirt handy in case it is needed.

The next section illustrates instances of visibility involving one medical interpreter during a doctor-patient interview. These instances were collected as part of a larger study.

THE STUDY

The larger study of which the transcript featured here is a part was conducted during 22 months in a county hospital, California Hope, in northern California.[1] Using an ethnographical approach, I observed 10 Spanish-English medical interpreters at California Hope. The interpreters worked for Spanish-speaking patients and English-speaking health care providers in face-to-face and over-the-speakerphone interpreted communicative events (ICEs).

During my time at California Hope, I recorded ICEs, took notes, interviewed the interpreters and the manager of Interpreting Services (IS) using semistructured protocols, and collected artifacts. From a total of 392 ICEs, 378 illustrated different instances of interpreters' visibility. Typical examples of openings, closings, and bodies of ICEs were analyzed using discourse and content analysis. The 30-minute interviews to discuss the interpreter's role were fully transcribed and analyzed for content. Five tapes were produced for each of the 10 interpreters. The ICE discussed in this chapter comes from Elda, one of the 10 full-time Spanish interpreters at California Hope.

The Site

California Hope emerged as a unique site for this study. The number of interpretations per day is higher than in any other medical site, and the hospital provides interpretation both face-to-face and over the speakerphone, which was unique at the time I conducted the study (other hospitals in California and Washington are presently looking into this technology, too).

California Hope is located in a city that is proud of the cultural and ethnic diversity of its population and workforce as well as of the rich cultural identity of its many neighborhoods. The residents speak more than 46 different languages (information from the area's unified school

1. All names of participants and places in the study are pseudonyms.

district). The population is currently higher than 800,000[2] and comprises African-Americans (4%), Asians or Pacific Islanders (19%), Hispanics (27%), others (1%), and Whites (50%). Seven universities and colleges as well as 11 school districts are located in the city.

Ever since 1876, California Hope has forged a long tradition of service and dedication to the health of the whole community. Each year, the demand for California Hope services grows. California Hope cares for thousands of hospitalized patients and provides a half-million outpatient and emergency visits annually. It is affiliated with six institutions (universities and others) all over the Bay Area, but it also enjoys a fine reputation for its own freestanding medical education programs.

California Hope has established a strong foundation as the community's health care provider. It is the only hospital in the county with an open-door policy that guarantees access to needed medical care regardless of ability to pay. As its mission states, "We are dedicated to the health of the whole community."

Although the hospital serves a population that ranges from the middle class to the working class, the average patient is poor. The community that uses the services of California Hope is made up from a diverse ethnic pool that reflects the population of the city. Most of the patients are African-American, Asian, and Hispanic, though in terms of interpreting, the Hispanic patients constitute the biggest group served by Interpreting Services at California Hope.

Because the hospital offers on-site interpreting over the telephone, the whole facility is wired to an advanced technology that allows for speakerphones within the rooms. When a non-English-speaking patient walks into a room, the health care provider calls Interpreting Services (IS) to connect with an interpreter. This step starts a three-party conversation in which two parties (patient and health care provider) are face to face and the third party (the interpreter) is removed, interacting through a speakerphone. Calls made from the different clinics and areas of the hospital come into IS through a central computerized system. Calls for face-to-face interpreting go to a dispatcher who assigns interpreters according to availability or other special requirements (e.g., special requests made on the basis of gender). Calls for "speakerphone" interpreting go into an automatic system, and those calls are assigned to available interpreters.

2. All figures are rounded to protect the identity of the site.

In a remote trailer, interpreters answer the calls in the order they are received. Health care providers and patients are instructed on how to talk by means of a speakerphone. Guidelines written by the IS manager explain how to communicate effectively using the speakerphone. In addition, California Hope staff members are also trained in the use of these "remote interpreters." Because the interpreter is physically removed from the communicative event and is deprived of eye contact, the parties compensate for this fact by making overexplicit statements.

Communication by means of speakerphone differs from face-to-face communication in several ways. Because the interpreter is not sharing the same context with the other two interlocutors, she or he has no access to body language. When an interpreter typically receives communication from an interlocutor who has been "trained" to speak through remote interpreters by rephrasing comments (e.g., the utterance "it hurts here" becomes "the patient is pointing at her right elbow"), the interpreter accesses only the explanation-interpretation of the kinesics from one of the two interlocutors, not the original message. The literature shows no consensus as to whether having a remote interpreter poses an advantage or a disadvantage to the ICE. Hornberger et al. (1996) found that having the interpreter physically removed from the doctor-patient encounter allowed the patient more privacy and improved communication. Garcia (2000) found increased productivity in the interpreting services when using speakerphones, which resulted in less waiting time for patients and providers. Benmaman (2001), while studying court interpreters, found that interpreters who were deprived of the context posited a threat to the integrity of the legal process and, thus, negatively affected communication. My data show no significant difference between the visible role of the interpreter during face-to-face ICEs and that role during over-the-speakerphone ICEs.

The Participants

The Spanish-speaking interpreting force at Interpreter Services (IS) is made up of 10 full-time interpreters plus 2 interpreters who work as extra or part-time help and 1 interpreter who works during night shifts in the Emergency Room. The IS department also uses 2 Chinese-speaking (Mandarin and Cantonese) and 2 Vietnamese-speaking interpreters who work full time and 1 Russian-speaking interpreter who works half time. Elda, the interpreter that we will encounter in this chapter, is one of the 10 full-time, Spanish-speaking interpreters who work between 9:00 a.m. and 5:00 p.m., Monday through Friday. Elda was born in Mexico where she also went to school. She is 52 years old and has been interpreting at California Hope for 12 years.

To work at IS, Elda met the following requirements: 2 years of experience in the field (as medical interpreter, translator, bilingual medical assistant, etc.), bilingual ability, and a passing score on the IS test. The test, which progresses from short phrases to complex paragraphs, measures medical vocabulary, interpretation skills, and memory retention in both directions (English into Spanish and Spanish into English). Elda, like all other interpreters at California Hope, facilitates communication between Spanish-speaking patients (mostly working-class immigrants) and English-speaking health care providers.

Data Collection

While collecting the data, I made an effort to minimize the intrusion of the researcher during the interaction and among the participants. By the time I started recording, I had already shadowed and monitored Elda (and the other Spanish interpreters) for more than 9 months. Two or three times per week, I arrived at IS at 8:30 a.m. and spent the day with Elda. I hooked a headset to her telephone, and she interacted with me as she did with other new interpreters who were in training. In a way, interpreters at California Hope were used to having "others" listening to (but never recording) their interpretations or going with them to do a face-to-face interpretation because that is the way in which new interpreters get training. Interpreters-in-training observed and asked questions, and so did I. At the time the recording started, my "intrusion" was evident by an additional cable on Elda's desk that connected my tape recorder to her phone. Consent for recording and observing was requested immediately before the interpreting started. During speakerphone interpretations, the parties (health care provider and patient) were requested to consent orally, and at that time, they were alerted to the presence of a researcher in the interaction. Sometimes the request involved just asking for consent; at other times, the participants engaged into a conversation about the nature of the study.

Data Analysis

ICEs vary widely in a health care institution in terms of length, time of the day, etc. Table 1.1 illustrates the variety of the 392 ICEs that were collected for the larger study (Angelelli, 2001) of 10 interpreters, including the share produced by Elda.

The ICEs produced by Elda varied from 1.5 minutes to 2 hours in length. She interpreted interactions face-to-face and over the speakerphone. The nature of the medical visits varied from hearings in a psychiatric ward to prenatal sessions to terminal diagnosis and end-of-life decisions to speech therapy.

The ICEs produced by Elda (and by the other nine interpreters) were first indexed. The index entries were used for unit analysis. The total number of units, or ICEs, found was 392 ICEs. Elda produced 40.

The analysis of the visibility-invisibility variable identified for Elda was carried out two separate times using unmarked index copies of the ICEs to ensure consistency in the identification procedure. Annotations were made in pencil beside each unit to allow for correction based on category fluctuation or solidification. These annotations (codes) constituted the basis of subsequent emerging categories and patterns (LeCompte & Schensul, 1999). The pattern of the nature of the ICE generated two categories: face-to-face and over-the-speakerphone. These categories were objective and did not need corroboration. Another unmarked index copy of the ICEs was used to analyze the intention of the interaction.

TABLE 1.1. *Inventory of Total ICEs*

Type of ICE	Total Number of ICEs (n = 392)	Percentage of Total ICEs	Percentage of Elda's Total ICEs (n = 40)
Visible	378	96.40	100.00
Invisible	14	3.57	0.00
Face-to-face	11	2.80	9.09
Speakerphone	381	97.19	10.23
Make an appointment	120	30.61	10.00
Place a phone call	10	2.55	0.00
Give results or news	4	1.02	0.00
Educational session	9	2.29	0.00
Visit or check in	230	5.86	12.17
Other (complain about bills, etc.)	19	4.84	0.00

Six categories emerged from patterns of the intention of the interaction of the ICE: make an appointment; place a phone call; deliver news or results; visit or check in; conduct an educational session; and other or miscellaneous. After analyzing the ICEs according to their nature and attempting a first classification according to intention of the interaction, I interviewed two of the informants (Elda was one of them). I asked them about the purposes of the interpretations that they are called to do (the kinds of calls they get) and took notes of their answers. Then, I offered my categories to them and got their feedback. In this way, I made sure that the etic perspective that I had initially gained coincided with the informants' perspectives and turned into an emic one (LeCompte & Schensul, 1999, p. 221). The process also served as corroboration for this category.

Another unmarked index copy of the ICEs was used for the last pattern that emerged, which involved the interpreter's intervention or lack of intervention during the ICEs and the reason behind the choice. Those interventions or behaviors were first coded in the margin. Those codes stated characteristics of the interpersonal role that transpired from the interaction across interpreters and across the nature and intention of the ICEs that I analyzed. Examples of those characteristics are solidarity and power (Tannen, 1984), editing by omitting or adding (Davidson, 1998), interpreter as principal interlocutor (Roy, 2000), and interpreter as facilitating understanding (Davidson, 1998). I called this pattern "visibility of the interpreter." Visibility means that the interpreter's role goes beyond the role of language switcher. The interpreter does not simply decode and encode the parties' messages cross-linguistically to bridge a communication gap (as generally described in the literature or prescribed by the professional associations). A visible interpreter expands beyond the "transparent language boom box" to the "opaque co-participant" and exercises agency within the interaction. Agency manifests itself, for example, when interpreters do one or more of the following: (a) introduce or position the self as a party to the ICE, thus, becoming a co-participant (Angelelli, 2001; Roy 2000; Wadensjö, 1998b) and co-constructionists (Davidson, 1998); (b) set communication rules (e.g., turn taking) and control the traffic of information (Angelelli, 2001; Roy, 2000); (c) paraphrase or explain terms or concepts (Angelelli, 2001; Davidson, 1998); (d) slide the message up and down the register scale (Angelelli, 2001); (e) filter information (Angelelli, 2001; Davidson, 1998); (f) align with one of the parties (Angelelli, 2001; Wadensjö, 1998b); or (g) replace one of the parties to the ICE (Angelelli, 2001; Roy, 2000).

To ensure that the categories were stable, I looked at the frequency and the stability of visibility across interpreters. Of the total 392 ICEs, 3.57% were invisible and 96.4% were visible. Behaviors of visibility were identified in all of the 10 interpreters observed. For 4 interpreters (Elda was one of them), all ICEs were visible. Invisibility found for each of the other 6 interpreters ranged from a minimum of 4% to a maximum of 12%.

The analysis of the visibility-invisibility variable identified for each interpreter was carried out two separate times using unmarked index copies of the ICEs to ensure consistency in the identification procedure. This analysis demonstrated a continuum of visibility for the interpreters' role (Angelelli, 2001). In this chapter, I present and analyze segments of one ICE from the whole corpus of Elda's ICEs (n = 40) to see how the interpreter's role manifests itself and how visible or invisible the interpreter becomes during the interaction. This example illustrates typical behaviors of the "visible" interpreter.

ANALYSIS OF VISIBILITY

Like any other communicative event, an ICE is characterized by having an opening, a body, and a closing. Like any monolingual medical consultation, an ICE also could be divided into the six phases that Byrne and Long (1976, in Heath, 1992, p. 237) identified in their study of verbal behaviors during 2,000 medical consultations. Those phases are (a) relating to the patient, (b) discovering the reason for attendance, (c) conducting a verbal or physical examination or both, (d) consideration of the patient's condition, (e) detailing treatment or further investigation, and (f) terminating. Contrary to a typical monolingual medical consultation, an ICE involves three participants, and the presence of the interpreter (the third participant) does affect these six phases.

Visibility occurs in the opening and closing of interactions as well as in the body or the different phases of the medical interview (e.g., in the exploratory phase or while examining the patient's condition, whether physical or mental, or when detailing treatment or further investigation). Visibility that occurs in openings and closings is highly ritualized (Goffman, 1981). During openings, if the health care provider does not introduce the interpreter, then the interpreter introduces and positions him- or herself. This behavior is what any co-participant to an interaction would do to claim participant status. During closings, the interpreter needs to close the relationship that has already been established. This behavior is expected of any co-participant. At California Hope, ICEs abide by conversational rituals that are very similar to those of monolingual communicative events.

In relating to the patient (phase one), for example, both the health care provider and the interpreter act independently and relate to the patient separately. So, all ICEs at California Hope start with either the patient or the health care provider (depending on who initiated the interaction) briefing the interpreter on the nature of the event for which they need help. If, for example, the health care provider initiates the call for an interpreter, then the health care provider customarily provides the interpreter with the name of the patient and the medical record number before a briefing of the case takes place. If the patient initiates the call, then the interpreter requests this information from the patient together with the health care provider or service the patient is trying to reach and follows by also requesting an assessment of the patient's needs.

During an ICE at California Hope, the identity of the health care provider and the patient are not the only identities that have to be revealed. The interpreter also introduces and positions him- or herself. In some cases, interpreters introduce themselves by merely stating their name. Sometimes, they add the fact that they are ready to help the parties communicate. At other times, interpreters state the fact that they work for California Hope and, thus, position themselves within the institution.

The following segments come from an interview between Ramira, a Spanish-speaking, working-class, elderly female patient, and Dr. Mien, a young, male neurologist at California Hope. Elda, a Mexican-American interpreter who is working on the speakerphone — thus, removed from the room — facilitates the communication between doctor and patient who are face-to-face in an office.[3]

In the first example (Segment 1.1), the interaction begins with the doctor calling in for an interpreter. Elda makes a point of greeting the doctor (lines 3–5) and claims her place as an interlocutor. As a staff interpreter, Elda frequently works for the same health care providers and has a cordial relationship with them. The doctor (D) tells Elda (I) the name of the

3. The level of detail in the transcripts is adequate for the kind of analysis performed. Again, the identity of participants all names used are pseudonyms.

patient (P) and her medical record number before the patient comes into the conversation (line 6).

SEGMENT 1.1

1	I	Language Services, can I help you . . . this is Elda.
2	D	Hi, my name is Peter Mien.
3	I	Is this Dr. Mien?
4	D	Yes.
5	I	How'you doing?
6	D	I'm good. I have a patient here . . . Rama . . . Ramira Cimarron.
7	I	Cimarron . . . name is Ramira . . . Dr., is this Woodpark?
8	D	I'm sorry?
9	I	What clinic is this?
10	D	This is neurology.
11	I	OK, and may I have the medical record number please?
12	D	The record number is . . . hmm . . . there's two numbers here . . . seven one zero three.
13	I	That is the one. Seven one?
14	D	Zero one two three four five.
15	I	Okay. . . . Ramira, buenas tardes. /Okay Ramira, good afternoon./
16	P	Buenas tardes. /Good afternoon./
17	I	Yo le voy a ayudar para interpretetar para el doctor Mien que está hablando con usted. /I am going to help you and interpret for Dr. Mien who is talking with you./
18	P	'Ta bien. /Fine./
19	I	Ready doctor.

After getting the patient's information from the doctor, Elda greets the patient (line 15) and states that her role is to *help* her communicate with the doctor. Elda characterizes her role as that of a helper (line 17). This line was not given to her. She chose to position herself as a helper in the opening of the ICE. A more neutral way of introducing herself and her role could have been by saying, "I am going to interpret between you and the doctor." But Elda positions herself as an active participant in this interaction and states that her role goes beyond switching between English and Spanish. She is there to help.

In 392 ICEs, three types of introductions took place during the openings. In the first type, interpreters chose to introduce themselves by stating their names and the fact that they would interpret during the interaction. In the second type, interpreters characterize the role as that of a helper by adding "I am here to help you communicate with. . . ." In the third type of introduction, the interpreter states the affiliation by saying "I am an interpreter at California Hope. . . ." In 392 ICEs, 83 examples of the second type of introductions were found, which was 21% of all possible introductions.

Interestingly, when the interpreters introduce themselves to the patients, the content of the lines is never given to them by health care providers (Angelelli, 2001). How interpreters decide to talk and what they want to say are under their own control. As co-interlocutors, they decide for themselves. They are not bound by the monolingual's discourse. They claim their position as co-interlocutors and have ownership in the text they use. A similar dynamic occurs at the closing of the ICE. Interpreters at California Hope are not given a line with which to close an ICE. They generate it themselves. But what is even more interesting in the closings is that interpreters bring the relationship they have developed with each of the monolingual interlocutors to a closing. In Segment 1.2, we can see an example of Elda closing the interaction with Ramira and with Dr. Mien.

SEGMENT 1.2

The visit is about to conclude. Doctor Mien has examined Ramira and has asked her to do one last thing for him as part of the neurological examination, to follow him with her eyes. After that, Dr. Mien thanks Elda for her work but does not say good-bye to his patient as he concludes the visit. Elda does.

330	D	I want her to do one more thing . . . to follow me.
331	I	A ver ahora él le va a hacer un examen más.
		/Let's see, now he is going to do one more test./
332	D	OK . . . great. . . .thank you very much . . . I really appreciate all your help.

333	I	You are welcome doctor. Have a good day . . . Ramira que tenga un buen día y muchas gracias.
		/Ramira, have a good day and thank you./
334	P	Gracias a usted.
		/Thank you./
335	I	Para servirle . . . OK, bye-bye doctor.
		/any time/
336	D	OK, bye.

Elda closes this interaction with the doctor (line 333) and then does the same thing with the patient as she wishes her a good day and thanks her. The patient (line 334), like the doctor, also thanks Elda for her help. This segment illustrates more than one thing about the interpreter's ownership at closing ICEs. First, interpreters at California Hope almost always create their own ways to say good-bye (line 333). Although health care providers close the ICE only by saying thank you or bye, interpreters express solidarity to patients by wishing them "que tenga un buen día" (hope you have a good day), "que le vaya bien" (hope everything is fine), "que se mejore" (hope you get better), or "mucha suerte" (good luck to you). In this sense, they are animators and authors of renditions (Metzger, 1999; Wadensjö, 1998b). Second, interpreters often take initiative on (author) not only the wording of the line but also the actual content of the utterance, and then they report to the other party once it is done, which is shown in this segment by line 335. Elda could have said to the patient "OK, great," but she chose to follow the rules of politeness of the patient and closed the ICE accordingly. The doctor did not give those lines to her. Elda created them.

In summary, this analysis of openings and closings shows that interpreters begin and end ICEs by using their own lines, not by using lines that have been given to them by the other interlocutors. In doing so, they become visible decision makers. The fact that health care providers may be in a hurry does not prevent interpreters from adequately closing an interaction (or closing it in the way that it is acceptable to the Spanish speakers with whom they are working). In my data, the occurrence of this behavior is frequent because interpreters and patients share a linguistic or ethnic background (Angelelli, 2001). Interpreters take ownership in ending the relationships that they constructed during the ICEs.

At California Hope, visibility does not occur only during openings (phase 1, relating, of the medical interview) and closings (phase 6, terminating). It also occurs during phases 2 to 5, that is, during the discovery, the examination, the consideration of the condition, and the detailing of the treatment or any further investigation (Heath, 1992). In Segment 1.3, we see an example of visibility during the discovery phase.

SEGMENT 1.3

Ramira is complaining about some pain. The doctor needs to find out whether it is related to any new medication or whether it is an old pain.

31	D	OK . . . Is this related to any new medication or is this . . . sudden?
32	I	¿Piensa usted que esto puede ser causado por alguna medicina . . . alguna medicina nueva que esté tomando o esto nomás le empezó de repente?
		/Do you think this is caused by any medicine . . . any new medication you are on or did this start suddenly?/
33	P	No, aquí me han . . . no . . . tiene mucho tiempo pero . . . me da de cuando en cuando . . . ya . . .
		/No, here I have . . . no . . . not for a long time, but . . . it's on and off . . ./
34	I	¿Entonces este mareo no es nada nuevo?
		/So this dizziness is not new?/
35	P	No.
36	I	¿Y ya lo tiene por mucho tiempo?
		/You have had it for a long time?/
37	P	Sí . . . porque la doctora me dio pastillas . . .
		/Yes, because the doctor gave me pills . . . /
38	I	¿para el mareo?
		/For the dizziness?/
39	P	Si, para el mareo . . . pos siempre me viene.
		/Yes, for the dizziness . . . because I always get it./
40	I	Ehhh . . . dicúlpeme que no le entendí lo último que me dijo.
		/Ah . . . sorry I did not understand the last thing you said./
41	P	Me dió . . . pastillas . . . la dotora . . . Mesarrocha . . . pero como quiera me viene.

		/She gave me . . . pills . . . doctor . . . Mesarrocha . . . but I get it anyway./

<table>
<tr><td>42</td><td>I</td><td>Le dio unas pastillas para lo del mareo.
/She gave you pills for the dizziness./</td></tr>
<tr><td>43</td><td>P</td><td>Sí.
/Yes./</td></tr>
<tr><td>44</td><td>I</td><td>Bero de todas maneras le vuelve.
/But you still get it./</td></tr>
<tr><td>45</td><td>P</td><td>Siiii.
/Yeees./</td></tr>
<tr><td>46</td><td>I</td><td>Doctor . . . actually . . . hmmm . . . this is an old problem, OK?</td></tr>
<tr><td>47</td><td>D</td><td>This is a . . . what?</td></tr>
<tr><td>48</td><td>I</td><td>An old problem . . . it is nothing new, nothing from today.</td></tr>
<tr><td>49</td><td>D</td><td>OK.</td></tr>
<tr><td>50</td><td>I</td><td>She's been having this problem before.</td></tr>
<tr><td>51</td><td>D</td><td>OK.</td></tr>
<tr><td>52</td><td>I</td><td>And she says . . . the doctor prescribed her some medication for the dizziness.</td></tr>
<tr><td>53</td><td>D</td><td>OK.</td></tr>
<tr><td>54</td><td>I</td><td>And . . . ehhh . . . the dizziness is on and off.</td></tr>
<tr><td>55</td><td>D</td><td>OK . . . has the medication helped?</td></tr>
<tr><td>56</td><td>I</td><td>Cuando se toma la medicina para el mareo señora ¿le ayuda?
/When you take the medicine for the dizziness, does it help?/</td></tr>
<tr><td>57</td><td>P</td><td>Sí . . . pa se (inaudible) la puedo tomar
/Yes . . . it seems . . . (inaudible) I can take it./</td></tr>
<tr><td>58</td><td>I</td><td>¿Mande?
/Excuse me?/</td></tr>
<tr><td>59</td><td>P</td><td>Sí . . . Pero se me acaba . . .
/Yes, but I run out of it . . . /</td></tr>
<tr><td>60</td><td>I</td><td>Hoy, ahorita no tiene.
/Today, now you are out of it . . . ?/</td></tr>
<tr><td>61</td><td>P</td><td>Me vuelve a dar.
/I get it again./</td></tr>
<tr><td>62</td><td>I</td><td>¿Ahorita no tenía medicina?</td></tr>
</table>

		/You did not have the medicine today?/
63	P	Tengo poquita.
		/I had a little./
64	I	¿Pero se la tomó esta mañana?
		/But, did you take it this morning?/
65	P	Sí.
		/Yes./
66	I	Yes doctor, she feels better when she takes the medication . . . but . . . hmm . . .
67	D	OK.
68	I	Sounds like she doesn't want to take it very much because she is very scared to run out of medication. She doesn't have too many pills . . . she says just a few.

Dr. Mien is looking for a yes-no answer. The patient does not conform to the answer expected and starts telling a story (line 33). Elda interrupts her (line 34) in search of the yes-no answer. Because Elda does not succeed in getting an immediate response, she explores from line 34 to 45 until she finally gets an answer for the doctor (line 46). The doctor did not give the lines to her. Another example of Elda exploring an answer is illustrated from lines 55 to 66. The doctor wants to know whether the medication has helped with the pain. Elda must make five attempts to get an answer. Similar examples of authoring text to explore are present in Segment 1.4.

SEGMENT 1.4

Dr. Mien wants to know how many seizures Ramira had in the last few months. Elda asks her the question and needs to interrupt Ramira when she starts telling a story (line 75) to bring her back "on track."

73	D	OK . . . ahmmm . . . can you ask her if she's been having a modest . . . how many seizures she's been having in the last few . . . per month . . . recently.
74	I	¿Cuántas convulsiones le han estado dando por mes Ramira?
		/How many seizures are you having per month, Ramira?/
75	P	No se porque a vec . . . a vez que voy pa'la cocina . . .

		y me pega . . . por un sólo día . . . porque asi me que'o en la silla . . .
		/I don't know because someti . . . sometimes I go t' the kitchen . . . and I get it for one day only . . . then I stay like this in a chair . . . /
76	I	Espéreme . . . dígame . . . ¿cuántas veces le dan por semana?
		/Hold on . . . tell me . . . how many times a week?/
77	P	Ehmmmm . . . tres veces.
		/Hmmm . . . three times./
78	I	¿Las convulsiones?
		/The seizures?/
79	P	Bueno . . . ¿ataques?
		/Well . . . attacks?/
80	I	Sí señora . . .
		/Yes./
81	P	Ahhhhhh . . . no se cuántas veces porque eh . . . ni . . . no me acuerdo.
		/Hmm . . . I don't know how many times . . . hmm . . . no . . . I don't remember./
82	I	¿No se acuerda . . . ?
		/You don't remember?/
83	P	No.
84	I	OK doctor . . . she says ehmmm . . . there is no way she can remember . . . I asked her even by week . . . but she doesn't remember.

Elda realizes that Ramira may not know the amount of seizures she has per month, so she helps her figure out the frequency by starting to count per week (line 76). She makes sure that Ramira cannot remember even that fact before she turns to Dr. Mien to report what she found out. Dr. Mien asked Elda for a fact on line 73. Elda broke that request into smaller pieces and presented it to Ramira. She also helps Ramira with the term *seizure* (lines 78–79), as she relates to the term the patient uses ("ataques"). The doctor did not ask Elda to take this approach. It was her own initiative. In Segment 1.5, we can see another example of visibility. Elda once again takes initiative, this time at describing a pain.

Dr. Mien needs to know more about the pain. He asks this question in one line and expects Ramira to better describe the pain for him.

161	D	. . . and . . . can she describe the pain better for me?
162	I	OK Señora . . . dígame qué tipo de dolor es . . . es como si le enterraran algo . . . como si le */OK . . . Tell me what kind of pain it is. Like if somebody were sticking something in there, like . . . /*
163	P	Siiiii. */Yesss./*
164	I	Apretaran la pierna . . . ¿o como con ardor? */Like if somebody were squeezing your leg . . . or does it itch?/*
165	P	Cooomooo */Liiiike/*
166	I	¿Mande? */Pardon me?/*
167	P	Cuando me pega la uña y que duele. */Like when I hit my nail and it hurts./*
168	I	Como adolorida. */Like sore./*
169	P	Sí. */Yes./*
170	I	Like sore . . . very sore.

Elda once again shows signs of solidarity as she helps Ramira describe the pain. Ramira does not produce the lines as much as she accepts or rejects the ones suggested by Elda. During eight exchanges, Elda helps Ramira find a description. Dr. Mien did not give these hints to Elda. She initiated them to help Ramira construct the answer.

DISCUSSION AND CONCLUSION

ICEs at California Hope (as is the case in many other medical settings) are very complex. At California Hope, when interpreters participate in the interaction, they are visible. As discussed in this chapter, visibility of the interpreter occurs in the opening and closing as well as in the body of the ICE. The opening and closing (which are in essence highly ritualized) show minor visibility instances in which the interpreter has occasional involvement as coauthor of the text (Segments 1.1 and 1.2). Higher degrees of visibility occur in places other than the opening and closing. Instances of higher degrees of visibility (i.e., highly consequential vis-à-vis the medical and personal information transmitted) occur in Segments 1.3 through 1.5 as the interpreter gradually replaces the monolingual interlocutor by determining the content of the text.

If we take a closer look at the segments through the lens of visibility, we can see examples of the manifestations of agency (as discussed on page 14). Segment 1.1 (lines 15 and 17) shows how Elda introduces and positions herself as she becomes a co-participant. She sets communication rules and controls traffic of information (Segment 1.3, lines 34–46) as she replaces the doctor in her line of questioning to find out whether Ramira's pain is related to a new medication. She paraphrases the term *sudden* and makes sure Ramira is giving her an answer with an understanding of the term (lines 32, 24, 36). In this segment, Elda also explores answers and filters information (lines 60, 62, 64). In taking this approach, she aligns with Ramira. The filtering of information is more evident in Segment 1.4 when she breaks up a question into small pieces to help Ramira seek an answer to the number of seizures she has had in the last month (lines 74, 76). Segment 1.5 is another example of filtering information as Elda and Ramira make eight attempts (162 to 169) to construct the description of the pain. Clearly, in this segment, Elda once again replaces Dr. Mien in her exploration of the pain.

At California Hope, interpreters are visible participants in the ICEs. Elda is an example of a visible interpreter. Interpreters become visible when they do the following: explore answers, expand and summarize statements, broker comprehension and explain technical terms, bridge cultural gaps, express affect, and replace interlocutors. As the interpreter determines the text, visibility increases. As visibility increases, the interpreter's role is more consequential. Understanding the complexities of a consequential and visible role is essential if we want to gain an understanding of how communication between speakers of more dominant and less dominant languages truly occurs. Perpetuating the myth of the invisible (Angelelli, 2001) and neutral (Metzger, 1999) interpreter will not help the field move ahead. Further research of dynamics such as visibility, however, will lead to important advances.

REFERENCES

Angelelli, C. (2000). Interpreting as a communicative event: A look through Hymes' lenses. *Meta* (Journal des Traducteurs, Les Presses de L'Université de Montréal [Translators' Journal, Translation Journal of the University of Montreal]), 45(4), 580–592.

Angelelli, C. (2001). *Deconstructing the invisible interpreter: A critical study of the interpersonal role of the interpreter in a cross-cultural/linguistic communicative event.* Unpublished doctoral dissertation, Stanford University, Stanford, CA.

Bakhtin, M. M. (1981). *The dialogic imagination: Four essays by M. M. Bakhtin* (V. W. McGee, Trans.). Austin: University of Texas Press.

Benmaman, V. (2001). *Telephone interpreting in American courts: Just reach out and ouch!* Paper presented at the American Translators Association 42nd Annual Meeting, October 31–November 3, Los Angeles, CA.

Berk-Seligson, S. (1990). *The bilingual courtroom: Court interpreters in the judicial process.* Chicago: Chicago University Press.

Davidson, B. (1998). *Interpreting medical discourse: A study of cross-linguistic communication in the hospital clinic.* Unpublished doctoral dissertation, Stanford University, Stanford, CA.

Garcia, A. (1999). *California Health Care Interpreters Association Newsletter,* May.

Goffman, E. (1981). *Forms of talk: Erving Goffman.* Philadelphia: University of Pennsylvania Press.

Heath, C. (1992). The delivery and reception of diagnosis in the general-practice consultation. In P. Drew & J. Heritage (Eds.), *Talk at work: Interaction in institutional settings* (Vol. 8, pp. 235–67). Cambridge: Cambridge University Press.

Hornberger, J., Gibson, C., Wood, W., Degueldre, C., Corso, I., Palla, B., & Bloch, D. (1996). Eliminating language barriers for non-English-speaking patients. *Medical Care, 34*(8), 845–856.

Hymes, D. (1974). *Foundations in sociolinguistics.* Philadelphia: The University of Pennsylvania Press.

Kaufert, J., & Putsch, R. (1997). Communication through interpreters in healthcare: Ethical dilemmas arising from differences in class, culture, language and power. *The Journal of Clinical Ethics, 8*(1), 71–85.

LeCompte, M., & Schensul, J. (1999). *Analyzing and interpreting ethnographic data* (Vol. 5). Walnut Creek, CA: Altamira.

Metzger, M. (1999). *Sign language interpreting: Deconstructing the myth of neutrality.* Washington, DC: Gallaudet University Press.

Michael, S., & Cocchini, M. (1995). Training college students as community interpreters: An innovative model. In S. Carr, R. Roberts, A. Dufour, D. Steyn (Eds.), *The critical link: Interpreters in the community* (Conference Proceedings, Vol. 19, pp. 237–248). Amsterdam: John Benjamins.

Prince, C. (1986). *Hablando con el doctor: Communication problems between doctors and their Spanish-speaking patients.* Unpublished doctoral dissertation, Stanford University, Stanford, CA.

Reddy, M. (Ed.). (1979). *The conduit metaphor: A case of frame conflict in our language about language.* Cambridge: Cambridge University Press.

Roy, C. (1989). *A sociolinguistic analysis of the interpreter's role in the turn exchanges of an interpreted event.* Unpublished doctoral dissertation, Georgetown University, Washington, DC.

Roy, C. (2000). *Interpreting as a discourse process.* New York: Oxford University Press.

Seleskovitch, D., & Lederer, M. (1989). *Pédagogie raisonnée de l'interprétation.* Brussels: Didier Erudition Opoce.

Shuy, R. (1976). The medical interview: Problems in communication. *Primary Care, 3*(3), 365–386.

Tannen, D. (1984). *Conversational style: Analyzing talk among friends.* Norwood, NJ: Ablex.

Wadensjö, C. (1995). Dialogue interpreting and the distribution of responsibility. *Hermes, Journal of Linguistics, 14,* 111–129.

Wadensjö, C. (1998a). Community interpreting. In M. Baker (Ed.), *Routledge encyclopedia of translation studies* (pp. 33–37). London: Routledge.

Wadensjö, C. (1998b). *Interpreting as interaction.* New York: Addison Wesley Longman.

Weber, W. (1984). *Training translators and conference interpreters.* New York: Harcourt Brace Jovanovich.

Turn Exchange

in an Interpreted Medical Encounter

Laura M. Sanheim

Turn taking is an integral part of our daily lives. We stop at red lights and allow other vehicles to cross while we wait for our turn. We stand in line at the checkout counter while we wait for the cashier to acknowledge that it is our turn to begin the process of totaling up and paying for our groceries. We also take turns when speaking to other people; this kind of exchange usually happens relatively smoothly between two or more people who speak the same language.

But what happens when two people need to communicate with each other but do not speak the same language? Often, an interpreter is called on to work as a go-between, as someone who is skilled in both languages that are involved in the interaction. Linguists have been studying the exchange of turns in monolingual conversations for approximately 30 years, but not until recently did researchers look at this phenomenon as it occurs in interpreted encounters.

The objective of this study is to add to the limited amount of research that examines the exchange of turns in interpreted encounters. Work in this area is needed because, as mentioned above, turns are an integral part of everyday life. In an interpreted interaction, the smoothness of turn exchange (or lack thereof) can affect, at the very least, how the parties perceive each other and, at the most, what information gets interpreted. Because of the life-and-death nature of the medical setting, one can argue that the import of interpreted information increases when the interpreted encounter takes place in that setting. For this reason, this study focuses on turn taking in data from a medical interpreted encounter.

Roy (1989, 2000) performed one of the only studies of turn exchange in an interpreted encounter between American Sign Language (ASL) and English, and the study discussed in this chapter is a replication of her initial work. Instead of analyzing an academic meeting as Roy's study did, however, the study discussed in this chapter will investigate the exchange of turns in an interpreted medical encounter. The replication of existing work is significant for several reasons. One reason is that later studies add to the general body of work in the field. Furthermore, findings in later studies can provide a basis for comparison and contrast. If findings are similar to the original study, theories can be strengthened. If findings are different, new questions can be raised and doors can be opened for further study.

Data for this study are taken from a previous study of an interpreted medical examination (Metzger, 1995, 1999). Turns in the data will be analyzed using Roy's (1989, 2000) categories of regular turns, turns with overlap, and turns with lag. The analysis is conducted under the assumption that turns occur between the users of one language; that is, turns occur in ASL between the deaf participant (or participants) and the interpreter, and turns occur in spoken English between the hearing participant (or participants) and the interpreter (see Metzger, 1995, 1999, for a discussion of interpreters and overlapping dyadic discourse). The results will then be compared to Roy's findings to see what similarities and differences exist across the two encounters (i.e., Roy's academic encounter and the medical encounter being examined here).

In addition, back channeling (signals indicating that an addressee is attending to the message without actually taking a turn) is briefly discussed as a way of confirming not only that the interpreted encounter consists of two overlapping dyads (one in each language; again, see Metzger, 1999) but also that the participants are cognizant of their position in one dyad or the other, but not in both.

LITERATURE REVIEW

Substantial research has been conducted on the discourse of spoken English (Sacks, Schegloff, & Jefferson, 1974; Tannen, 1984, 1986, 1990, to name just a few), and more research is being done every day to explore the discourse of American Sign Language and other signed languages (Baker, 1976a, 1976b, 1977; Baker & Padden, 1978; Martinez, 1995). However, very few studies have applied concepts of discourse style to the process of signed language interpreting (Metzger, 1995, 1999; Roy, 1989, 2000), and it is this latter category that will be the focus of the current study.

Laying the foundations for the study of turn exchange were Sacks, Schegloff, and Jefferson (1974), who collected a large corpus of audiotaped data for analysis. One of their many findings was that, for successful turn taking to occur, interactants must follow and attend to the utterances made by the speakers who were speaking just before the interactants claim a turn for themselves. This finding is in keeping with the idea of the importance of context in understanding language from a sociolinguistic viewpoint (Sacks, Schegloff, & Jefferson, 1974; Schiffrin, 1994; Shuy, 1987). In addition, Sacks, Schegloff, and Jefferson found parallels in the "one turn at a time" style of English turn taking in other languages and in other situations that were not directly related to the use of language.

Tannen (1984, 1986, 1990) has conducted a variety of studies that focus more specifically on conversational style in English. One of her most in-depth studies (1984) details the interaction among six friends at a Thanksgiving dinner get-together. Some interesting observations were made by Tannen related to the conflicting styles of different interactants at the dinner table. Tannen noted that Sally, a participant from England, had a different style of joking that was lost on the American dinner guests. The American interactants may have been left with the idea that Sally did not really know how to make a joke when, in reality, her joke-telling style may be something that works in her culture but not in theirs. In addition, Tannen recounts a story in which she was eager to get another interactant's opinion on the works of a certain author, but her own conversational style—showing her enthusiasm with a series of interruptions (referred to in later works as overlap)—inadvertently thwarted that effort.

Baker (1976a, 1976b, 1977) did some of the pioneering work in identifying the features of ASL conversations, focusing predominantly on the role that eye gaze and other eye movements play in ASL discourse. She began by explaining that ASL has five channels through which language information can potentially be expressed: eyes, face, head, body, and hands (Baker, 1976b). Baker emphasized that these five channels are used simultaneously, not segmentally, and in making this important distinction, she also reiterated the fact that, in ASL users, the hands, when considered alone, are not analogous to the mouth for speakers of English.

After establishing the unique elements of ASL channels for communicating linguistic information, Baker (1977) explained that one of the most important roles of eye gaze in ASL is to regulate the turns between speaker and addressee. To subdivide the concept of regulation, Baker uses the terms *initiation, continuation, shift,* and *termination* after Wiener and Devoe (1974). Baker observed that, in an interaction, the addressee almost always maintains a +GZ (gaze) focus on the speaker, attending to the message and waiting for cues that signal constituent boundaries or turn exchange (shift). Baker found that "proper timing of turn exchanges requires an ability to 'read' and respond to each other's shift regulators" (1977, p. 232). The addressee's maintenance of +GZ is so important, in fact, that Baker said it is "socially rude in ASL discourse for an addressee not to maintain eye gaze on the speaker's face" (1977, p. 222).

Baker (1977) also identified some of the specific actions that the addressee used to indicate the desire to claim a turn. Some of these actions included raising one hand to in front of the addressee's torso, with palm out, facing the speaker; an increase in the size of head nodding; and an increase in the quantity of head nodding performed by the addressee.

Various back-channeling mechanisms were also found in Baker's research (1977). She found that the deaf interactants in the study, in addition to manually producing signs, would use movements of the head, face, and upper body (alone or in combination) to react to things that the speaker had said. When the addressee manually produced signs that overlapped with the speaker's (whether back-channeling or not), 42% of the time, the signs were short repetitions of the signs made by the speaker. In addition, Baker's study showed that when sign overlap did happen, its duration was anywhere from 1.5 seconds to 4.3 seconds, significantly longer than the overlaps found in spoken languages.

Although several exhaustive works have been done about the principles of signed language interpreting, the code of ethics for interpreters, how to stand, and even what to wear (Frishberg, 1990; Humphrey & Alcorn, 1995), not enough attention has been paid to working with the discourses of both languages. A relatively simple statement from someone who is a linguist and not an interpreter best summarizes the situation: "Interpretation goes far beyond the mere translation of words" (Shuy, 1987, p. 2).

The most detailed work to study discourse and then apply that knowledge to signed language interpreting has been done by Metzger (1995, 1999) and Roy (1989, 2000). As an interpreter and a linguist, Metzger focused on the discourse in a medical interview and looked at the frames and expectations brought by each party in the interaction. In stark contrast to the feeling of many in the interpreting field that the interpreter must remain a completely neutral interactant in interpreted discourse, Metzger's findings show that, in fact, "provision of 'extra' information or utterances in order to provide equal information actually minimizes the interpreter's influence on the interaction" (1995, p. 233). She summarized the current situation by saying, "The fact remains that interpreters do influence interactive discourse" (1995, p. 270). Because the study described in this chapter is based on part of Metzger's data, a fuller description of the medical interview will be provided in the methodology section of this chapter.

Roy, another linguist and ASL-English interpreter, performed a study of turn taking in an academic encounter between a Deaf student, a hearing professor, and an ASL-English interpreter (Roy, 1989, 2000). Roy found three broad categories of turns occurring in her data (regular, turns with overlap, and turns with lag). After analyzing these turns, Roy also came to the conclusion that the interpreter is not a neutral party in interpreted encounters but, instead, is an active participant. Because the study described in this chapter is meant to be a replication of Roy's work, her findings will be discussed in more detail in the methodology and data analysis sections of this chapter.

INTERPRETED MEDICAL ENCOUNTERS

When doctors and patients come together for a medical interview, each comes with a unique perspective and agenda about the meeting that will take place. Doctors come with many years of technical training behind them, ready to ask all the right questions so a certain set of symptoms and ailments can eventually be narrowed down into a definitive diagnosis. The patient approaches the situation from a personal point of view: the "certain set of symptoms and ailments" that the doctor wants to investigate are things that are most likely affecting the patient's daily life and, consequently, are the reason for the appointment. Patients generally do not have years of medical training and, thus, are able to describe what's bothering them only by using everyday language.

This delicate balance wherein each party brings information that the other party needs can be difficult enough when the doctor and patient speak the same language. But what happens when doctor and patient do not speak the same language? If an interpreter is used, how does his or her presence have an effect on the flow of information between doctor and patient? This issue will be addressed in the analysis portion of this study.

To get a picture of what an interpreted medical situation looks like, however, one must begin by investigating communication in medical settings in general. Thus, this study will begin by looking at language use in medical settings where doctors and patients speak the same language and interpreters are not used (Ainsworth-Vaughn, 1992; Fisher, 1982). Next, this study will look at two studies that are representative of the growing body of work that focuses on communication issues in medical settings where spoken language interpreters are used (Davidson, 1998; Diaz-Duque, 1989). Finally, the focus will shift to the communication issues that have been identified in medical settings when using a signed language interpreter (Metzger, 1999), and consider how these studies inform the way we look at the exchange of turns in an interpreted medical encounter.

Fisher (1982) compared two clinics and the resulting diagnoses and treatments made by the physicians in each. She studied women who had received abnormal Pap smear results and who were referred to the clinics for further testing and treatment. Some women were referred by their private physicians to a "Faculty Clinic," which was staffed by a gynecological oncologist who was also a professor of medicine (1982, p. 55). Because of this staffing dynamic, no "student" doctors came in and out of the clinic, so patients were able to develop an ongoing relationship with only one physician. In contrast, women who received regular medical services from one clinic were referred for further testing to another "Community Clinic" where residents do their rotations to learn about this particular area of medicine. As a result, patients may see one resident on one visit and a new resident at their next appointment. Aside from the staffing differences between the two clinics, Fisher also mentions that the clinics even differed in their physical layouts: the Faculty Clinic was set up with separate waiting rooms, examination rooms, and consultation rooms. In this way, the physicians were able to examine patients in one room and then move to a formal office setting in another room to discuss their results. In contrast, the Community Clinic had no waiting room, and patients who were waiting in the halls often overheard results being delivered to other patients—a situation that compromised the privacy of the patient being consulted and served to frighten the patient who was waiting.

Logistics aside, Fisher's (1982) main finding was that "women with abnormal Pap smears referred to the Community Clinic were more likely to receive nonconservative treatment (i.e., to receive hysterectomies) than were women referred to the Faculty Clinic" (p. 51). She identified three strategies used by physicians when working with patients in making their treatment decisions: questioning strategies, presentational strategies, and persuasional strategies (1982, p. 60).

Questioning strategies were used by physicians to gauge the competence of patients about their specific medical problem. When physicians asked these questions, a slot was opened into which the patients could insert their response, thus showing the doctor their knowledge (or lack thereof) about their medical condition. Patients could also use that opportunity to ask further questions and to give input about treatment options. Among the cases provided by Fisher, a pattern is revealed: the physicians at the Community Clinic seemed to use these questioning strategies less often with their patients, thereby giving patients less of an opportunity to display their competence about their condition and less of an opportunity to ask questions and give input about which treatment option they preferred.

Presentational and persuasional strategies were used by physicians when presenting patients with various treatment options. Fisher (1982) explains that physicians not only presented patients with information about options but also used presentational strategies that "*suggested* how that information should be understood" (p. 76, italics in the original). An example of a presentational strategy is to say that something is *usually* done in a certain way. When physicians went beyond suggesting to adding overt information about which option would be best—for example, "No more uterus, no more cancer, no more babies, no more birth control, and no more periods" (1982, p. 60)—they were using persuasional strategies and exercising a considerable amount of control over the decisions their patients made.

In summary, Fisher's study shows that physicians come to the medical interview with strategies in mind that will allow them to get information from their patients and to influence their patients' decisions. Although we often think about interpreting as conveying the *meaning* behind an utterance (Seleskovitch, 1978), we now must consider that, even in monolingual medical settings, participants come not only with meanings to be exchanged but also with very specific ways for exchanging them.

In another study of monolingual medical interviews, Ainsworth-Vaughn (1992) looked at how male and female physicians produced topic transitions in their discourse with patients. She explains that speakers can transition from one topic to the next in one of two ways: with reciprocal activities or with unilateral activities (1992, p. 415). Reciprocal activities are "sequences in which both speakers contribute a move" (West & Garcia, 1988, in Ainsworth-Vaughn, 1992, p. 419) during topic transition. The balance in contribution that takes place during reciprocal activities implies a more equal balance of interactional power between participants.

Unilateral activities, in contrast, are topic transitions performed primarily by one of the participants. As their name suggests, unilateral activities show the balance of power tipped more heavily in favor of one participant than the other. These activities are divided into three categories: links, minimal links, and sudden topic changes. Links are "attempts by a participant to refer explicitly to the content of the previous turn before changing a topic" (Ainsworth-Vaughn, 1992, p. 419). So, the participant using a link makes some acknowledgment of the other's contribution before moving on. Minimal links are defined as "markers such as *Okay, M-hm,* or, *Alright* followed immediately by a change of topic by the same speaker" (1992, p. 419). The participant using minimal links still provides an acknowledgment of the previous turn but is more unilateral in doing so. Finally, sudden topic changes are the most unilateral of the topic transition activities and take place when "cohesion with a previous utterance is absent, and there are no reciprocal activities, links, or minimal links" (1992, p. 419) before the topic is changed.

Ainsworth-Vaughn (1992) cited several studies that showed "no differences between men and women physicians in actual therapeutic actions taken" (p. 410) and, therefore, concludes that, when patients rated themselves as being more satisfied with the care they received from female physicians, ways of communicating must have been a decisive factor. Her findings support this theory. Her data support not only the idea that "physicians realize far greater interactional power than patients in medical discourse" (1992, p. 423) but also the finding that female physicians used reciprocal topic transition activities five times more than they used unilateral activities whereas male physicians used reciprocal activities only 1.4 times more than unilateral ones. According to the power implications that go along with reciprocal activities, this finding would mean that female physicians established a more "even playing field," so to speak, when interacting with their patients. This interactional difference is another fascinating example of how monolingual communication can differ from one medical setting to another and provides us with even more reason to investigate what an ASL-English interpreted medical encounter looks like.

Two studies from the field of spoken language interpretation are also particularly applicable to the current study; these are Diaz-Duque (1989) and Davidson (1998). Diaz-Duque's work is the culmination of 15 years of personal Spanish-English interpreting experience in a large university hospital medical setting and analysis of a number of tape recorded medical interviews that were gathered over a 15-year period. Davidson's work is an in-depth analysis of 20 recorded medical interviews, chosen from a grand total of 50, which were collected over a 6-month period at a hospital-based, outpatient General Medicine Clinic in northern California. Both studies add to our understanding of the issues facing spoken language and signed language interpreters alike.

Both Diaz-Duque (1989) and Davidson (1998) touch on one of the main communication issues facing spoken language interpreters: deciding what gets interpreted and what does not. Diaz-Duque mentions that "a flowery or anecdotal style is characteristic of the discourse of some Hispanics," (1989, p. 96) and that these "anecdotal presentations have served to alleviate nervousness felt by patients in relaying information to the physician" (1989, p. 96, 97). When faced with the overbooked schedules of busy physicians, interpreters must decide how much of the seemingly "extra" information they should interpret. One of Davidson's main findings was that the interpreters at the General Medicine Clinic seemed to act as "filters," deciding how much of the patient's contribution was worth interpreting into English for the physician who wants concise answers. Both authors point out, however, that this filtering process is not as beneficial as it may seem. In particular, Diaz-Duque says that, in his study, "at times, the seemingly irrelevant material has contained key details in the patient's medical history" (1989, p. 96).

Davidson (1998) noted that, while interpreters performed this filtering, they engaged in a dialogue with the patients in an attempt to get the pertinent information before expressing an answer to the physician. This approach often left the physician "out of the loop" of conversation for several turns while the interpreter and patient had their own exchange. Davidson's explanation of this phenomenon is worth quoting at some length:

[I]t is the interpreter who determines which utterances will be conveyed immediately, and which utterances to which she will reply directly, thus engaging in conversation rather than interpretation. Exactly when she makes these choices, and which of the two interlocutors she chooses to engage in conversation (rather than maintaining a strict conversational rhythm of "utterance-interpretation"), will become crucial to the analysis of how interpreters function within medical interviews. (1998, p. 111)

In looking at Metzger's (1999) study of two ASL-English interpreted medical interviews (one mock, student-interpreted interview and one real, professionally interpreted interview), we see something strikingly similar to the "conversation" described by Davidson. Metzger noted that the interpreters in both interpreted interactions produced a number of nonrenditions in their interpretations. Metzger (1999) uses Wadensjö's (1992) concept of nonrenditions to refer to "an additional utterance, generated by the interpreter, that has not originated with anyone else" (Metzger, 1999, p. 98). The nonrenditions in Metzger's data manifested themselves in various forms, including the following: source attributions (when the interpreter informs a participant about the source of an utterance); explanations (when the interpreter explains information related to the interpreted event, for example, someone else entering the room or the addressing of the interpreter by the doctor); and repetitions (when an interpreted utterance originates with one of the participants but then is repeated by the interpreter).

In the real-life interpreted medical interview, Metzger (1999) noted that a full "three-quarters of the interpreters' nonrenditions are accessible only to the Deaf participants" (p. 157). This addition of nonrenditions by the ASL-English interpreter is remarkably similar to the intra-turn conversations between the interpreters and patients in Davidson's (1998) study. Also important to note is that these "extra" utterances are directed at the patients in both cases (really, the mother of the patient in Metzger's study), and that both of these individuals are, linguistically and culturally speaking, in the minority in the medical interviews.

A crucial difference between spoken language and signed language interpreting is revealed here, however. Metzger's (1999) analysis of the interpreter's nonrenditions (keeping in mind that Metzger's "nonrenditions" and Davidson's (1998) "conversations" are not totally equivalent) attributes them to the unique nature of working between a signed and a spoken language. Most of the source attributions, for example, seem to have been made by the interpreter in an attempt to compensate for the fact that the Deaf interlocutor does not hear who is taking a turn in the discourse. Metzger (1999) proposes that additions of this kind "are an essential part of the interpretation of interactional equivalence" (p. 199), and actually serve to minimize the interpreter's influence on the interpreted event.

METHODOLOGY

The following sections describe the situation in which the data were collected and how the data were transcribed.

The Medical Encounter

The data for the study discussed in this chapter were taken from a previous study of interpreted medical discourse by Metzger (1995, 1999). The medical encounter takes place in a pediatrician's office where a Deaf mother has brought her 18-month-old son to be examined by the doctor. This occasion is the first time that this child has been brought to this particular physician, and it is also the first time that this interpreter has worked with the mother, child, and physician. Also present at certain points during the interaction is a nurse, who becomes a primary participant in the interaction as the physician needs her. Finally, the researcher associated with the initial study was in the room for the entire interaction to monitor the video camera.

One paradox that comes from collecting data of interpreted encounters comes from the fact that video-recording the situation and its participants is necessary for analysis purposes, but finding people who are willing to participate and be recorded is extremely difficult. Perhaps, if the results of studies like this one can be shared with the participants' respective groups (Deaf, medical, and interpreting communities), these people can see how confidentiality and respect for those involved is maintained and how valuable the participants' time and efforts are, not only for researchers but also for the communities being researched.

Dealing With the Data

The entire medical encounter was 26.31 minutes from start to finish. It was transcribed using the musical score format to show all of the participants and the relationship of one (or more) of the participant's utterances to another's over time. A sample of the transcription appears in Example 2.1.

EXAMPLE 2.1

142

Mother: UP-TO-NOW NO (head shake)
Doctor: = no penicillin allergy that she knows of?
Nurse:
Child:
Interpreter (English):   Not so far . . . no.
Interpreter (ASL): = NONE PENICILLIN ALLERGY PRO.2 KNOW PRO.2?

The interpreter is represented twice in the transcription to more clearly express her switching back and forth between English and ASL. In the remainder of the examples provided, the participants will be represented by the first letter of their label (i.e., M, D, N, C, I, and I). The number or number range that precedes each example indicates line numbers from the transcript.

Next, it is important to mention how turns are defined in the data. Roy (1989) looked at a turn as being the complete exchange from the hearing participant (through the interpreter) to the deaf participant—as something that happens between interlocutors across languages. She explains that a smooth exchange happens when "one primary speaker talks, and the interpreter begins interpreting; the speaker stops, after a few seconds the interpreter stops, and the next speaker begins talking" (1989, pp. 259–260).

Roy's analysis continues on to make the groundbreaking point that the interpreter is indeed a third participant in the interaction and that conduit models of interpreting that dictate that interpreters must be neutral third parties need to be eliminated in light of her findings. Roy's perspective about the interpreter's role in regulating interpreted discourse has been further developed by Metzger (1999), who concluded:

The interpreter is having a direct conversation with each of the participants, who are unable to have a direct conversation with each other.

Thus, three-party interpreted interaction is not a dyadic conversation between the Deaf and hearing participants. Nor is it a triadic conversation between the Deaf participant, the hearing participant, and the interpreter. Instead, the three-party interpreter-interactive discourse is comprised of two overlapping dyads. (p. 180)

Metzger uses the example of a greeting exchange between the doctor and interpreter (in English) and the interpreter and the mother (in ASL) to show how turn exchange in an interpreted interaction results in an overall adjacency pair in one language that can be completed only after an embedded adjacency pair in the other language has taken place between the interpreter and one of the primary participants.

In Roy's (2000) more recent work, she reflects on the research of other linguists who have studied interpreted interactions and acknowledges that, "although it may be possible at times for speakers to feel as if they are talking directly to each other, they are not. They are always exchanging speaking turns with the interpreter" (p. 67).

The combination of Roy's (2000) and Metzger's (1999) findings provide the framework used in analyzing the data for this study. Roy's categories of turns (regular, overlapping, and those with lag) will be applied to the data while using Metzger's perspective in considering each turn as something that happens between the interpreter and one of the primary participants within only one language.

Data Analysis

The data were divided into three main categories of turns for analysis: regular turns, turns with overlap, and turns with lag. The overlap category was then subdivided according to Roy's classification of these turns and will be analyzed in depth in following sections. Likewise, turns with lag were also separated into two categories based on Roy's two different kinds of lag: regular and lengthy. Table 2.1 shows the distribution of the various kinds of turns in the data.

REGULAR TURNS

Roy (2000) defined regular turns in interpreting as those that "resemble regular turns in ordinary face-to-face conversation" (p. 68). Regular turns are smooth exchanges between speakers that have no overlap, extended pauses, or gaps.

TABLE 2.1. *Distribution of Turns*

Type of Turn	Number of Occurrences (*n* = 186)	Percentage
Regular	132	70.9%
Overlap 1	0	0.0%
Overlap 2	26	14.0%
Overlap 3	9	4.8%
Overlap 4	3	1.6%
Lag—Regular	12	6.5%
Lag—Lengthy	4	2.2%
Totals	186	100.0%

Of the 186 total turn exchanges identified in the data, 132 (70.9%) were classified as regular turns. Example 2.2 includes a regular turn in English that occurs between the doctor and the interpreter (shown by the line in the example). Remember that the interpreter's turns, for the most part, are motivated by something said by the primary speaker. (See Metzger, 1999, for an analysis of interpreter turns that are not motivated by either of the primary speakers.)

EXAMPLE 2.2

142

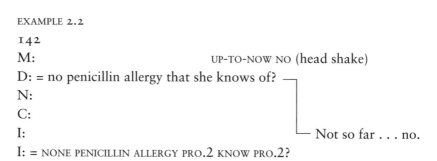

M: UP-TO-NOW NO (head shake)
D: = no penicillin allergy that she knows of?
N:
C:
I: Not so far . . . no.
I: = NONE PENICILLIN ALLERGY PRO.2 KNOW PRO.2?

In this example, the doctor creates his English message, and the interpreter begins interpreting into ASL. This interpreter tends to maintain a relatively short lag time while interpreting, and as a result, she finishes her ASL interpretation just after the doctor finishes his turn in English. The mother then responds in ASL, and the interpreter begins interpreting right away, allowing for a very natural, regular turn exchange between the doctor and the interpreter in English.

Another way in which to determine that this exchange is, in fact, a regular turn is by listening solely to the English message that is produced.

This technique was used by Zimmer (1989) to gauge the naturalness of the English portion of an ASL-English interpreted exchange. When the ASL portion of the exchange in Example 2.2 is ignored, the English message still sounds natural; a pause occurs between the doctor's turn and the interpreter's turn of less than one second, and no overlap occurs as the turn is exchanged.

Example 2.3 is an example from the data of a regular turn in ASL between the interpreter and the Deaf mother.

EXAMPLE. 2.3

```
70-71
M:                                           ┌─ NO++
D: So far though they don't suspect anything. │
N:                                            │
C:                                            │
I:                                            │    No, huh-uh.
I:           #SO FAR NOT SUSPICIOUS NOTHING? ─┘
```

In this example, the doctor and the mother are discussing the baby's ability to hear. The doctor asks the mother a question about this topic, which is interpreted into ASL and then answered by the mother, creating a regular turn between the interpreter and the mother in lines 70–71. As in the English example, we can see that this sequence is a regular turn by watching only the ASL message, without the English source message. When looking only at the ASL portion, we see that the interpreter asks a question that is almost immediately responded to by the mother, creating a regular turn in ASL with no gaps, pauses, or overlap.

TURNS WITH OVERLAP

In her data, Roy (2000) identified four ways in which the interpreter handled overlap when both primary speakers were talking at the same time. Her categorizations are as follows:

1. An interpreter can *stop* one (or both) speakers and allow the other speaker to continue. If an interpreter stops both speakers, then either the interpreter indicates who speaks next or one of the primary speakers decides who talks next.
2. An interpreter can *momentarily ignore* one speaker's overlapping talk, hold the segment of talk in memory, continue interpreting

the other speaker, and then produce the "held" talk immediately following the end of a speaker's turn. Decisions about holding talk in one's memory lie within the interpreter's ability to do so and the interpreter's judgment regarding the importance or impact of the talk to be held in memory.

3. An interpreter can *ignore* overlapping talk completely.

4. An interpreter can momentarily ignore overlapping talk and upon finishing the interpretation of one speaker, *offer the next turn* to the other speaker, or indicate in some way that a turn was attempted. (2000, p. 85, italics in the original)

These categorizations were motivated by the ways that the interpreter handled overlap in Roy's data from an academic meeting. By showing the range of options available to the interpreter, Roy illustrated that the interpreter really does have the potential to have an effect on the interpreted encounter. In the data from the current study, described in this chapter, similar types of overlap were found, with the exception of the first kind—stopping one or more of the speakers. No examples of the interpreter stopping one or both of the speakers were found in the data. The following sections discuss examples of each kind of overlap that are present in the interpreted medical encounter (Overlap 2, 3, and 4 from Roy's list).

Overlap 2—Momentarily ignoring overlapping talk.

Overlap that was momentarily ignored and then inserted by the interpreter happened 26 times in the data (14%). Example 2.4 is an example in which the doctor and mother are talking at the same time. The mother has just finished saying that it does not seem like her child has gotten any better since his last visit (during the previous week), and she is concerned as to why. The doctor responds by saying that the child's symptoms during this visit are entirely different from the ones he presented with during the last visit, and the mother overlaps with the doctor in disagreement.

EXAMPLE 2.4

82

M: NO NOT-NOW-NO BEFORE LAST-WEEK HAVE #FEVER PRO.1 =

D: = we're talkin' about fever and vomiting. Last time we were talkin' about cold symptoms.

N:
C:
I: No, last week, he had fever, too,
I: = #STUFFY NOSE. NOW TALK ABOUT #FEVER

In keeping with Roy's description of this kind of turn, the interpreter momentarily ignores one speaker (the mother) and continues interpreting. She then ends her ASL interpretation and inserts the mother's disagreement ("No . . .") along with the continuation of the mother's response to the doctor. Again, this kind of overlap is related to the interpreter's judgment about her ability to retain the momentarily ignored talk and her judgment about the effect or importance of the ignored talk. In this example, the interpreter may have felt comfortable "holding" the mother's general disagreement ("NO . . . NOT- . . . " etc.), but may have realized the effect of the mother's message when the mother went beyond simple negation and into a full-fledged explanation.

Overlap 3—Ignoring overlapping talk completely.

Of the 186 total turns identified in the data, the interpreter completely ignored a portion of overlapping talk in only 9 of them (4.8%). The same example shown in Example 2.4 is repeated here as Example 2.5 to illustrate a portion of the medical encounter in which the interpreter ignored the talk of one participant completely.

EXAMPLE 2.5
82
M: NO NOT-NOW-NO BEFORE LAST-WEEK HAVE #FEVER PRO.1 =
D: = we're talkin' about fever and vomiting. Last time we were talkin'
    about cold symptoms.
N:
C:
I: No, last week, he had fever, too,
I: = #STUFFY NOSE. NOW TALK ABOUT #FEVER

Here, the interpreter has already handled one portion of the overlapping talk by momentarily ignoring the mother's message, continuing with the doctor's, and then inserting the "held" information. In inserting the "held" information, however, the interpreter makes a judgment about which participant's message takes priority, and the second half of the doctor's message ("Last time we were talkin' . . . ") gets ignored completely and is never inserted at a later point in the encounter. The combination of these two strategies for dealing with overlap occurring in one line of the data provides us with even more insight as to the kinds of choices interpreters are faced with every day.

Overlap 4—Offering the next turn to a speaker after overlapping talk.

The final kind of overlapping talk found in Roy's data that was also found in the study described in this chapter is that in which the next turn is offered to one of the speakers by the interpreter. One clear example of the use of this strategy was found in the data; two more possible occurrences were also found, but, in those, it is difficult to determine whether or not the next turn at talk was "encouraged" by an offer from the interpreter or would have happened regardless. The one clear example of the interpreter offering the next turn to a speaker following overlapping talk is shown in Example 2.6.

EXAMPLE 2.6

179
M: BEC- BECAUSE PRO.1 HUSBAND #WAS SAY THAT PRO.3 YEL-
D: = draining down from his nose and his ears. If we clear up the ears, we'll clear up the cough.
N:
C:
I:
I: = JUST DRIP-FROM-EAR FROM EARS NOSE #IF #IF CLEAR EARS FUT- COUGH =

180
M: OH-I-SEE BECAUSE PRO.1 HUSBAND #WAS SAY =
D:
N:
C:
I: 'Cause my husband was saying that
I: = FUTURE CLEAR SAME (leans forward)

In this example, the interpreter begins by using the third strategy for dealing with overlapping talk in line 179. She continues interpreting the doctor's message into ASL while ignoring the mother's ASL message. Once the interpreter is finished in ASL, however, she leans forward, as a signal to the mother that she may now take a turn. In addition, the interpreter folds her hands at her waist in what could be considered (for this interpreter) "full-rest" position, a signal identified by Baker (1977) as indicative that one speaker's turn is finished. We can see that the mother understood the interpreter's lean forward as a signal to take a turn because she immediately jumps in and repeats what she was attempting to express in line 179, this time with an English interpretation produced by the interpreter.

TURNS WITH LAG

The following section focuses on the third and final category of turns in the data, turns with lag.

Regular lag. Roy (2000) identifies two kinds of lag that affected the exchange of turns in the interpreted academic meeting. She labeled the first kind of turn as one with "regular lag" and defined this kind as a turn in which the "interpretation *lags,* or is delayed, several seconds behind a primary speaker's message" (p. 76, italics in the original). Roy (2000) goes on to explain that this lag can happen in one of two ways: when the interpreter waits a minute before beginning her interpretation or when the primary speaker has finished speaking but the interpreter has not finished yet.

Because this interpreter seems to have a very short "process" or "lag" time when producing her interpretations, the latter kind of regular lag became the focus of this part of the study. Regular lag, caused by an interpretation that continues beyond a primary speaker's source message, occurred 12 times (6.5%) in the data. An example of regular lag between the turns in English is provided in Example 2.7.

EXAMPLE 2.7

65
M:
D: = something there. One more question, how recently has he had
    fever?
N:

C:
I:
I: = SEE CAN FIND SOMETHING. ONE MORE QUESTION. HOW- (gaze to Dr.) =

66
M: (begins answer; blocked by Dr.)
D:
N:
C:
I: The most
I: = PRO.3 (baby) HAVE FEVER #WHEN BEFORE RECENT?

Here, the doctor asks a question of the mother, and the interpreter's ASL rendition extends beyond the doctor's English message. Four seconds pass from the time the doctor's question is complete in line 65 to the time the interpreter begins rendering the mother's response back into English in line 66. This period is considered regular lag primarily because the participants "go along with" the process. The doctor does not say anything more until he receives the mother's answer, and by saying nothing, he communicates that he is willing to allow the process of interpreting to take place in the interest of getting the information he requested.

Lengthy lag. When participants are not willing to wait during a period of lag, however, they send a "message" of sorts that communicates their discomfort. Roy (2000) found that

> [f]rom regular lag, another type of lag can develop—a delay that becomes too long for one of the speakers. Lengthy lag occurs when a speaker perceives that the ensuing verbalizing or silence is taking too much time and reacts verbally or nonverbally. Typically this produces one of two results. The speaker who is uncomfortable begins to talk again, creating a pause, or exhibits some discomfort while waiting. (p. 77)

Although this finding is an excellent descriptive analysis of lag, it is extremely difficult to determine when lengthy lag has happened without actually asking the participants.

In her study, Roy (2000) was able to have a "debriefing" conference with each of the three participants following the academic meeting and was able to glean their opinions of the gaps in the discourse. During the interview with the professor, Roy was able to get a better sense of how the professor viewed some of the segments with lag. At one point, the professor felt that she had more to say and simply added more information before the Deaf student had an opportunity to see and respond to the professor's first utterance. In another instance, the professor shifted in her chair after waiting 3 seconds for a response and hearing none. She told Roy during the follow-up interview, "'If I'm really going to have to wait this long, I'll just settle in here'" (2000, p. 83). Although Roy noticed that the professor's tolerance for lag increased significantly from the beginning to the end of the interpreted event, some of the gaps were still too long for her to handle without some display of unrest.

Unfortunately, there was no opportunity to interview the participants in the interpreted medical encounter once the data collection was finished. In looking at the videotape and transcript, four possible instances of lengthy lag might occur in the data; confirmation is difficult to determine because one cannot say for sure whether the participant was uncomfortable and added an utterance to fill a gap or simply had more to say, as was the case with the professor in Roy's study.

One example from the data that seems to show a period of lengthy lag is provided in Example 2.8. Just a few lines before this segment occurred, the mother was explaining the child's symptoms to the doctor. The mother responded in ASL, and the interpreter translated the mother's response into English, using the first person to match the mother's message (i.e., "I tried to give him something"). The doctor became confused and inquired as to who tried to give the child something to drink, the mother or the interpreter. The lines in Example 2.8 follow a response from the mother about the role of the interpreter.

EXAMPLE 2.8

59
M: = CONFUSE TRUE TALK PRO.1, #AS #IF PRO.3 PRO.1
D: I'm just interested in the pronoun, that's all.
N:
C:
I: = confuses, you, the interpreter's really speaking as if-
I: PRO.1 (REALLY) INTEREST =

60

M: #OK PRO.1

D: You're not taking care =

N:

C: (cries)

I:

I: = WORD "I" (*I* on chest) PRO.#(left hand)I (*I* on chest)

In this example, 6 seconds pass from the end of the doctor's utterance in line 59 ("I'm just interested in the pronoun, that's all.") to the time he starts speaking again in line 60. Although the mother has just finished an explanation of the role of the interpreter, the doctor adds a final comment (which could possibly be understood as an indirect request for information) to which there is no response in English. Hearing no response, the doctor fills the silence (one of the characteristics of lengthy lag) by adding a statement about his understanding of the situation.

Back Channeling

As this chapter has established earlier, the interpreter does, in fact, take turns with each participant in their two respective languages during the interpreted medical encounter. One final way to provide support for this view is to look at the back-channeling events that took place throughout the medical encounter. These events are defined here as verbal or nonverbal signals to the current speaker that the addressee is either listening and following along or listening and needs clarification. Back-channeling events are not attempts to take the floor but merely efforts to show the current speaker that the addressee is, in a sense, "with them" as far as the current message is concerned.

Wadensjö (1998) refers to the work of Jönsson (1990), who analyzed back channeling during interpreted encounters in a courtroom setting. Wadensjö explains that Jönsson found that "the content of what is said is conveyed between the attorneys and lawyers on the one hand and the layperson on the other, yet more or less *without* the back-channeling signals" (Wadensjö, 1998, p. 76, italics in the original). She goes on to say that "these signals, according to research on conversation in general, are essential for interlocutors' understanding of how to act" and that "Jönsson concludes that interpreter-mediated interaction in court could—

in part—be described as two simultaneously ongoing dialogues between the interpreter and the respective parties" (1998, p. 76). This point—that back channeling contributes to a view of the interpreted interaction as two separate but overlapping dyads—will be examined here.

BACK CHANNELING IN THE ASL DYAD

Back channeling in ASL regularly occurred in the data, and it shows that both the mother and the interpreter were working solely in one language during segments when one or both women were using ASL. An example of a back channel from the mother is shown in Example 2.9.

EXAMPLE 2.9

145

M:

D: treatment of- of uh vomiting, like with diarrhea is the diet. Uh, and, the diet, basically

N:

C: (starts crying)

I:

I: = DO-DO? TO HELP-TO (baby) VOMIT SAME WITH DIARRHEA SAME #DIET

146

M: (head forward, brows raised)

D: with vomiting the diet is small quantities, of clear liquids, frequently.

N:

C:

I:

I: = IMPORTANT WHAT EAT IMPORTANT WITH VOMIT MUST PROVIDE =

In this segment of the data, the interpreter fingerspells the word *diet*, which the doctor uses in his English message. Immediately following the fingerspelled word, the mother tilts her head forward and raises her eyebrows to back-channel to the interpreter and let her know that something about the message needed clarification. Perhaps the mother did not catch the fingerspelled word, or perhaps she did not understand its relationship to the previous talk ("diet" is the topic of a new utterance for the doctor). The exact reason is not as important as the fact that the mother realizes that the interpreter is working in ASL at the moment and that her back-channel signal about needing clarification will be attended to.

The interpreter, in turn, sees the mother's signal and realizes that something about the message needs to be more clear. Instead of fingerspelling the English word *diet* again, the interpreter provides an interpretation of what the word means, and the interaction continues without the interpreter ever "leaving" the ASL dyad for the English dyad with the doctor.

BACK CHANNELING IN THE ENGLISH DYAD

In the same way that the mother and the interpreter form a dyad in ASL, the doctor and the interpreter form a dyad in English. An example of back channeling that supports this idea is provided in Example 2.10.

EXAMPLE 2.10

43

M: FLU

D: what kind of symptoms.   Okay,

N:

C:

I: First he was sick in his stomach,

I: STOMACH   WANT EXPLAIN WHAT WRONG =

Here we see two things happening. The interpreter has just finished interpreting the mother's message into English with "First he was sick in his stomach" and has dealt with the overlapping message of the doctor by using the second kind of overlap (momentarily ignoring one speaker and inserting the message in at the next opportunity), which allows the interpreter to interpret the doctor's question about symptoms into ASL immediately after her English interpretation is finished.

At the end of the interpreter's English utterance, just before she switches to ASL, she uses a slightly rising intonation to indicate the beginning of a list of items. While she quickly interprets the "held" information into ASL, the doctor signals that he is following the English message with "okay," as a back channel. He may or may not be aware of the interpreter's brief switch to ASL, but he does show through his back channeling that he is following what is happening in the English dyad of the interpreted encounter.

CONCLUSION

The primary finding of this study is that, of the seven kinds of turns found by Roy (2000) in an interpreted academic meeting, six occurred in the data from the medical encounter. This finding reinforces the grouping of turn exchange categories established by Roy while also adding strength to the conclusions made in her study—mainly, that the interpreter is not a neutral party in the interpreted encounter.

The only kind of turn that did not occur was "Overlap 1" in which the interpreter stops both overlapping participants and decides who may have the next turn. This kind of turn may not have occurred because of the relative power and status associated with the role of physician in American society. Perhaps the interpreter—though willing to have an effect on the interaction by means of other kinds of turn management—decided that the power differential between doctor and patient was too significant for the interpreter to feel she could stop the interaction. Further investigation is needed, however, to determine whether this finding is a pattern across interpreted medical discourse or is unique to the interaction studied here.

In addition, several occurrences of back channeling in both languages help to clarify the notion advanced by Metzger (1999) that the interpreted interaction consists of two overlapping dyads of participants, with the interpreter holding "dual membership" status. Back channeling helps to explain this view of the encounter because it shows that the participants have an understanding of "how to act" (Wadensjö, 1998) when the interpreter is working in their respective languages (dyads).

Finally, this study provides further support for the idea that the interpreter not only is involved in two overlapping dyads but also is a very active participant in both. The interpreter—especially by means of her handling of overlapping talk—does make choices about what gets interpreted, and these choices can have an effect on the outcome of the interpreted medical encounter (Davidson, 1998; Diaz-Duque, 1989).

Areas for further research could include a more in-depth study of how turn exchange and interpreters' decisions about turns affect what information is interpreted and what is omitted. In addition, more investigation into the structure of regular turns in both ASL and English would help interpreters, educators, and students to understand what will be accepted as normal discourse when working in both dyads while interpreting.

An ideal project for future research would be to analyze an interaction between a deaf doctor, a hearing patient, and an interpreter, a study that would help us to understand more fully the dynamics of the interpreted medical encounter. A scenario of this kind could provide insight on many levels, including how the interpreter deals with the deaf physician as the person in the "one-up" role who, because of medical training and expertise, has more power but who at the same time is someone in a linguistic and cultural minority. Does a deaf doctor use questioning strategies and topic transitions in ASL similar in structure to those found by Fisher (1982) and Ainsworth-Vaughn (1992), respectively? If so, knowing what those strategies and transitions look like would be invaluable to interpreters who are working in or planning to work in medical settings.

Finally, simply replicating the current study would be of value to the field because the replication could look for not only potential patterns in turn exchange that are similar to those found here but also potential differences. More studies like this one and further investigation into the areas of research suggested above need to be done to provide linguists, interpreters, interpreter educators, students, and consumers with a clearer understanding of interpreting and the discourse process at work therein.

APPENDIX 2.A

Transcription Conventions

SMALL CAPITAL LETTERS	Used for English glosses of signs
F-I-N-G-E-R-S-P-E-L-L-I-N-G	Fingerspelling
#LETTERS	The gloss that follows is lexicalized spelling
HYPHENATED-WORDS	Represent a single sign
++	Duplication of a sign
PRO.1	PRO = pronoun, 1 = first person, 2 = second person, 3 = third person
POSS.1	Possessive pronoun (and person)
CL	Classifier predicate
Bob-ASK-TO-Mary	Indicating verbs include the subject-object referents
(actions)	Indicate visual-spatial information and some contextual information
...	Pause of half-second or more
-	Interrupted utterance
(?)	Unclear from the video recording
.	Sentence final prosody
,	Clause final intonation

?	Rising intonation (English) or nonmanual signals indicating a question form
=	Utterances continuing to the following or from the preceding line

REFERENCES

Ainsworth-Vaughn, N. (1992.) Topic transitions in physician-patient interviews: Power, gender, and discourse change. *Language in Society, 21,* 409–426.

Baker, C. (1976a). Eye openers in ASL. In *California Linguistics Association conference proceedings* (pp. 1–13). San Diego: San Diego State University.

Baker, C. (1976b). What's not on the other hand in American Sign Language. In S. S. Mufwene (Ed.), *Papers from the twelfth regional meeting of the Chicago Linguistic Society* (pp. 24–32). Chicago: Chicago Linguistic Society.

Baker, C. (1977). Regulators and turn-taking in ASL discourse. In L. A. Friedman (Ed.), *On the other hand: New perspectives on American Sign Language* (pp. 215–241). New York: Academic Press.

Baker C., & Padden, C. (1978). Focusing on the nonmanual components of American Sign Language. In P. Siple (Ed.), *Understanding language through sign language research* (pp. 27–57). New York: Academic Press.

Davidson, B. (1998). *Interpreting medical discourse: A study of cross-linguistic communication in the hospital clinic.* Unpublished doctoral dissertation, Stanford University, Stanford, CA.

Diaz-Duque, O. (1989). Communication barriers in medical settings: Hispanics in the United States. *International Journal of the Sociology of Language, 79,* 93–102.

Fisher, S. (1982). The decision-making context: How doctors and patients communicate. In R. DiPietro (Ed.), *Linguistics and the professions* (pp. 51–81). New Jersey: Ablex.

Frishberg, N. (1990). Interpreting: An introduction. Silver Spring, MD: RID Publications.

Humphrey, J., & Alcorn, B. (1995). So you want to be an interpreter? An introduction to sign language interpreting (2nd ed.). Amarillo, TX: H & H.

Hymes, D. (1972). Models of the interaction of language and social life. In J. Gumperz & D. Hymes (Eds.), *Directions in sociolinguistics: The ethnography of communication* (pp. 35–71). New York: Holt, Rinehart and Winston.

Jönsson, L. (1990). Förmedlade samtal: Om atkerkoppling I tolkade rättegangar. In U. Nettelbladt & G. Hakansson (Eds.), *Samtal och undervisning. Studier till Lennart Gustavssons minne* [Linköping Studies in Arts and Science 60] (pp. 71–86). Linköping, Sweden: Linköping University,

Department of Communication Studies.

Martinez, L. (1995). Turn-taking and eye gaze in sign conversations between deaf Filipinos. In C. Lucas (Ed.), *Sociolinguistics of deaf communities* (pp. 272–307). Washington, DC: Gallaudet University Press.

Metzger, M. (1995). *The paradox of neutrality: A comparison of interpreters' goals with the reality of interactive discourse.* Unpublished doctoral dissertation, Georgetown University, Washington, DC.

Metzger, M. (1999). Sign language interpreting: Deconstructing the myth of neutrality. Washington, DC: Gallaudet University Press.

Roy, C. (1989). *A sociolinguistic analysis of the interpreter's role in the turn exchanges of an interpreted event.* Unpublished doctoral dissertation, Georgetown University, Washington, DC.

Roy, C. (2000). *Interpreting as a discourse process.* Oxford: Oxford University Press.

Sacks, H., Schegloff, E., & Jefferson, G. (1974). A simplest systematics for the organization of turn-taking in conversation. *Language, 50*(4), 696–735.

Schiffrin, D. (1994). *Approaches to discourse.* Malden, MA: Blackwell.

Seleskovitch, D. (1978). *Interpreting for international conferences.* Washington, DC: Pen and Booth.

Shuy, R. (1987). A sociolinguistic view of interpreter education. In M. McIntire (Ed.), *New dimensions in interpreter education—curriculum and instruction: Proceedings of the sixth National Convention of the Conference of Interpreter Trainers* (pp. 1–8). Silver Spring, MD: RID Publications.

Tannen, D. (1984). *Conversational style: Analyzing talk among friends.* Norwood, NJ: Ablex.

Tannen, D. (1986). *That's not what I meant! How conversational style makes or breaks relationships.* New York: Ballantine.

Tannen, D. (1990). *You just don't understand: Women and men in conversation.* New York: Ballantine.

Tannen, D. 1993. Interactive frames and knowledge schemas in interaction: Examples from a medical examination/interview. In D. Tannen (Ed.), *Framing in discourse* (pp. 57–76). New York: Oxford University Press.

Wadensjö, C. (1992). *Interpreting as interaction: On dialogue-interpreting in immigration hearings and medical encounters.* Linköping, Sweden: Linköping University, Linköping studies in Arts and Sciences.

Wadensjö, C. (1998). *Interpreting as interaction.* London: Longman.

Wiener, M., and S. Devoe. 1974. *Regulators, channels, and communication disruption.* Research proposal, Clark University, Worcester, MA.

Zimmer, J. (1989). ASL/English interpreting in an interactive setting. In D. Hammond (Ed.), *Proceedings of the 30th Annual Conference of the American Translators Association* (pp. 225–231). Medford, NJ: Learned Information.

Analysis of Interactive Discourse

in an Interpreted Deaf Revival Service:

Question-Answer Adjacency Pairs

Initiated in an ASL Sermon

Mary Ann Richey

Research on religious interpretation is limited at best and, for the most part, has been concerned with defining the role of the interpreter in church settings or with making general recommendations to address logistical or environmental issues. However, few empirical studies have been made of interpreted religious events, either from English to ASL or vice versa. In particular, there have been no published data-based linguistic analyses on a discourse level of an interpreted ASL sermon nor has there been research on interactions in a Deaf[1] worship service. Therefore, this case study will focus on a discourse analysis of an interpreted ASL sermon and interaction in a Deaf worship service.

Consequently, this study examines a new genre of ASL discourse and of interpretation. It also builds on research focusing on the use of formal ASL as used by native signers in a majority-status role as compared to a minority-status role. Therefore, the findings of this study will contribute to a growing body of research related to the structure of ASL monologic discourse (see, e.g., Bahan & Supalla, 1995; Gee, 1986; Liddell & Metzger, 1998; Mather & Winston, 1998; Metzger, 1995; Roy, 1989a; Wilson, 1995;

---

1. In this paper, the protocol used by Padden and Humphries (1988) will be followed. The word *deaf* in lowercase letters is an adjective describing an audiological condition of not being able to hear whereas the word *Deaf* in uppercase letters is an adjective describing a community of deaf people who are users of American Sign Language (ASL) and members of a distinctive culture (Padden & Humphries, 1988, p. 2).

Winston, 1992, 1993; Zimmer, 1989b), and to a growing body of empirical research related to interpreted interaction (see, e.g., Angelelli, 2001; Berk-Seligson, 1990; Metzger, 1995, 1999; Roy, 1989b, 2000; Wadensjö, 1992, 1998; Zimmer, 1989a, and others in this volume). In addition, this study both builds on previous work and extends it, focusing on, in Hymes's (1972) sense, a unique "speech" situation (a religious gathering), event (a revival service), and "speech" act (questions).

This case study consists of an analysis of a preexisting videotaped worship service conducted by a guest Deaf pastor to a Deaf, predominantly Caucasian, Protestant congregation. The main thrust of this case study is to examine the question of whether or not interactive discourse occurs in this most formal of settings. In these data, the speaker and audience do interact with one another, despite the fact that a church worship service is considered a formal setting where, typically, little or no speaker-initiated interaction occurs between a pastor and the congregation. The pastor-congregation interaction also affects the interpretation. Although research has been conducted on the interpretation of one-on-one interviews (Angelelli, 2001; Berk-Seligson, 1990; Metzger, 1995, 1999; Roy, 1989b, 2000; Wadensjö, 1992, 1998; Zimmer, 1989a), little research has been conducted on the pragmatics of multiparty interaction such as that found in discussion groups, in counseling sessions or elsewhere. Here, the interaction is both multiparty and formal, being constrained by the structure of the religious event taking place. This interactive element must be considered in addition to the fact that the translation of religious discourse is a unique undertaking.

Religious interpreters regularly confront challenging source material. The Bible is fraught with figurative language, and religious discourse itself is replete with concepts that can be experienced and understood on a multitude of levels. Joos (1967), in his work *The Five Clocks*, describes how frozen text can be read and reread with new considerations or insights occurring with each new reading (Joos, 1967, p. 41). Moreover, the sermon itself is more than a monologic speech event; it is a divine connection. In *The Practice of Preaching*, Wilson (1995) claims that "preaching is an event in which the congregation meets the living God" (p. 21). In consideration of the monologic and religious aspects of a sermon, the task facing religious interpreters is extremely challenging and requires a wholehearted dedication to preparation. Gaining a better understanding of the interactive features of religious discourse can only serve to make the task faced by interpreters more manageable.

This case study will examine the intricacies of interaction between speaker and audience in a Deaf-Deaf religious setting. The reader may wonder why interpretation would be necessary in a Deaf-Deaf setting. In this case study of a church revival service, interpreters were provided to ensure equal access to all participants, including but not limited to hearing coworkers, acquaintances, and extended family members who were invited to the worship service by Deaf members of the congregation. Of paramount importance to the congregation would be the free and unencumbered sharing of the gospel of Jesus Christ, regardless of hearing status or linguistic preference.

Religious interpretation is a formidable task and deserves an in-depth examination. The goals of this paper are to examine the type of interaction elicited by the Deaf pastor, possible functions for these interactions, and finally, an analysis of the interpretation of these interactions. Before proceeding with this examination, however, the reader will benefit by first gaining insight into what is typical of group behavior in a religious setting.

LITERATURE REVIEW

An examination of group behavior will help us understand how it is manifested in a religious setting and how certain kinds of special events may play a role in the participants' behavior compared to the role a typical religious event plays. Unfortunately, a paucity of research exists on the behavior of people in public places. Typically, psychologists have concentrated their studies on inappropriate behavior exhibited by individuals instead of on the social mores and conventions intrinsic in any society (Goffman, 1963, p. 3). Recognizing this deficiency, Goffman proposes a "framework" with which to examine societal conventions in an effort to define socially acceptable behavior, which would, in turn, provide groundwork to examine deviations therefrom (Goffman, 1963, p. 4). One of the sources for his study is the use of etiquette manuals, which have traditionally defined typical American behavior in polite circles, although they lack empirical data to corroborate their findings and fail to dissect these cultural mores (Goffman, 1963, pp. 5–6). Nonetheless, etiquette manuals possess a certain value as a source or starting point from which Goffman constructs his observations of various public events or "gatherings" (Goffman, 1963, pp. 5, 9, 11).

Goffman's analysis leads to his definition of a "gathering," which refers to "any set of two or more individuals whose members include all and only those who are at the moment in one another's immediate presence" (Goffman, 1963, p. 18). In this case study of a Deaf worship service, the people who were present at that location and who attended the worship service for any portion of the allotted time constituted a "gathering." Defining a gathering is only part of the picture that Goffman paints of social encounters. Another facet is that of "situation."

A "situation" refers to "the full spatial environment anywhere within which an entering person becomes a member of the gathering that is (or does then become) present" (Goffman, 1963, p. 18). In other words, once a person entered the Deaf chapel that evening, whether before or after the worship service began, he or she then became part of the "situation" and, therefore, a member of the "gathering." One could say that the "situation" is the location for the "gathering" and that the purpose for the gathering can be defined by the term "social occasion."

A "social occasion" occurs in a specific location at a specific time and date and normally makes use of equipment that is permanently installed (Goffman, 1963, p. 18). Furthermore, it provides "the social context in which many situations and their gatherings are likely to form, dissolve, and re-form, *while a pattern of conduct tends to be recognized as the appropriate and (often) official or intended one*" (Goffman, 1963, p. 18, italics added). The revival service can be classified as a "social occasion" according to the criteria established by Goffman. The Deaf revival service occurred at a specific church at an appointed date and time. The pastor and congregation made use of permanently affixed equipment such as pews, lights, tables, podium, etc. Therefore, this Deaf revival service is a social occasion as defined by Goffman. The question then, is this: Is the Deaf code of conduct different from the hearing code of conduct in a worship service? This paper will address that question.

What behavior is expected of participants in a traditional church worship service as compared to a revival setting? Typical attendees of mainstream American church services are dignified and worshipful. Indeed, according to Emily Post, well-known expert on American manners and customs, "Reverence is the quality that guides one's behavior at all religious services, and while it is expressed in various ways, in most faiths quiet, attentiveness, and dignity are the ingredients" (Post, 1992, p. 102). Even the clergy take note of the congregation's behavior, which in turn affects the clergy's pulpit behavior. Clyde Reid (1967) analyzes preaching as communication in *The Empty Pulpit*, and he asserts that preaching lacks the interactive element present in early New Testament churches and that "preaching as traditionally practiced is basically monologue" (pp. 82, 85). This view is further corroborated by Bishop Ken Untener in his analysis of preaching styles in *Preaching Better: Practical Suggestions for Homilists* (Untener, 1999). Untener notes that, although interactive or dialogue homilies have a certain appeal, an open-ended format can result in loss of control and subsequent loss of audience interest (Untener, 1999, pp. 111–113). One of his parishioners cannily observed, "All we get to do is say 'Amen' or go to the bathroom" (Untener, 1999, p. 111). Interestingly then, speech is limited to the pastor, and apparently, movement in the congregation is restricted. Although no one can speak for all churches at all times, the general pattern of behavior in American society is that participants in a traditional church worship service are expected to listen quietly and attentively while the pastor conducts a monologue. Would the same behavior be expected in a revival service? Let us examine a brief history of revivals in America and the hallmarks of a revival that differentiate it from a typical church worship service.

McLoughlin (1978), in his book, *Revivals, Awakenings, and Reform*, recognizes "five great awakenings" in the United States since 1607 that had a profound influence on American society (McLoughlin, 1978, p. 8). According to the *Concise Encyclopedia of Preaching* (Willimon & Lischer, 1995), these "great awakenings" were characterized by the widespread use of revivals focusing on individual spiritual transformation (p. 406). Thus, revivals have a psychological effect on the individual by converting his or her spirit to one of obedience to God's will (McLoughlin, 1959, pp. 86–87).

During colonial times, revivals were a way of increasing church membership by adding new believers (Willimon & Lischer, 1995, p. 407). In the early to mid 18th century, itinerant preachers such as George Whitefield started traveling from church to church, preaching to thousands of people regardless of religious affiliation (Willimon & Lischer, 1995, p. 407). The practice of preaching across denominational lines no doubt led to the cross-pollination of ideologies and to greater cohesion as a society from a religious perspective. Revivals or "camp meetings" also cut across racial lines. In *The Negro Church in America*, Frazier (1971) notes that the Methodist and Baptist preachers struck a chord in the hearts of slaves:

[T]he slaves who had been torn from their homeland and kinsmen and friends and whose cultural heritage was lost, were isolated and broken men, so to speak. In the emotionalism of the camp meetings and revivals some social solidarity, even if temporary, was achieved, and they were drawn into a union with their fellow men. . . . Not only did religion draw negroes into a union with their fellow men, it tended to break down barriers that isolated them morally from their white masters. (pp. 8–9)

As the years passed, revivals developed into a traditional event characterized by special music, personal testimony, and impassioned speech (Willimon & Lischer, 1995, p. 407–408). The purpose of revivals has always been to preach the gospel of Jesus Christ to the uninitiated, but their purpose also is to strengthen and encourage the longtime believer, including those who desire to recommit their lives after a time of personal rebellion against God (Willimon & Lischer, 1995, p. 408). Sermons preached during a revival serve as a stimulus for repentance and typically incorporate explicit comparisons such as heaven and hell (Willimon & Lischer, 1995, pp. 408–409). Revivals have become an annual event in many denominations, including the Pentecostals, the Baptists, and others (Willimon & Lischer, 1995, p. 408). Furthermore, revivals differ from traditional worship services in that a guest speaker or traveling evangelist is the keynote speaker of a special event in which he or she uses impassioned speech, personal testimony, and music to elicit a spiritual awakening in both the unacquainted and the longtime believer (Willimon & Lischer, 1995, pp. 408–409).

Some churches, for example, Pentecostal or African-American churches where the congregations frequently interject spoken comments throughout the sermon, are perceived as being more emotional in their regular worship services than other denominations. Melva Wilson Costen (1993) investigates and documents many aspects of African-American congregations in *African-American Christian Worship*. Costen is quick to point out that not all African-American churches can be lumped together in a single category of "typical" worship patterns (Costen, 1993, p. 15). African-American worship services can include an entire spectrum of responses to God, although the congregation members generally express themselves in an external rather than internal fashion. (Costen, 1993, p. 18). An insight into the meaning of this expression can be seen in Costen's description of a "prayer event" in the early African-American church:

Rather than passively listening to a prayer, the gathered community becomes involved with the prayer (prayer leader), using a variety of responses. There might be verbal "witnessing" to what is being prayed, such as "Amen!"; "Thank you, Jesus!"; or "Yes, Lord!" There might be direct urging or nudging of the leader to "pray your prayer!" or "tell it to the Lord!" There are often injections of admonitions to God to "Come by here"; "Oh, help him, Jesus"; "Hear us . . . "; or "Help us now, Lord!" Some participants moaned or hummed in perfect cadence with the prayer leader. Some rocked, swayed, cried softly, or merely nodded their heads in assent. The "prayer event" often reached full intensity as the leader and congregation, filled with the Spirit, demonstrated that everyone's heart was spiritually "in tune."(Costen, 1993, p. 42)

This description of a "prayer event" shows that the congregation is actively participating in the worship experience along with the prayer leader in a vertical expression of oneness in the Holy Spirit. Or in other words, the members of the congregation are expressing their innermost feelings to the presence of the Lord. Their comments are directed upward to God. The comments from the congregation members are spontaneous and are not answers to questions directed to them from the worship leader to obtain needed information to continue with his or her sermon. Certain aspects of African-American worship also can be recognized in Pentecostal and Charismatic churches.

Like the early African-American churches' "prayer event" (Costen, 1993, p. 42), the early Pentecostal church had worship services in which "a person could, if he wished, clap his hands, tap his feet, cry, pray audibly, speak forth in tongues if he 'felt the spirit leading,' dance, or exhort his brethren during the testimony meeting" (Nichol, 1966, p. 65). Quebedeaux also draws this comparison in his examination of the Pentecostal movement:

So as not to "quench the Spirit," Pentecostals felt free to exercise the *charismata* at just about any time during a service, which itself might be characterized by repeated outbursts of enthusiasm—spontaneous testimonies, shouting, screaming, and dancing—not untypical of the black worship experience as a whole. (Quebedeaux, 1976, p. 30)

Although both African-American and Pentecostal churches have been characterized as conducting "emotional" worship services (Bradfield, 1979, p. 18–19; Costen, 1993, p. 16; Nichol, 1966, pp. 226, 235), these attributes of shouting, bodily movements, and vociferous prayers are deemed as being spontaneous and led by the Holy Spirit and directed to God (Costen 1993, p. 18; Nichol, 1966, p. 75). Consequently, the question arises: Does the Deaf church differ from the African-American, Pentecostal, or mainstream Protestant churches in discourse format?

Parvin (1992) reports in her book, *That All May Understand*, that the congregation actively participates in their worship experience at Christ United Methodist Church of the Deaf in Baltimore, Maryland (Parvin, 1992, p. 44). She agrees that hearing worship services are rigidly formal events where the congregation is discouraged from commenting aloud unless it is the time for announcements (Parvin, 1992, p. 44). However, in this Deaf congregation, the pastor asks members of the congregation questions at the conclusion of the sermon. The reason for this practice is twofold. First, it is an attempt to verify their understanding of the points of the sermon and to hear their reaction to the sermon (Parvin, 1992, p. 44). The pastor encourages straightforward comments from the congregation and appreciates the opportunity to address any issues (Parvin, 1992, p. 44).

So, in Parvin's experience with Deaf worship, the service concludes with a question-and-answer session in which the members of the congregation have the opportunity to clarify questions they may have about the sermon's content, and they may also share their point of view with the pastor with respect to points made during the sermon (Parvin, 1992, p. 44). This type of dialogic interaction between the pastor and congregation is clearly different from the African-American or Pentecostal churches where attendees react spontaneously in a vocal or physical manner to the presence of the Holy Spirit (Blackman, 2002, pp. 1, 10; Costen, 1993). Blackman describes the emotional responses of the congregation as interactional, but her description differs from the one used in this chapter. In this chapter, the interaction specifically takes the form of question-answer adjacency pairs in which the pastor asks direct questions of audience members to get needed information before proceeding (Blackman 2002, pp. 1, 10–11). Furthermore, the worship service described by Parvin differs from the study described in this chapter in that Parvin does not provide empirical data, and the interaction between speaker and audience occurs after rather than during the sermon.

The case study described in this chapter examines interaction during a sermon between the Deaf pastor and the Deaf congregation in a revival service. The pastor questions the congregation directly about regional sign usage and other needed information before proceeding with his sermon. This question-and-answer strategy represents a difference between Deaf pastors and hearing pastors in similar revival situations for hearing congregants. The data also include an ASL-to-English interpretation of the pertinent sections of the ASL sermon. This paper examines the interaction between the pastor and congregation as well as the interpretation of this interaction.

METHODOLOGY

A preexisting videotape of a Deaf church revival service was examined to determine the existence and function of discourse strategies, specifically, question-answer adjacency pairs[2] initiated by the pastor to the congregation. The preexisting videotape was chosen to lessen the influence of "Observer's Paradox" (Labov, 1972, pp. 209–210), which occurs when the systematic collection of data on a particular community's language use influences how the participants use the language (Labov, 1972, pp. 209–210; Wardhaugh, 1998, pp. 8, 149). Sociolinguists have discovered that, in a prescribed experimental setting, the use of video cameras or audiotapes might cause the participants to alter their language choices in response to the presence of the researcher and the equipment (Labov, 1972, pp. 209–210; Wardhaugh, 1998, pp. 8, 149). Granted, one could argue that the mere presence of the video camera at this church revival service could have had some effect on the participants' language use. However, the purpose of videotaping the event was not for linguistic research but, rather, for the edification of church members who were unable to attend the event; thus, the "Observer's Paradox" should have been minimized. The data were transcribed and coded as described in the next section.

2. Adjacency pairs (Schegloff & Sacks, 1973) refer to what is typically a two-part feature generally found in conversational discourse. These could include, for example, greetings, conversational closings, and question-answer pairs.

Data

In this case study, a previously recorded videotaped sermon of a pre-dominantly Caucasian Deaf revival service was examined. The data in this study are based on the ASL sermon and on the ASL-to-English interpretation of this sermon. The data were coded by the hearing researcher with the assistance of an outside and uninvolved Deaf pastor, documenting the Deaf preacher's use of questions during the sermon to elicit a response from the congregation. Although the camera does not record the congregation members, some information about their response can be deduced on the basis of the speaker's pauses and reactions.

After noting the occurrences of questions directed to the congregation, the questions were analyzed according to their form and function. The transcriptions of the questions in ASL were provided by native Deaf signers. Native English speakers who are also interpreters provided the italicized English translations and coded the transcriptions of the interpreter's target utterances.[3]

Participants

The Deaf pastor in this study was a guest speaker at a revival service and was serving as a pastor to a Deaf congregation in a state other than his home state. The pastor, ordained for more than 20 years, has been a pastor to Deaf congregations in several areas. His educational background includes both college and theological seminary.

Two interpreters, one male and one female, provided services at this revival. Only one interpreter's voice is heard on the tape, that of the male interpreter. In addition to being an interpreter, he has also served as a hearing pastor to Deaf people in the same denomination and has college degrees in religious education. The Registry of Interpreters for the Deaf, Inc., awarded him the Comprehensive Skills certificate (CSC) in the 1970s. At the time of the videotaping, he had been personally acquainted with the Deaf speaker for more than 20 years.

The second interpreter who worked this event was a hearing female graduate student and member of that Deaf congregation for 5 years. She had worked with the male interpreter in the past but was unacquainted with the Deaf speaker until the event.

---

3. For transcription conventions used here, see Appendix 3.A.

During the sermon, 10 different instances of speaker-audience interaction were noted. These interactions between the Deaf speaker and Deaf audience consist of questions generated by the speaker and answered by one or more of the members of the audience. The questions asked by the speaker assumed two different types: yes-no (Y/N) questions and WH questions (defined in the next paragraph). The direct questions that the speaker asks of the congregation fulfill several functions. For example, the answers to his questions help the speaker to determine local sign usage, to elicit other needed information, or to establish solidarity and rapport with the members of the congregation. In this section, these three functions will be examined after a brief discussion of basic question forms in ASL.

Questions in ASL can assume several forms. One form is known as WH questions. Valli and Lucas (1992) describe WH questions in ASL as utterances using the manual signs glossed as WHO, WHAT, WHEN, WHERE, and WHY in combination with the appropriate nonmanual signal of eyebrow squint and head tilt accompanied by raised shoulders and forward tilting of the body (Valli & Lucas, 1992, p. 278). Another question form is that of yes-no (Y/N) questions. These are questions that necessitate a yes or no response and are marked by particular nonmanual signals, including raised eyebrows, eyes wide open, and tilted forward movement of the head and body; occasionally, the expression of Y/N questions also involves the inclusion of raised shoulders or the holding of the last sign (Valli & Lucas, 1992, p. 277). In this sermon, 70% of the questions take the form of Y/N questions and 30% are WH questions (see Table 3.1).

In the videotape, the speaker used direct questions to serve one of three purposes (see Table 3.2). Questions about local sign usage or regional variations in ASL constitute nearly half (40%) of the questions asked. Another 40% of the questions pertain to requests for other types of information such as names of local attractions. Finally, questions to establish solidarity and rapport or to ensure audience understanding of speaker comments generated 20% of the questions. The following sections will discuss, using specific examples, these three functions found for questions initiated by the pastor to the congregation.

TABLE 3.1 *Percentage of Questions (n = 10) Divided by Question Form*

Example Showing the Question	Y/N Questions (*n* = 7)	WH Questions (*n* = 3)
Example 3.1		X
Example 3.2	X	
Example 3.3	X	
Example 3.4	X	
Example 3.5		X
Example 3.6		X
Example 3.7	X	
Example 3.8	X	
Example 3.9	X	
Example 3.10	X	
Total Percentage	70%	30%

Local Sign Usage

Several studies have identified lexical variation in ASL based on a variety of factors, including ethnicity, gender, socioeconomic status, and specific topic such as signs for sexual behavior or for drug use (Bridges, 1993; Lucas, Bayley, & Valli, 2001; Mansfield, 1993; Shapiro, 1993; Shroyer & Shroyer, 1984; Woodward, 1976, 1979, 1980). The identification of regional variation at the lexical level, in particular, was the focus of the Shroyer and Shroyer (1984) study in which 1,200 sign forms are reported for 130 words, as documented from more than 35 signers across 25 states in the United States.

Further, in the largest study of variation in ASL to date, Lucas et al. (2001) examined variation in 207 ASL signers from seven different sites around the United States who were grouped not only by region but also by age, race, and socioeconomic status. In addition to other forms of variation (phonological, morphosyntactic) and in keeping with earlier studies' findings, Lucas et al. (2001) found evidence of lexical variation in ASL. Interestingly, the study found that, although regional variation does occur at the lexical level, a large number of lexical variants were shared across all seven sites studied. The authors suggest that this finding reflects close social ties in the American Deaf community. For example, residential schools and their relationship to one another historically as well as the "powerful role played by sports, civic, and religious organizations in the deaf community" (p. 185) bring signers (and their sign choices) from various regions into contact. Thus, the fact that a visiting pastor

TABLE 3.2 *Percentage of Questions (n = 10) Divided by Question Function*

Example Showing the Question	Question to Verify Local Sign Usage (*n* = 4)	Question to Request Other Information (*n* = 4)	Question to Establish Solidarity or Understanding (*n* = 2)
Example 3.1	WH-Q		
Example 3.2	Y/N-Q		
Example 3.3	Y/N-Q		
Example 3.4	Y/N-Q		
Example 3.5		WH-Q	
Example 3.6		WH-Q	
Example 3.7		Y/N-Q	
Example 3.8		Y/N-Q	
Example 3.9			Y/N-Q
Example 3.10			Y/N-Q
Total Percentage	40%	40%	20%

would be aware of sign variation and that the sharing of sign variants would emerge within a Deaf religious service is not at all surprising.

In the case study here, nearly half (40%) of the questions were requests for clarification of that congregation's use of a particular sign. The pastor's questions about local sign usage are asked to ensure that the congregation understands the lexical item signed by the pastor and, therefore, that the congregation can understand the sermon. That is, if a particular sign that the pastor chose had a number of regional variations and if the congregation members were unfamiliar with the sign the guest pastor or evangelist used, then they would very likely miss the point of the entire story. To prevent this communication breakdown from happening, a pastor might express an idea using the sign most familiar to him or her and then fingerspell an English translation of the sign used. Then the pastor could ask the congregation whether or not his or her lexical sign is the sign used by the congregation. Another possibility would be for the pastor to simply fingerspell an English word and ask the members of the congregation to respond with their lexical variant for it.

One example that illustrates the importance of verifying local sign usage within sermon discourse comes from the late Clifford Bruffey, a well-known Deaf evangelist and missionary. He told the following story about a traveling evangelist who failed to inquire about local sign usage:

A pastor to the Deaf from Texas or Oklahoma went to a nearby state to preach at a Deaf church. He announced that he would be preaching on the topic "How to Overcome Disappointment." When he finished his sermon, the congregation asked him why he had not preached about overcoming disappointment? He insisted that he had preached on that subject. The congregation disagreed; it so happened that he had used their sign for STEP-MOTHER instead of their sign for DISAPPOINTMENT. (Personal correspondence from C. Bruffey, 28 October 1999)

The visiting pastor in this anecdote failed to question congregation members about their local sign usage and, as a result, they misunderstood the entire sermon. Clearly, a traveling evangelist to the Deaf community must verify local or regional signs to ensure audience understanding.

Examination of the data here provides evidence that the pastor in this study is also aware of the issue of lexical variation and of its relevance while preaching a sermon in a new locale. Example 3.1 takes place about halfway through the sermon. The speaker uses his variation of the sign for GOAT and also fingerspells the English word *goat*. Then, the speaker asks the audience members to demonstrate their sign for G-O-A-T.

EXAMPLE 3.1
Pastor:

_____(WH-Q)
GOAT$_1$ G-O-A-T PRO.2 SIGN G-O-A-T
Goat. G-o-a-t. What is your sign for the English word goat?

GOAT$_2$++ (feels beard)
You say goat . . . and your sign is goat, hmmm . . . .

PRO.1 ONE T-H-E-M
I seem to be a goat myself.

NO++ HAND-WAVING NOT
No, no, not really!

Interpreter:
You know, goats . . .goat.
I'm one of them because I have a . . . I have a goatee.

The pastor uses his sign for *goat*, then fingerspells the English word *goat*. He explicitly asks the congregation members for their sign for the term, repeats what he sees, and then moves on to joke about his resemblance to a goat, given the small beard on his chin. Here is a clear example of a dialogic interaction between a speaker and an audience. A direct question is asked and answered in a formal setting, specifically, a sermon during a Deaf church worship service that, in a typical hearing setting, is perceived as being monologic in nature (Parvin, 1992, p. 44; Post, 1992, p. 102). The information requested by the speaker was necessary to ensure that audience members would understand the message without being hindered by unfamiliarity with a nonlocal sign. Furthermore, this question takes the form of a WH question, which is an open-ended question that allows the audience to interact with the speaker for a longer period of time than a simple yes-no response. Perhaps because open-ended questions tend to require a longer response time than Y/N questions, the other three examples of questions on local sign usage take the form of Y/N responses. In particular, Examples 3.2 and 3.3 show the speaker using Y/N questions for verification purposes to avoid the possibility of misunderstandings because of local sign usage.

EXAMPLE 3.2
Pastor:
MANY CHILDREN LOOK-UP++ S-P-O-R-T-S PLAY-PERSON
Many children look up to athletes

$$\underline{\qquad}\text{Y/N-Q}$$
BASEBALL FOOTBALL$_1$ FOOTBALL$_2$ FOOTBALL$_1$
From such sports as baseball, football—or do you sign football this way? Football.

Interpreter:
Where are children,
who today are starving to look for those to give them proper example,
like sports figures.

In Example 3.2, the pastor is discussing the issue of athletes as role models in the lives of children. As he identifies various sports that bring these role models to American youth, he signs FOOTBALL, then signs a second variant, asking with a Y/N question as indicated nonmanually, whether that variant is preferred by the congregation. He then returns to the first variant.

EXAMPLE 3.3
Pastor:
MEET DIFFERENT++ PEOPLE CULTURE OF-COURSE
I have met many people from a variety of cultures.

UNDERSTAND MANY DEAF FLOCK GALLAUDET
You know, a lot of deaf people choose to go to Gallaudet . . .

DIFFERENT++ STATE S-T-A-T-E-S
They come from all different states, s-t-a-t-e-s

                        Y/N-Q
_____
RIGHT SIGN STATE++ (head nod)
Is this your sign? States? Alright.

Interpreter:
I have met several people.
I have seen the cultural influences of the city including Gallaudet University.
And how the university represents deaf people from all over the United States.

In Example 3.3, the pastor is discussing the fact that Gallaudet serves students from all over the United States. As he mentions that these students are from different states, he first uses one sign variant and then fingerspells the English word *states*. He next asks the congregation with a Y/N question whether they use the same sign variant he is using.

Example 3.3 illustrates the ease with which a pastor can initiate and conclude a question-answer adjacency pair in a visual language such as ASL. The question is asked and answered quickly and smoothly, and he scarcely misses a beat in the sermon flow.

In both Examples 3.2 and 3.3, the speaker questions the audience to verify the linguistic accuracy of a sign. In Example 3.2, he offers the option of a second variant. In Example 3.3, he does not; he simply uses one variant, STATE, then fingerspells S-T-A-T-E and asks whether the lexical sign demonstrated is a variant acceptable to the congregation. Clearly, the speaker wishes to make sure of the audience's sign preference and avoid misunderstandings.

In Example 3.4, the final example of questions related to local sign usage, the pastor once again offers two variants for a particular sign. Interestingly, in this example, the second variant is actually initiated by someone else during the course of the sermon.

EXAMPLE 3.4
Pastor:
POSS.1(pl) IDEA
Our idea,

POSS.1(pl) PHILOSOPHY
Our philosophy,

POSS.1(pl) EXPERIENCE
Our experience,

POSS.1(pl) TRADITION
Our tradition,

POSS.1(pl) CULTURE$_1$
Our culture,

POSS.1(pl) CULTURE$_2$
Our culture (uses a different sign)

THANK-YOU CORRECT PRO.1
Thanks for correcting me.

Y/N-Q
CULTURE$_2$ C-U-L-T-U-R-E (looks at audience member and head nods)
Is this your sign for culture? The English word c-u-l-t-u-r-e, yes.

Interpreter:
We try to develop Christians in the church.
And what we . . . we try to develop them in the way we want them or the way we think they should develop and grow.
Traditionally, we say our culture or (Interpreter's name) adds the *r* at the end.
Culture. Our culture. We'll spell it.

In Example 3.4, the pastor receives a lexical variant suggestion from someone in the midst of his sermon. As a result, and similar to the signing of two variants for FOOTBALL in Example 3.2, he offers two variants for CULTURE, and accepts the variant shown by the interpreter.

These four examples are evidence of this speaker's desire to be sure the audience is familiar with the signs he uses. In this way, he avoids the problem mentioned in the earlier anecdote about the visiting pastor using the local sign for STEP-MOTHER instead of DISAPPOINTMENT. The way that this Deaf pastor avoids misunderstanding is to ask the congregation directly, even though a sermon is a formal discourse genre.

The four examples of questions initiated by the pastor to the congregation in this section consist entirely of questions about local sign usage. One example represents an open-ended WH question, and three are Y/N questions. In one of these three examples, the pastor simply uses his variant, STATES, and asks whether it is the sign used by the congregation. In the remaining two Y/N questions, the pastor actually signs two different variants as he asks whether one of them is the lexical variant that the congregation prefers.

OTHER INFORMATION REQUESTS

In addition to questions about local sign usage, the Deaf pastor directly questions the congregation to derive other needed information. One example of this questioning may serve to ask congregation members about their knowledge of a particular scriptural reference before using it during the sermon.

The late Reverend Bruffey shared the following example of this kind of question function. If he planned to preach a sermon based on John 3:14–16 and intended to incorporate a reference to Moses and the brazen serpent, he would first ask congregation members whether they were familiar with the story before proceeding with the sermon. If that scripture reference were unknown, he would briefly tell the story of Moses and the serpent before proceeding with the sermon. In this way, he would avoid confusing the audience and risking the possibility that they would fail to grasp the point of the story (Personal correspondence from C. Bruffey, 1 November 1999). In the current study, 40% of the questions were asked to obtain information other than sign or lexical variants. This category was evenly split on question format, with two of the questions being Y/N and two being WH questions. All were requests for verification of proper names: two for names of individuals, one for an organization's name, and one for a local attraction's name.

In Example 3.5, the speaker struggles to recall the singer who introduced a sign for *helpless* in the song that preceded the sermon. The speaker scans the audience in search of the face and is directed to the singer, whom he then acknowledges.

EXAMPLE 3.5

Pastor:

H-E THAT PERSON MAN SAW PEOPLE STUN (point to audience with questioning look)

This man recognized that people were helpless.

           WH-Q

WOMAN SIGN SHOCK H-E-L-P (head nods, index right) H-E-L-P-L-E-S-S

Where is that lady who showed us the sign STUN *for* HELPLESS? *Oh yes, there she is!*

SHOCK

Yes, we are helpless.

Interpreter:

As this gentleman would see people who were helpless.

As (name of singer) has shared with us the sign before she sang.

As he would see helpless people . . .

In Example 3.5, the pastor uses a WH question to ask the congregation the location of a member who demonstrated a sign earlier in the revival service. The pastor-initiated question receives a response from the congregation, and the pastor then uses the information by acknowledging the woman with a point and a nod.

Example 3.6 is another case of searching for information related to a proper name. In this utterance, the pastor struggles to recall the name a of famous talk-show host. Eventually the audience indicates recognition of the personality, and the speaker is satisfied with the name he had been using for her. The actual talk-show host's name is Sally Jessie Raphael, which was what the interpreter spoke, although the speaker called her Sally Jessica. The Deaf audience recognizes the person he was talking about by way of her physical description. However, the hearing audience members recognize the allusion only after hearing her true proper name, which was what occurred in the interpretation (see next section for a more detailed discussion of this example).

EXAMPLE 3.6
Pastor to the audience:
NOW TALK S-H-O-W
She is with a talk show . . .

J-E-S-S-I-C-A   NO++
Jessica—no, no

<u>   WH-Q</u>
S-A-L-L-Y   J-E-S-S-I-C-A
Her name is Sally Jessica . . . what is her name?

RIGHT++
Yes, yes.

WOMAN RED H-A-I-R Cl:5 (2h) (hair slicked back)
She's the one with red hair

Cl: open 9 (2h) (at the eyes indicating large glasses) GLASSES (2h)
And big glasses

Interpreter:
Movie stars, uh . . . Jessica . . . Jessica . . . the woman . . .
she has red . . . . .red hair. I forget. . . .
big . . . big glasses.
Sally Jessie Raphael. The talk program.

In Example 3.6, the pastor asks the congregation what the last name is of the talk-show host to whom he refers. Although he does not get an answer to the content of his question, he does get a response from Deaf members of the congregation indicating that they understand whom he means. This response is sufficient for him to continue with his sermon.

Example 3.7 is distinct from the previous two because the speaker directs a question to a particular audience member to verify his use of an appropriate acronym for an organizational unit within the church.

EXAMPLE 3.7
Pastor to audience member:
BUT PRO.1 (pl) STORY GOOD HAPPEN THINGS
We would talk about some of the positive things that were going on.

S-B-C-D FLOCK INDEX (rt)
When people gathered at SBCD

F-M-P-D WOMAN INDEX AND M-A-P-S (lt)
There were two auxiliary groups that meet also FMPD and MAPS

<u>   Y/N-Q</u>
CORRECT PRO.1
Am I right?

RIGHT++ (nods)
Yes, that's right.

Interpreter:
Obviously, we'd share good things that were going on.
Then at SBCD (Southern Baptist Conference of the Deaf),
we had a Fellowship of Missionaries and Pastors for the Deaf [FMPD].
And then there was uh . . . (name of a woman in congregation) might have to correct me, but uh, the Fellowship of Missionary and Pastor Wives [MAPSF].

In Example 3.7, the pastor directs his question to a specific member of the audience who he believes will be able to answer his question about the name of the organization for which the acronym is *MAPSF*. Locker McKee (1992) describes this type of insert in nonreligious, monologic, formal ASL discourse and describes it as an aside. This example provides evidence that these asides also can happen in the midst of an ASL sermon.

The final example in the category of other requests for information, Example 3.8, deals with a question about the name of a local attraction, RFK stadium. The speaker tries to remember whether the area he is visiting has a stadium and what the name of the stadium is. In fact, this example contains several questions in one example.

EXAMPLE 3.8
Pastor:
MAYBE GO R-F-K (looks up and to the right thinking)
Maybe go to RFK stadium . . .

<u>   Y/N-Q</u>
PRO.1 WRONG
Do I have that right?

RIGHT++
Yes.

<u>   Y/N-Q</u>
R-F-K HERE
Where is RFK, is it local for you all?

RIGHT++ WONDERFUL S-T-A-D-I-U-M
Yes . . . it's a great stadium!

<u>   Y/N-Q</u>
RIGHT R-F-K PRO.2
Your local stadium is RFK stadium, isn't it?

HAND-STOP RELIEVE
Whew, that's what I thought!

Interpreter:
Did you have . . . ? Do you have a stadium? RFK stadium? Right!
I was think . . . I was thinking you did.

For the first of the three questions in Example 3.8, the speaker asks himself whether the area in which he is preaching is indeed the location for RFK stadium. This question is not the first part of an interactional question-answer adjacency pair. The next question is asked of the audience and then basically repeated for clarification. The third question is a Y/N question that is clearly directed to the audience and that receives a clear response.

Four examples of questions requesting information other than that related to lexical variation are described here. Of these four, two are WH questions and two are Y/N questions. Interestingly, although these requests are not for lexical signs per se, they all relate to requests for names of people and places, both of which, like local sign preferences, are predictably unfamiliar to a visiting pastor.

ESTABLISHING SOLIDARITY AND RAPPORT

Establishing audience rapport or solidarity is another reason that the Deaf pastor in this study uses direct questions. When a Deaf evangelist comes into a town to preach, he or she wants to establish a bond with the audience, so the evangelist may mention the names of local people with whom he or she is acquainted and ask audience members whether they also know those individuals. In a similar fashion, the evangelist may mention points of interest in the local area that he or she has visited and ask audience members whether they have also seen those places. Similarly, the visiting pastor may bring up a subject such as sports to capture the attention of the audience before proceeding with the sermon. In this way, the evangelist is able to establish a common bond with the people in that area (Personal correspondence from C. Bruffey, 1 November 1999). In this case study, 20% of the questions were asked to establish solidarity or audience rapport.

In Examples 3.9 and 3.10, the speaker asks questions to establish a rapport with the audience. Example 3.9 could even be labeled an icebreaker; the speaker asks whether the members of the congregation enjoy politics, and that question becomes a springboard into his later comments.

EXAMPLE 3.9

Pastor:

LIKE PEOPLE LIKE POLITICS (shoulders shrug)
I like . . . well.. people like politics.
_____Y/N-Q

PRO.2 LIKE POLITICS?
Do you like politics?

DISCUSS++
People get into heated debates about politics.

Interpreter:

As we view the political scene, we can't believe how, not only in D.C., but all over the world, how politics has been brought to a new priority in people's lives and our country's lives.

In this example, the pastor asks the audience whether they have an interest in politics. This question is a strategy the pastor uses to involve the audience, and he refers to it later in the sermon, adding cohesion to the discourse as a whole.

Example 3.10 provides evidence for the pastor's desire for solidarity as he talks about Lamaze classes. One of the ways in which this question searches for solidarity and rapport is by verifying audience understanding of the topic being discussed. As described earlier, when preaching in an unfamiliar church, Rev. Bruffey would intentionally mention sports or local attractions to establish a common bond with a congregation. In a similar way, this visiting pastor wants to relate to the audience through a shared awareness of Lamaze, but he wants to be sure the audience was familiar with Lamaze before proceeding with his sermon. Audience rapport and understanding are keys to a successful discourse strategy in this case, and the speaker uses this question to effectively accomplish that goal.

EXAMPLE 3.10

Pastor:

CLASS PRO.1 TAKE-UP WITH WIFE
My wife and I once took a Lamaze class

FIRST BABY AWKWARD CALLED L-A-M-A-Z-E
Because we had no experience with infants before the birth of our first child

---
                                Y/N-Q
PRO.2 (pl) WOMAN KNOW TALK ABOUT?
Perhaps some of you women know what I am referring to?

YES++ (both hands) (laughs and nods head)
Yes, I see that you do.

Interpreter:
When our first child was conceived, we were awkward,
and we didn't know what to expect.
We went to Lamaze classes.
Some of you are laughing.
You did the same thing.

In the third line of Example 3.10, the pastor asks some of the women in the congregation whether they have heard of Lamaze classes. They respond affirmatively, and the pastor laughs, and reiterates their affirmative response, emphasizing it, in fact, by signing the normally one-handed sign YES with both hands. The pastor has successfully made a connection with these members of the congregation and has confirmed that at least some of the audience members are familiar with the topic at hand.

SUMMARY OF QUESTION FUNCTIONS
The questions initiated by the pastor during this sermon in a Deaf church assumed several forms, including both Y/N and WH questions. Furthermore, the questions served a number of purposes: verifying local sign usage, gathering needed information about the local area, as well as establishing audience solidarity and rapport. The author has personally and informally observed the use of these devices also at other Deaf churches around the United States, including churches in Virginia, Missouri, and Texas. The use of question forms and functions in the sermons of Deaf pastors at churches in a variety of regions is an area for further study.

The use of questions during a sermon in a Deaf congregation can be contrasted with what happens during a sermon in a hearing church.

Seldom, if ever, do pastors in hearing churches ask direct questions of the congregation. According to Doug Munton, pastor of First Baptist Church of O'Fallon, Illinois (Personal correspondence from D. Munton, November 28, 1999), the rationale for this approach can be attributed to the sheer numbers of people involved. The situation in which one questioner might interact with large numbers of people giving a response would be awkward. Another reason not to use questions during a sermon is that someone may give an incorrect answer that would necessitate a detailed rebuttal and consume valuable time (Personal correspondence from D. Munton, November 28, 1999). As a result of these factors, hearing pastors are reluctant to ask the congregation questions during a sermon, which is perceived as strictly a monologic event. The examples found in these data were relatively rapid interactions and added little in the way of distraction or added time to the sermon itself. A possible reason for this dynamic is the mode of the discourse itself; a visual language such as ASL lends itself more readily to a quick interaction in the midst of the formal discourse.

ISSUES RELATED TO THE INTERPRETATION OF QUESTION-ANSWER ADJACENCY PAIRS IN AN ASL SERMON

If Deaf pastors, as compared to hearing pastors, frequently use questions during their sermons, how should the interpreter handle this source utterance? These kinds of interpreting questions have often been answered in theory but rarely have been examined through empirical study. Some of the issues that an interpreter faces are the same issues that interpreters and translators have faced for centuries (compare Lefevre, 1992). One central concern to interpreters and translators focuses on the issue of form as compared to meaning. For example, in the current data, the pastor uses both WH and Y/N questions. In some schools of thought, the interpretation might attempt to maintain the form of the source by translating the pastor's questions into a similar syntactic question form in the target language, using a WH question in the target language to represent one in the signed source message. For the purpose of this paper, the assumption will follow the notion that, for signed language interpreters in the United States, an interpretation is a meaning-based translation whereas a transliteration is a form-based translation (see, e.g., Frishberg, 1990; Metzger & Fleetwood, 1997; Siple, 1997). That said, a meaning-based interpretation such as the one performed in these data must face a second issue that is central to interpretation and translation—that of equivalence.

Equivalence is likely the most important goal of an interpreter. However, since the time of Aristotle, disagreements about the nature of equivalence have been documented (Wadensjö, 1992). Equivalence of form leads back to the question of meaning as compared to form discussed above. If an interpreter were to translate a poem and maintain the form of it, the poem in the target language might end up as a sequence of words that do not carry the linguistic and cultural intent of the poet (see Metzger, 1999, for a more in-depth review of the issue of equivalence). Equivalence of form relates to the phonologic structure of a language, the most basic level at which languages are apt to differ. At the same time, focusing on the meaning of a source text may be equally problematic; the meaning of a text is reflected not only by the speaker of it but also by the audience and all the world knowledge, cultural biases, and social experience that the audience brings to the task of comprehension (see Nida, 1964). Nida's (1964) focus on the importance of equivalence and effect are of especial importance when discussing interactive interpretation. In the case of this study, what effect would the pastor's requests for local sign variants have on the hearing audience? How would two sign variants representing one English word be interpreted into English? With these questions in mind, we will now turn to an analysis of the ways in which the interpreters translated the questions examined in the previous section.

Interpretation of Local Sign Usage

As seen earlier, the pastor initiated four questions to the congregation that related to local sign usage. Of these, one is a WH question and three are Y/N questions. Of the three Y/N questions, one includes a single lexical variant, and the other two include two lexical variants.

Translation of linguistic-related questions can be quite challenging. In Example 3.1, the WH question, the interpreter would have difficulty mentioning the discussion about the two different signs for GOAT. That is, a literal interpretation of the discussion between speaker and congregation about sign variations of GOAT might look something like, "What's your sign for GOAT? This is my sign for GOAT. What's your sign for GOAT? Oh! That's your sign for GOAT." To the uninitiated, "this sign" and "that sign" mean no more than any other sign generated by the speaker. Thus, the inclusion of the regional sign variation question into the target language of English is not a matter of a simple translation if the interpreter is trying to express an equivalence of meaning. In the sample translation about the sign for GOAT, the hearing audience would clearly not get the same effect as the Deaf audience.

According to the interpreters at the event under examination, they chose for this reason to omit the question about lexical variation while managing to incorporate the joke made by the speaker in a way that the hearing audience could understand. The visual joke of the speaker being a goat because he has a beard is amusing to the Deaf audience. The speaker first mentions goats and then strokes his own beard before making the comment that he is a goat, too. Thus, the Deaf audience member makes the visual connection between the goat's tuft of fur under its chin and the speaker's beard—an amusing visual joke.

Despite the fact that the joke is a visual one, the interpreter is able to capture the humorous concept for the target hearing audience by saying that the pastor is a goat because he has a goatee. This visual joke is an implicit reference that the Deaf congregation has understood on a level that native English speakers would not, but it can translate into an English pun of sorts; because the speaker has a *goat*ee, he is a goat! Here, the interpreter makes use of expansion techniques—to translate the visual joke into an acoustic one—to bring about the cultural mediation necessary for the target audience to get the point of the joke. If the interpreter had not added the phrase "because I have a goatee," then the hearing members of the audience would most likely not have understood the humor in the pastor's comment, particularly because the interpretation does not overlap in time with the moment at which the pastor touches his beard. In this case, the exclusion of the question about the local sign GOAT does not produce any interactional difficulties, and explication of the reference to the pastor's goatee is necessary to understand the humorous remark.

In two of the three Y/N questions, the interpreter applies a similar strategy. In Examples 3.2 and 3.3, the interpreters simply omit the question-answer adjacency pairs that relate to the signs for FOOTBALL and STATES. As in the first example, no evidence indicates that this omission causes any difficulties or problems with the sermon or the interpretation. However, in the third Y/N question, which occurs in Example 3.4, the interpreters do incorporate the interaction (Example 3.4 is repeated on the next page for convenience).

EXAMPLE 3.4
Pastor:
POSS.1(pl) IDEA
Our idea,

POSS.1(pl) PHILOSOPHY
Our philosophy,

POSS.1(pl) EXPERIENCE
Our experience,

POSS.1(pl) TRADITION
Our tradition,

POSS.1(pl) CULTURE₁
Our culture,

POSS.1(pl) CULTURE₂
Our culture (uses a different sign)

THANK-YOU CORRECT PRO.1
Thanks for correcting me.

Y/N-Q
CULTURE₂ C-U-L-T-U-R-E (looks at audience member and head nods)
Is this your sign for culture? The English word c-u-l-t-u-r-e, yes.

Interpreter:
We try to develop Christians in the church.
And what we . . . we try to develop them in the way we want them
or the way we think they should develop and grow.
Traditionally, we say our culture or (Interpreter's name) adds the *r* at
the end.
Culture. Our culture. We'll spell it.

In this example, the translation of the question causes some potential
awkwardness in the target utterance. To the extent that interpreters strive
toward naturalness in their target utterances (and they do; see e.g., Gile,

1995; Hatim & Mason, 1990, 1997), this target utterance could be less than understandable to the target audience. They may have questions about what it means to say, "We'll spell it," particularly because, in the English target utterances, the word is spoken and not spelled.

With respect to local sign usage then, evidence shows that an interpreter might include an interpretation of the interaction or exclude it. Because the goal of interpretation is to provide equivalence, using exclusion as a strategy seems counterintuitive. Perhaps excluding translation of the question-answer interactions here seems to suffice because the hearing audience likely has experience with hearing pastors in hearing churches where that kind of interaction is not typical. Signed language interpreters can choose from a number of strategies that could be used in a metalinguistic situation such as the request for local sign usage. These include spoken, physical descriptions of signs; general summary of the content; and collaboration with the speaker to coordinate their relevant signs within the spoken translation:

· Physical description (e.g., "signed with hand near face or down near chest")
· General summary (e.g., "I know of two different signs to represent the game of football. What is your sign? I will use your sign.")
· Working with speaker (e.g., "I sign football like this [point to pastor and ask for repetition of sign variant 1]. You sign it this way? [Again ask for repetition, this time of sign variant 2.]")

Because the issue of sign variation involves linguistic information within the discourse itself, it is somewhat unique. The interpreters' decision to exclude some of these questions is quite different from their handling of other requests for nonlinguistic information as can be seen in the following section.

Interpretation of Other Information Requests

The pastor initiates four requests for information other than lexical variants. Of these, two are WH questions and two are Y/N questions. Of the four, the content of all are included in the target utterance in one form or another. Content for some requests are included in the target utterance using a question form, and other requests are included in target utterances in such a way that the question carries pragmatically. Other target utterances exclude the question-answer interaction entirely but incorporate the relevant information that the pastor obtains.

The latter approach can be seen in the interpreter's utterance in Example 3.5 where the question—asking for the name of the singer who informed the congregation of a sign before singing—was omitted (the line from Example 3.5 is repeated here for convenience).

Interpreter:
As this gentleman would see people who were helpless. As (name of singer) has shared with us the sign before she sang.

Despite the omission of the question-answer pair, the woman's name is included in the interpreter's target utterance. In this case, equivalence of meaning and equivalence of effect is achieved. Interactional equivalence is not achieved because the hearing audience has not received an interpretation of the interactive element. However, in a sense, for hearing revivalists, the informational element without the interactional element may provide a measure of equivalence in terms of discourse genre because, as we have seen, hearing revivalists are used to pastors who engage in these kinds of interactions infrequently, if ever.

In Example 3.6, again, the interpreter provides no explicit interpretation of a question directed to the congregation about the name of the talk show host. However, at a pragmatic level, the interpreter does incorporate the speaker's hesitancy and uncertainty with respect to her name (the interpreter line from Example 3.6 is repeated here for convenience).

Interpreter:
Movie stars, uh . . . Jessica . . . Jessica . . . the woman . . . she has red . . . red hair.
I forget . . . big . . . big glasses.
Sally Jessie Raphael.

The interpreter then uses the actual name of the talk show host, despite the fact that the pastor does not. Once again, this approach may seem counter to the notion of equivalence. However, it is important to contextualize the pastor's use of a physical description of the talk show host, including hair color and eyeglasses as descriptors. In many signed language communities, the use of name signs is often and, in some cases, primarily a descriptive phenomenon based on physical characteristics or features of the person to whom the name sign refers (Locker McKee & McKee, 2000). For this reason, a common approach for interpreters is to regularly make translations between signed name signs and spoken proper names. The interpreters' choice to do so in this example allowed the interpretation to provide what Nida (1964) calls "dynamic" equivalence, equivalence in effect for both the source and target audiences.

The third request for information other than local sign usage, Example 3.7, is the one in which the speaker directs a question to a particular audience member to verify the use of an appropriate acronym for an organizational unit within the church. In this case, the interpreter does not include the question per se but retains an element of uncertainty as to the veracity of the comment (the interpreter line from Example 3.7 is repeated here for convenience).

> Interpreter:
> Obviously, we'd share good things that were going on.
> Then at SBCD, Southern Baptist Conference of the Deaf,
> we had a fellowship of missionaries and pastors for the Deaf.
> And then there was uh . . . (name of a woman in congregation) might have to correct me,
> but uh, the fellowship of missionary and pastor wives.

Although the form of the question does not appear in the target utterance, the interpreter does include an explicit invitation for the woman being addressed to correct the pastor. Once again, the meaning is equivalent despite the difference in syntactic form.

The final question in this category is Example 3.8 in which the pastor requests confirmation that RFK is the name of the local stadium. In this example, the interpreters do interpret Y/N questions to represent the question initiated by the pastor (the interpreter line from Example 3.8 is repeated here for convenience).

> Interpreter:
> Did you have . . . ? Do you have a stadium? RFK stadium? Right!
> I was thinking you did.

This example in which both the syntactic form and the pragmatic function of the question appear in the translation is the clearest case of equivalence.

In the category of requests for information other than local sign usage, evidence has shown that the interpreters include the content, in one form or another, for all of the pastor-initiated questions. Interestingly, the source Y/N questions are more related to question forms in the target message than are the source message's WH questions. This finding certainly provides an area ripe for further research in any type of interactive interpretations. Also of interest is the fact that these questions are included at one or another level of equivalence, unlike those related to local sign usage.

Interpretation of Questions for Establishing Solidarity and Rapport

The pastor asks two questions to establish solidarity and rapport with his audience. Both of these take the form of Y/N questions. As described earlier, each of these questions is asked to establish solidarity and rapport with the members of the congregation. Interestingly, the interpreters do use English-based involvement strategies to establish rapport, and these pragmatically consistent strategies result in a meaning-based interpretation that differs in syntactic form; no questions appear in the target utterances.

In Example 3.9, the pastor directly asks the congregation whether they have an interest in politics. The interpreter does not include a question form in the translation (the interpreter line from Example 3.9 is repeated here for convenience).

Interpreter:
As we view the political scene, we can't believe how, not only in D.C., but all over the world, how politics has been brought to a new priority in people's lives and our country's lives.

Rather than use a question in the target language, the interpreter commiserates with the congregation in the manner of ritual complaints as discussed by Tannen (1986). Tannen shows that, in English, ritual complaints are one strategy that speakers use to establish a bond with their interlocutors. Thus, the interpretation can be seen to carry equivalence at the discourse level because it applies an involvement strategy common in the target language to accomplish the same effect as the strategy used in the source message.

The pastor also uses a Y/N question in Example 3.10 to establish a bond with members of the congregation, although once again, no question form appears in the translation (the interpreter line from Example 3.10 is repeated here for convenience).

Interpreter:
When our first child was conceived, we were awkward,
and we didn't know what to expect.
We went to Lamaze classes.
Some of you are laughing.
You did the same thing.

Here, the interpretation includes an explicit mention of the bond by mentioning that some of the audience members have clearly had similar experiences. The target utterance maintains equivalence at the discourse level despite the absence of syntactic equivalence.

In both Example 3.9 and Example 3.10, the effect of creating a bond between the speaker and audience is achieved through both the source and target languages. In Example 3.9, the speaker is able to commiserate with audience members about the powerful political arena, and in Example 3.10, he laughs with them about taking classes where adults learn how to "breathe" and "focus." In the target messages, the speaker alternates between sharing ritual complaints and sharing lighter moments with the audience members. The dynamic effect is the same for both Deaf and hearing members because the audience is drawn into a closer relationship with the speaker through shared experiences.

In the 10 examples of pastor-initiated questions, nearly three-quarters (70%) were interpreted with clear evidence of equivalence at some level. Seleskovitch (1978) points out that, most of the time, words do not have direct equivalents in other languages:

> There are words that have direct equivalents in other languages, just as there are words that are "untranslatable." This is a cliché which, for once, is true, but with one small correction: untranslatable words are the rule, and words that always have exact translations the exception. (Seleskovitch, 1978, p. 73)

If a question were asked about local sign usage, the vocalization of that question could be confusing to a hearing audience member who is unfamiliar with the language, and it could even be considered a linguistic intrusion in the target message. Regional sign variation questions are not readily a meaningful part of the interpretation for hearing audience members. In fact, an attempt to interpret these kinds of questions could result in so literal an interpretation that a spoken description of the signed phonology of the variant would be necessary. This type of situation can be compared to trying to interpret into American Sign Language a difference in accent or pronunciation of a word spoken in English. Clearly, instances involving the inclusion of direct questions to the audience about local sign usage were the most problematic because they comprised 30% of questions that were intentionally omitted from the interpretation.

CONCLUSION

In this case study, documentation has been provided to support the hypothesis that a Deaf speaker and Deaf audience members interact even in formal settings such as church worship services, which are typically monologic events in similar hearing Caucasian settings. The pastor-initiated questions, both WH and Y/N in form, had three functions in this case: verification of lexical information, requests for other kinds of information, or questions to establish solidarity or rapport with the audience. Examination of these pastor-initiated questions and the ways in which they are interpreted has implications for the fields of linguistics and interpretation as well as for the religious setting itself.

Linguistic implications relate to the general finding that, in this case at least, an ASL sermon incorporates interactive features not typically found in hearing sermons. As is true in any case study, one needs to recognize the limitations of the study. Thus, in this case, the fact that the pastor is a visiting pastor is noteworthy with respect to at least two categories of question types: lexical variants and other requests for information. Because revival services may often be conducted by visiting pastors, it is pertinent to this setting and genre to identify the frequency and types of questions that are asked by visiting pastors. In fact, it would be worthwhile to extend this study with a larger corpus of data, including sermons for revival services from many pastors giving sermons around the United States. This study also raises a question about the role of question-answer adjacency pairs in sermons given by local pastors; that is, do local pastors also use question-answer adjacency pairs as an interactional strategy? If so, how do their questions differ from those found in this study? These questions indicate another area for further research.

Additional research is warranted to study a variety of types of religious discourse, including sermons from services other than revival services and from a variety of churches and denominations. Finally, future research is needed to study discourse strategies such as question-answer adjacency pairs in any formal ASL lecture or presentation. Studies that provide a better understanding of the use of question-answer adjacency pairs in ASL discourse could be useful not only for pastors and other lecturers and presenters but also for linguists who want to understand variation in ASL at the discourse level.

The use of direct questions by the Deaf speaker in this Deaf religious setting also demonstrates the need to consider these discourse tools in the practice of interpreting. Further research such as that just mentioned is needed to better understand the discourse styles of Deaf preachers in Deaf churches. To achieve equivalence at the discourse level, interpreters in hearing churches may be able to use these discourse devices in their English-to-ASL interpretations. Apparently, despite the formality of the setting, Deaf audiences crave a more interactive style than is found in hearing settings. With a better grasp of the needs of Deaf consumers in formal settings such as the religious arena, interpreters could provide a more satisfactory interpretation.

Moreover, interpreters are often called to interpret for hearing speakers in formal platform situations where a large number of Deaf audience members may be present. Being sure that the audience members understand the signs being used is crucial to the success of the interpretation. Perhaps, further research on this interpretation issue can be designed to parallel this study of a Deaf speaker in a Deaf setting. This research could attempt to determine whether the use of questions and interaction on the part of interpreters with audience members can become a viable interpreting strategy to achieve naturalness and equivalence. For example, in research on English-to-ASL interpretation, a study could be made to determine whether interpreters use the discourse strategies demonstrated by the Deaf speaker in the examples discussed here in which the interpreter directs a question to audience members about signs that are subject to regional variation. Clearly, more research along these lines could positively influence the quality and effectiveness not only of interpretation but also of interpreter education.

The pursuit of equivalence and the related avoidance of misunderstanding is crucial in any setting but is especially important in the religious setting that has special challenges because of the complexities inherent in the type of language used in the Bible (see Nida & Reyburn, 1981, for more on Bible complexities). Using the wrong sign can cause gross misunderstanding or failure to understand the entire message, which occurred when the visiting pastor from Texas used the wrong sign for DISAPPOINTMENT in the anecdote described earlier. A simple question about local sign usage would have avoided this problem.

Even one single error can cause misunderstanding of the entire message, and the consequences can be disastrous. Sampley (1990) cites an example of how even one wrong sign can skew the entire message. A hearing pastor stated that Jesus' blood is "precious"; however, the interpreter did not sign PRECIOUS but, instead, signed WORTHLESS, a sign with similar attributes. The result was a skewing of the message in a catastrophic, even heretical way (Sampley, 1990, p. 62). The importance of having a qualified interpreter working in the church cannot be overstated (Parvin, 1992, p. 35) because, although consumers in a medical situation may be concerned that errors will affect their health and consumers in a legal setting may have concerns that errors will affect their freedom, consumers in a religious setting may be concerned that errors will have eternal consequences. As evidenced in example of the interpreter using the sign WORTHLESS instead of PRECIOUS, the potential exists for gross misunderstanding of the message. Indeed, a comment often heard among religious interpreters is that church interpreting errors have the potential for the most devastating results for the Deaf consumer.

Because, historically, relatively little attention has been paid to signed language interpretation in religious settings, perhaps a comparison of worst-case scenarios may help the reader understand the point that every setting requires preparation and dedication to excellence. For consumers, a concern might be that, in a medical setting, the worst-case scenario of an interpreting error would be their death; in a legal setting, their imprisonment or execution. However, a consumer who is subjected to a major error in a church setting might be concerned that he or she could spend eternity in hell. Clearly, from a consumer perspective, the outcomes of interpretation in a religious setting have the potential to be the longest lasting.

The point here is not to offend or frighten potential religious interpreters but to point out the fact that, whether working with adults or children in a medical office, a courtroom, or a church, every setting requires interpreters to prepare themselves. Furthermore, in every setting, the possibility exists for repercussions resulting from interpreting errors, repercussions that are of great concern to consumers. As he or she would do in other settings, the novice religious interpreter should seek out a seasoned interpreter-mentor who has the appropriate expertise and who can provide the training necessary to work effectively in this setting.

ACKNOWLEDGMENTS

Special thanks to Dr. Val Dively for her technical expertise and advice, to Holly Roth for contributing her time and many talents, and to Dr. Melanie Metzger for her willingness to share her knowledge and for her boundless encouragement. In addition, a commemorative thanks to the late Clifford Bruffey for countless fascinating hours of discussion on this topic and for sharing his insight into the Deaf church. And last, but certainly not least, thanks for the good Lord, without whom none of this work would have been possible!

APPENDIX 3.A
Transcription Conventions

Transcriptions in ASL	
SMALL CAPITALS	The English word commonly glossed to express that ASL concept
FOOTBALL$_1$	One variant of that sign
F-I-N-G-E-R-S-P-E-L-L	A fingerspelled word
(looks to the right)	Describes physical actions of the speaker
Cl:5 claw (on eyes)	Classifier predicate describes handshape (e.g., 5 claw hand) and action or location of classifier
(2h)	Speaker signs using both hands

++	Speaker repeats sign

<u>WH-Q</u> WHY	Who, what, where, when, why questions
<u>Y/N-Q</u> LIKE POLITICS	Question that requires a yes or no response
Translation	English translation of ASL transcriptions

English Transcription Details

. . .	Speaker pauses or hesitates or incomplete sentence

REFERENCES

Angelelli, C. (2001). *Deconstructing the invisible interpreter: A critical study of the interpersonal role of the interpreter in a cross-cultural/linguistic communicative event.* Unpublished doctoral dissertation, Stanford University, Stanford, CA.

Bahan, B., & Supalla, S. (1995). Line segmentation and narrative structure in American Sign Language. In K. Emmorey & J. Reilly (Eds.), *Language, gesture, and space* (pp. 171–191). Hillsdale, NJ: Lawrence Erlbaum.

Berk-Seligson, S. (1990). *The bilingual courtroom.* Chicago: University of Chicago Press.

Blackman, M. J. (2002). Interactive interpretation in African American Pentecostal churches. *Views, 19*(11), 1, 10–12.

Bradfield, C. D. (1979). *Neo-Pentecostalism: A sociological assessment.* Washington, DC: University Press of America.

Bridges, B. (1993). *Gender variation with sex signs.* Unpublished manuscript, Gallaudet University Department of Linguistics and Interpreting, Washington, DC.

Costen, M. W. (1993). *African-American Christian worship.* Nashville, TN: Abingdon Press.

Frazier, E. F. (1971). *The Negro church in America* (6th ed.). New York: Schocken Books.

Frishberg, N. (1990). *Interpreting: An introduction.* Silver Spring, MD: RID Publications.

Gee, J. (1986). Units in the production of narrative discourse. *Discourse Processes, 9,* 391–422.

Gile, D. (1995). *Basic concepts and models for interpreter and translator training*. Amsterdam, Netherlands: John Benjamin.

Goffman, E. (1963). *Behavior in public places*. New York: The Free Press.

Gumperz, J. J., & Hymes, D. (1986). *Directions in sociolinguistics: The ethnography of communication*. Oxford, UK: Blackwell.

Hatim, B., & Mason, I. (1990). *Discourse and the translator*. London: Longman.

Hatim, B., & Mason, I. (1997). *The translator as communicator*. London: Routledge.

Hymes, D. (1972). Models of the interaction of language and social life. In J. Gumperz & D. Hymes (Eds.), *Directions in sociolinguistics: The ethnography of communication* (pp. 35–71). New York: Holt, Rinehart, and Winston.

Joos, M. (1967). *The five clocks*. New York: Harcourt Brace Jovanovich.

Labov, W. (1972). *Sociolinguistic patterns*. Philadelphia: University of Pennsylvania Press.

Lefevre, A. (Ed.). (1992). *Translation/history/culture: A sourcebook*. London: Routledge.

Liddell, S., & Metzger, M. (1998). Gesture in sign language discourse. *Journal of Pragmatics, 30,* 657–697.

Locker McKee, R. (1992). *Footing shifts in American Sign Language lectures*. Unpublished doctoral dissertation, University of California, Los Angeles.

Locker McKee, R., & McKee, D. (2000). Name signs and identity in New Zealand Sign Language. In M. Metzger (Ed.), *Bilingualism and identity in Deaf communities* (pp. 3–40). Washington, DC: Gallaudet University Press.

Lucas, C., Bayley, R., & Valli, C. (2001). *Sociolinguistic variation in American Sign Language*. Washington, DC: Gallaudet University Press.

Mansfield, D. (1993). Gender differences in ASL: A sociolinguistic study of sign choices by Deaf native signers. In E. Winston (Ed.), *Communication forum 1993* (pp. 86–98). Washington, DC: Gallaudet University Department of Linguistics and Interpreting.

Mather, S., & Winston, E. (1998). Spatial mapping and involvement in ASL storytelling. In C. Lucas (Ed.), *Pinky extension, eye gaze, and other sign language intricacies: Language use in Deaf communities* (pp. 183–210). Washington, DC: Gallaudet University Press.

McLoughlin, W. G. (1959). *Modern revivalism*. New York: The Ronald Press.

McLoughlin, W. G. (1978). *Revivals, awakenings, and reform: An essay on religion and social change in America, 1607–1977*. Chicago: The University of Chicago Press.

Metzger, M. (1995). *The paradox of neutrality: A comparison of interpreters' goals with the realities of interactive discourse*. Unpublished doctoral dissertation, Georgetown University, Washington, DC.

Metzger, M. (1999). *Sign language interpreting: Deconstructing the myth of neutrality*. Washington, DC: Gallaudet University Press.

Metzger, M., & Fleetwood, E. (1997). *What is transliteration, anyway?* Paper presented at the Florida RID conference, Tampa, FL.

Nichol, J. T. (1966). *Pentecostalism*. New York: Harper & Row.

Nida, E. (1964). *Toward a science of translating with special reference to principles and procedures involved in Bible translating*. Leiden, Netherlands: E. J. Brill.

Nida, E., & Reyburn, W. D. (1981). *Meaning across cultures*. Maryknoll, NY: Orbis Books.

Padden, C., & Humphries, T. (1988). *Deaf in America: Voices from a culture*. Cambridge, MA: Harvard University Press.

Parvin, D. W. (1992). *That all may understand*. St. Louis, MO: Christian Board of Publication.

Post, E. (1992). *Emily Post's etiquette* (15th ed.). New York: Harper Collins.

Quebedeaux, R. (1976). *The new charismatics: The origins, development, and significance of neo-Pentecostalism*. New York: Doubleday.

Reid, C. (1967). *The empty pulpit: A study in preaching as communication*. New York: Harper & Row.

Roy, C. (1989a). Features of discourse in an American Sign Language lecture. In C. Lucas (Ed.), *Sociolinguistics of the Deaf community* (pp. 231–251). San Diego: Academic Press.

Roy, C. (1989b). *A sociolinguistic analysis of the interpreter's role in the turn exchanges of an interpreted event*. Unpublished doctoral dissertation, Georgetown University, Washington, DC.

Roy, C. (2000). *Interpreting as a discourse process*. New York: Oxford University Press.

Sampley, D. (1990). *A guide to Deaf ministry: Let's sign worthy of the Lord*. Grand Rapids, MI: Zondervan Publishing.

Schegloff, E., & Sacks, H. (1973). Opening up closings. *Semiotica, 7*(4), 289–327.

Seleskovitch, D. (1978). *Interpreting for international conferences*. Washington DC: Pen and Booth.

Shapiro, E. (1993). Socioeconomic variation in American Sign Language. In E. Winston (Ed.), *Communication forum 1993* (pp. 150–175). Washington, DC: Gallaudet University Department of Linguistics and Interpreting.

Shroyer, E., & Shroyer, S. (1984). *Signs across America*. Washington, DC: Gallaudet University Press.

Siple, L. (1997). Historical development of the definition of transliteration. *Journal of Interpretation, 7*(1), 77–100.

Tannen, D. (1986). *That's not what I meant!* New York: Ballantine.

Untener, K. (1999). *Preaching better: Practical suggestions for homilists.* New York: Paulist Press.

Valli, C., & Lucas, C. (1992). *Linguistics of American Sign Language.* Washington, DC: Gallaudet University Press.

Wadensjö, C. (1992). *Interpreting as interaction: On dialogues-interpreting in immigration hearings and medical encounters.* Stockholm, Sweden: Linköping University, Linköping Studies in Arts and Sciences.

Wadensjö, C. (1998). *Interpreting as interaction.* New York: Longman.

Wardhaugh, R. (1998). *An introduction to sociolinguistics* (3rd ed.). Malden, MA: Blackwell.

Willimon, W., & Lischer, R. (Eds.). (1995). *Concise encyclopedia of preaching.* Louisville, KY: Westminster John Knox Press.

Wilson, P. S. (1995). *The practice of preaching.* Nashville, TN: Abingdon Press.

Winston, E. A. (1992). Space and involvement in an American Sign Language lecture. In J. Plant-Moeller (Ed.), *Expanding horizons: Proceedings of the 12th National Convention of the Registry of Interpreters for the Deaf* (pp. 93–105). Silver Spring, MD: RID Publications.

Winston, E. A. (1993). *Spatial mapping in comparative discourse frames in an American Sign Language lecture.* Unpublished doctoral dissertation, Georgetown University, Washington, DC.

Woodward, J. (1976). Black southern signing. *Language in Society, 5,* 211–218.

Woodward, J. (1979). *Signs of sexual behavior.* Silver Spring, MD: T. J. Publishers.

Woodward, J. (1980). *Signs of drug use.* Silver Spring, MD: T. J. Publishers.

Zimmer, J. (1989a). ASL/English interpreting in an interactive setting. In D. Hammond (Ed.), *Proceedings of the 30th Annual Conference of the American Translator's Association* (pp. 225–231). Medford, NJ: Learned Information.

Zimmer, J. (1989b). Toward a description of register variation in American Sign Language. In C. Lucas (Ed.), *Sociolinguistics of the Deaf community* (pp. 253–272). San Diego: Academic Press.

Part II **Monologic Discourse**

A Sociolinguistic Analysis

of the Occurrence and Types

of Omissions Produced by Australian

Sign Language-English Interpreters

Jemina Napier

This chapter presents the findings of a study that explored the linguistic coping strategies of Australian Sign Language (Auslan)-English interpreters (Napier, 2001). The intention of the study was to introduce, for the first time, a sociolinguistic analysis of interpreters working between Auslan and English. Although many academic studies have been completed that focus on signed language interpreting from a sociolinguistic point of view (e.g., Cokely, 1985; Davis, 1990; Metzger, 1995; Roy, 1989), all of them concentrate on the practices of interpreters working between American Sign Language (ASL) and English. Reference to these studies no doubt provides a wider scope of knowledge, and assumptions can be made about the validity of research in relation to Auslan interpreting. Nonetheless, an in-depth sociolinguistic study of Auslan interpreters and their approach to interpreting was much needed to examine this group's practices in an Australian context.

Signed language interpreting has often been referred to as an "emerging profession" (Fenton, 1993; Ozolins & Bridge, 2000; Scott Gibson, 1992), which explains the dearth of research in the area. This study, therefore, contributes to expanding the little knowledge that is available not only about signed language interpreting in general but also about Auslan-English interpreters and their linguistic coping strategies in particular.

Coping strategies can be defined as those methods or techniques adopted by interpreters to ensure that they are best equipped to cope with the variety of different factors that may affect their interpreting.

Interpreters respond to demands from various sources that arise from linguistic factors associated with the languages being used and from nonlinguistic factors such as environmental, interpersonal, and intrapersonal demands (Dean & Pollard, 2001). Coping strategies generally can be considered as those strategies that are used by interpreters to deal with the demands associated with nonlinguistic factors, for example, teamwork and preparation techniques. Notwithstanding, linguistic coping strategies are those strategies that specifically deal with linguistic factors influencing an interpretation. Examples of linguistic coping strategies used by interpreters would include the use of linguistic transference (Davis, 1990), communication management (Roy, 1989), application of linguistic and cultural knowledge (Metzger, 1995), translation style (Napier, 1998a), and the use of additions within an interpretation (Siple, 1995).

The study described here specifically focused on (a) the types of omissions that Auslan-English interpreters made as linguistic coping strategies while interpreting for a university lecture and (b) the extent to which sociolinguistic factors affected the number and types of omissions made. One of the linguistic demands placed on interpreters when interpreting in a university lecture is the lexical density of the text. University lectures are often presented using a structure of language that is more characteristic of written rather than spoken language (Halliday, 1978), meaning that more use of lexical (content) words than functional (grammatical) words is customary. The segment of the university lecture used in the study was, therefore, lexically dense.

One of the unique aspects of the study was that it analyzed the metalinguistic awareness of interpreters by assessing how conscious the interpreters were of what omissions they made and why they made them. Thus, rather than simply identifying erroneous or strategic omissions, the study defined five specific categories of omissions that are based on whether interpreters were conscious of the omissions and whether they made omissions intentionally.

Although the process of identifying levels of metalinguistic awareness could be argued as psycholinguistic, the key point of interest in the study was the sociolinguistic factors that influenced interpreters' decision making in producing omissions. By identifying interpreters' levels of metalinguistic awareness about any omissions made, one could discern the extent to which sociolinguistic factors such as educational background, familiarity with the discourse environment, language register, lexical density of text, and familiarity with terminology affected the number and types of omissions made by the interpreters. The findings related to sociolinguistic factors affecting occurrence and types of omissions during an interpretation of a university lecture could possibly apply to discussion of the sociolinguistic dynamics of other contexts, which may have a different effect on the occurrence and types of omissions made by interpreters. The study is particularly useful in that it presents a new omission taxonomy that can be used by interpreter educators to analyze the "omission potential" of interpretations, thus leading to a heightened metalinguistic awareness among interpreting students and working interpreters.

Before detailing the methodology involved, this chapter provides an overview of the theoretical foundation of the study, including discussion of interpreting from a sociolinguistic point of view, consideration of discourse environmental factors that may influence an interpretation, and exploration of interpreting omissions as errors and as linguistic coping strategies. After this literature review, the chapter describes the methodology used for data collection and analysis, followed by presentation of the results, discussion of the implications of the findings in relation to interpreting in different contexts, and suggestions for future research.

INTERPRETING: A SOCIOLINGUISTIC-SOCIOCULTURAL APPROACH

Various authors (e.g., Cokely, 1985, 1992b; Frishberg, 2000; Metzger, 1995, 1999; Neumann Solow, 2000; Pergnier, 1978; Roy, 1989, 1992, 1996, 2000a) have stated that any study of interpretation should apply a framework of sociolinguistic parameters because interpreters can be seen to mediate not only between two individual languages but also among distinct communities and cultures. Any interpretation, therefore, needs to be based on a linguistic and cultural understanding of the participants within an interaction as well as on their differing norms and values. Scott Gibson (1992) asserted that interpretation involves more than just comprehension of a message. She stated that any interpretation should reexpress the thoughts of one language into another, incorporating the same intent and style that a native speaker of the second language would use.

By adopting a sociolinguistic approach to interpreting, the focus is not on the decoding and reencoding of information in different languages but, rather, on the message that is delivered and the meaning it expresses. A sociolinguistic perspective emphasizes that the crux of any interpretation is to achieve "dynamic equivalence" (Hatim & Mason, 1990), that is, to get the message right by ensuring that the target-language audience derives the same meaning from a message as is intended by the source-language presenter. According to Metzger (1995),

> texts often depend on prior textual experiences in order to evoke significant meanings (intertextuality). When recipients of the discourse have not had experience with language and thus, the relevant prior texts, it becomes the responsibility of the translator to provide a translation that allows the recipients to infer the ideological stances intended in the source. (p. 28)

For an interpreter to provide discourse participants with a sociocultural framework in which to make inferences about "ideological stances," he or she must be bilingual and bicultural. Being bicultural and bilingual is not enough, however, because interpreters also need to have the tools to determine what something means to their target audience and the best way to meaningfully interpret a message so it makes sense with respect to the audience's cultural norms and values. Therefore, interpreters not only need to understand sociolinguistic and sociocultural contexts of their audiences' worldview but also need to use appropriate interpretation methods to ensure that they have the facility to express the meaning of a message within a sociocultural framework.

The premise of "frame theory" provides a foundation for interpreters to make inferences about what is meaningful to interlocutors between whom they are interpreting, a foundation that then provides interpreters with the tools to use a process of "free interpretation" as they apply this frame theory to the interpreting process. These two concepts will now be discussed in depth.

Frame Theory

As previously stated, every communicative interaction is influenced by the people involved and, inevitably, by the life experiences those people have had. The kind of experiences people have had throughout their life and the culture to which they feel they belong will lead them to develop a set of assumptions about the world and the people with whom they interact. Frame theory is one way to explain how people categorize their knowledge according to their experiences with similar situations and, thus, may consciously or unconsciously use lexical, grammatical, and experiential knowledge to make judgments about a discourse situation and its participants.

Several writers, including Goffman (1974), Gumperz (1982), Hatim and Mason (1990), Metzger (1995, 1999), Roy (2000b), Schiffrin (1993), Tannen (1979, 1993), and Wilcox and Wilcox (1985) have referred to "frame" or "schema" theory in relation to discourse. Schema theory is defined by Wilcox and Wilcox (1985) as "a theory about knowledge" that offers an explanation of how comprehension takes place and how it is influenced by prior knowledge and contextual influences. Schema, or frame, theory claims that the meaning of a message is not decoded, as described in cognitive models of language; rather, it is constructed. Essentially, frame theory describes "frames" of concepts on which people "hang" information, and on these frames, people base their assumptions about objects, people, and places. The frames are constructed of different values, which will vary from person to person depending on his or her life experience. When put together, the values give rise to a concept.

In the same way that individuals make assumptions about people, objects, and places, they assume "scripts" for "unwritten" rules of behavior. Schank and Abelson (1977) defined scripts as a "standard event sequence" (p. 38) whereas Hatim and Mason (1990) referred to scripts as "stabilised plans with pre-established routines" (p. 160). These scripts are used to guide a person through particular forms of social intercourse according to certain expectations of behavior within any particular discourse environment, which, again, will depend on the types of social interactions to which one has been exposed while growing up.

New information is given and received according to an assumption of what is already known, and bridging inferences are made between frames and scripts to make further assumptions about information that is being received. Therefore, interpreters enter into an interpreting assignment with their own frames and scripts about the people, the subject, the event, and so forth. All other participants, whether Deaf or hearing, will also have their own assumptions that may influence the interaction. Consequently, the assumptions held by the interpreter inevitably will have some kind of influence over the interpretation itself, meaning that, when considering models of the interpreting process, this dynamic must be a central factor.

The Application of Frame Theory to the Interpreting Process

A sociolinguistic-sociocultural approach to interpreting has the capacity to incorporate the "interpreter as participant" into the interpretation process and, therefore, to acknowledge that the interpreter and primary interlocutors will have an influence on any interaction that takes place.

By using their contextual knowledge of both communities, including those groups' languages and cultures, and by subsequently making assumptions and judgments about what their audiences mutually understand, interpreters can ensure that any interpretation they make will be linguistically and culturally effective for all participants. Interpreters will make specific language choices according to (a) their frames of reference, (b) what certain concepts mean to them, and (c) inferences they make about what concepts will mean to their source- and target-language audiences from a cultural perspective (Napier, 1998a, 1998b, 2000, 2001). Thus, interpreters will construct the meaning of a message according to the perspective of the listener-receiver (Frishberg, 2000) by considering the "cultural realities" of the interlocutors (Cokely, 1995).

To ensure that their audiences are making the same inferences about the message they are receiving, interpreters need to search for linguistic and cultural equivalents. It is not sufficient to search for directly translatable words in each language because sociocultural contexts may alter the way certain expressions are used. Hatim and Mason (1990) stated that the interpretation process is "an evolving entity, a process whereby producers and receivers cooperate and communicate by making assumptions about a shared cognitive environment" (p. 100), and Roy (2000a) described interpreting as a "discourse process." Therefore, to best deal with the sociolinguistic and sociocultural contexts of interpreting, interpreters need to recognize their linguistic abilities and cultural knowledge as well as the fact that their interpretations can be enhanced by using their knowledge. In this way, interpreters can positively contribute to any communicative interaction. The idea posited here is that the most appropriate and dynamic interpretation method to use to apply the fundamentals of frame theory and perform effectively as a linguistic and cultural mediator is one that incorporates a search for semantic equivalence (Baker, 1992).

The principle of "free interpretation" provides interpreters with the scope to apply their linguistic and cultural knowledge to an interpreted event. An interpreter must have a deep understanding of the potentially opposing cultural norms and values and should make judgments about his or her interpretation accordingly. Thus, an interpreter has to be prepared for the different assumptions held by the different cultures. Each interpreter will take one piece of information and interpret it differently, according to what that piece of information means to him or her, but what each interpreter also has to consider is what that information will mean to the participants using the target language once the message has been received.

The key to "free interpretation" is in the assumptions brought to and the inferences made during any interpreting assignment. To make assumptions about the target audience, the interpreter needs to be bicultural and bilingual. Familiarity with the community and its culture will expose the interpreter to knowledge about the kind of information to which community members have been exposed and about the nature of language use alongside cultural norms and values. The interpreter can make considered choices throughout the translation by making inferences about the members' cultural and linguistic understanding of the topic being discussed and can transpose cultural meaning appropriately (Hatim & Mason, 1990). The ability to paraphrase the meaning of an utterance and, thus, impart cultural significance can be more important than the ability to translate word for word by concentrating on the form of the message. Free interpretation, therefore, can be deemed as a method of interpretation whereby "the linguistic structure of the source language is ignored, and an equivalent is found based on the meaning it conveys" (Crystal, 1987, p. 344) as opposed to a literal interpretation, which means that "the linguistic structure of the source text is followed, but is normalised according to the rules of the target language" (Crystal, 1987, p. 344). For example, if interpreting from English into Auslan, the literal delivery of Auslan would incorporate English word order or lip patterns while also using Auslan features.

In recognizing the influence of additional sociolinguistic and sociocultural factors, Crystal (1987) stated that, in addition to being bilingual and bicultural, interpreters must thoroughly understand the discourse being used in the interpreting context and, thus, any social, cultural, or emotional connotations that may influence the intended effect of the message. To effectively evaluate the influence that the discourse environment has on the interpretation output, interpreters, while interpreting, need to simultaneously engage in a process of monitoring interpreted renditions by drawing on their metalinguistic awareness.

METALINGUISTIC AWARENESS

The concept of metalinguistic awareness is usually discussed within the context of language acquisition and development of literacy skills. Several writers have discussed the metacognitive skills that children acquire, the metalinguistic awareness they have about their own language development, and how this awareness affects their bilingualism, translation skills, or literacy skills (Clark, 1978; Karmiloff-Smith, 1986; Malakoff & Hakuta, 1991; Perner, 1988; Tunmer & Bowey, 1984; Tunmer & Herriman, 1984).

Garton and Pratt (1998) defined metalinguistic awareness as "the ability to focus attention on language and reflect upon its nature, structure and functions" (p. 149), and they stated that "those who work with language must be able to focus attention on it" (p. 150). Therefore, the concept can be applied to interpreters and the skills they have to self-regulate and monitor their abilities in the languages between which they interpret (Peterson, 2000; Smith, 2000).

Bialystok and Ryan (1985a, 1985b) and Bialystok (1991) asserted that metalinguistic awareness involves key skills. These skills include the ability to analyze linguistic knowledge and organize it into categories, the capability to control attentional procedures that select and process specific linguistic information, and the facility to intentionally consider what aspects of language are contextually relevant. One can argue, therefore, that interpreters should have metalinguistic awareness to be able to perform their function as interpreters because they are constantly having to analyze the linguistic structure of language and consider sociocultural contexts of language use. This concept has been alternatively referred to as "meta-competence" (Nord, 2000) or as the use of "meta-strategies" (Hoffman, 1997).

One focus of this study was on the level of metalinguistic awareness or "metacognition" (Peterson, 2000) that the interpreters had about the linguistic choices they made while interpreting in university settings. The goal was to discover the level of consciousness or metalinguistic awareness of Auslan-English interpreters when they interpreted for a lexically dense university lecture in relation to the types of omissions they made and why. Darò, Lambert, and Fabbro (1996) noted that the conscious monitoring of attention during simultaneous interpretation might affect the number and types of mistakes made by interpreters. Thus, the goal of the research was to demonstrate what types of omissions were made by interpreters and the "metacognitive strategies" (Smith, 2000) they used in making certain omissions.

INTERPRETING OMISSIONS

The majority of people who know the English language would consider the word *omission* to refer generally to something that has been left out. For the purposes of this study, an omission is defined as "something that has not been included or not been done, either deliberately or accidentally" (Fox, 1988, p. 547). This definition identifies that the act of omission can be accidental or deliberate or, to put it another way, unconscious or conscious. Conscious omissions would be those that are made by an interpreter, either deliberately or not, for a variety of reasons. An interpreter may be conscious of the fact that he or she has made an omission, but it was not necessarily a deliberate decision. Alternatively, a conscious decision can be made to not embrace certain concepts within the interpretation, that is, to omit either those that have no relevance to the receivers of the interpretation or those that are not central to the message and would be more detrimental to understanding if left in. These conscious omissions, when used strategically by interpreters, can be considered as means to cope with lexical density as well as linguistic and cultural relevance. Typically, however, studies of interpreting have deemed omissions as errors.

Omissions as Errors

Kopczynski (1980) concentrated a large part of his writing on errors made by interpreters. In establishing a context, he defined an error as "any utterance of the speaker-learner which deviates from the adopted norm" (p. 63). He identified two different kinds of errors: those that violate the rules of the norm that are not known to the learner (systematic errors) and those that violate the rules known to the learner (mistakes). Kopczynski (1980) distinguished between systematic errors and mistakes. Systematic errors, also referred to as errors of competence, were defined as those errors committed regularly by people at the same level of proficiency and with the same learning experience. However, mistakes, otherwise known as errors of performance, were explained as occurring because of other influencing factors such as inattentiveness, stress, and fatigue.

In introducing the notion of error analysis, Kopczynski (1980) stated that the only utterances that can be considered as erroneous are those that violate the known rules (i.e., errors of performance). He defined a taxonomy of errors, which categorizes three major types of errors by which an interpreter may depart from the original source-language message. These are omissions, additions, and substitutions, each of which are broken down into certain types. The category of additions includes qualification, elaboration, relationship, and closure additions whereas the category of substitutions incorporates mild and gross semantic errors based on lexical items or chunks of speech (such as phrases or sentences). The taxonomy for the category of omissions details four types of errors: skipping errors (exclusion of a single lexical item); comprehension errors (omission of a larger unit of meaning as a result of an inability to comprehend the source-language message); delay errors (omission of a larger unit of meaning because too great a lag exists behind the speaker); and compounding errors (a conjoining of elements from different clauses or sentences).

Kopczynski (1980) conducted a study in an attempt to determine the borderline between correct and erroneous translation, afterward, acknowledging that the qualitative outcome of a translation and the assessment of that outcome depends on the context. He delineated three contextual categories of translation: (a) literary, where the "goal is aesthetic and the translator has to take into consideration the poetic form of the message in addition to the content" (p. 72); (b) anthropological, where the goal is "an explication of the cultural content of the source message" (p. 72); and (c) informative, where "the primary goal is the transfer of information, i.e., the presentation of the content" (p. 72).

Kopczynski (1980) made the distinction between "obligatory" and "optional" omissions, with obligatory omissions arising as a result of differences between the structure of the two languages being interpreted (p. 85). These types of omissions were deemed more or less appropriate according to whether key words within a piece of text are translatable. Kopczynski defined omissions under two umbrellas: errors of performance and errors of receptive competence. He claimed that omissions could be deemed as performance errors because they can be affected by memory lapses, failure to choose the optimal moment of interpreting, time pressure, fatigue, etc.; however, they also could be deemed as receptive competence errors if they occur because the interpreter fails to understand the source-language message.

In detailing Kopczynski's (1980) perspective on omissions as well as on how and why they occur, one can see clearly that he deemed omissions as errors that occur during an interpretation. No indication is given within his writing that omissions may be used as a conscious part of the interpreting process or as a linguistic coping strategy. His work expresses no consideration that omissions may be used effectively to ensure that cultural equivalence is obtained as part of a successful interpretation.

One can gain insight into the interpretation process by breaking down any interpretation and analyzing it for meaning and accuracy. Other writers (e.g., Altman, 1989; Cokely, 1985, 1992a, 1992b; Moser-Mercer, Kunzli, & Korac, 1998; Russell, 2000) have adopted an approach similar to Kopczynski's (1980) in that they have looked at errors made by interpreters and have categorized omissions as mistakes rather than as strategies. This study, however, highlights the different types of omissions made by interpreters—those that could be defined as strategic and others that could be identified as potential errors.

Enkvist (1973) questioned whether analysis of interpretation should count the number of errors or measure the success in communication. In supporting a goal-oriented approach to analysis, Enkvist suggested the concept of contextual appropriateness as a yardstick by which to assess the seriousness of an error, which involved looking at the appropriateness of an utterance in the context of situation. Enkvist claimed that, because interactions are goal related, errors should be considered only in relation to functionally relative objectives rather than simply as errors. Baker (1992) has also recognized the occasional need for interpreters to "translate by omission." The following section discusses the contextual appropriateness of interpreting omissions, which can be considered as conscious strategic omissions.

Conscious Strategic Omissions

In giving an account of interpreter-mediated communication, Wadensjö (1998) explored the responsibilities of the interpreter and the expectations of both the participants and the interpreter involved in an interaction. Wadensjö suggested her own taxonomy for use in determining the successful outcome of an interpreted event, a classification that incorporated components similar to those of Barik (1975) and Cokely (1985, 1992a, 1992b).

First, Wadensjö (1998) established the interpreter's utterance as a *rendition* that relates in some way to the immediately preceding original utterance. The relation between the rendition and the utterance of the originator can be classified into distinct subcategories. She stated that source texts can be considered as "context(s) in a chain of utterances" (p. 106) that condition and influence additional discoursal and contextual development. Wadensjö claimed that, although "original" utterances are heard (or seen in signed language) in a particular context, interpreters need to decontextualize each original utterance to a certain extent so it is a separate unit and can be recontextualized as a new utterance in the "flow of talk" (p. 107).

Thus, to compare interpreters' utterances with the originals, Wadensjö (1998) defined a taxonomy comprising eight subcategories of renditions: close renditions, expanded renditions, reduced renditions, substituted renditions, summarized renditions, multipart renditions, nonrenditions and zero renditions. These subcategories enable the analyst to explore the successful nature of an interpretation by looking at the appropriateness of particular renditions in the context of the interpreted interaction.

In relation to conscious strategic omissions, the subcategory of most interest is that of reduced renditions, otherwise termed *condensing strategies* (Sunnari, 1995) or *selective reductions* (Hatim & Mason, 1990). Wadensjö (1998) defined reduced renditions as "less explicitly expressed information than the preceding 'original' utterance" (p. 107). As noted earlier, omissions can be deemed as strategies whereby a conscious decision is made to leave something out or to reduce the amount of information included from the source-language message into the target-language interpretation. Therefore, Wadensjö's approach—wherein an interpreter decides to provide a reduced rendition—applies positive connotations to the concept of making deliberate omissions because those omissions are used to meet the communicative goals of any interaction.

Livingston, Singer, and Abramson (1994) came to the same conclusion. In analyzing successful ASL interpretations and transliterations of a lecture, Livingston et al. noted that omissions did not necessarily lead to less understanding of the message. In fact, they reinforced the concept of omissions being used consciously as part of a strategic linguistic process. They explained that certain information might be omitted from an interpretation for two reasons. First, the interpreter might make a conscious decision to delete information because he or she feels that an equivalent message would be difficult to find. Second, the interpreter makes an omission based on his or her estimation of what would be meaningful to the particular audience he or she is serving. Livingston et al. condoned the use of omissions as part of a strategic linguistic process that can enhance an interpretation. They stated that "omissions were not necessarily indications of a poor interpretation. . . . [In fact,] . . . it appeared to be just the opposite" (p. 28).

Winston (1989) also studied transliteration of a lecture and focused on "conscious strategies used by transliterators during analysis and production of the target form, rather than random productions or errors" (p. 152). She highlighted particular strategic choices that are used to achieve certain types of transliteration. These strategies included conceptual sign choice, use of additions and omissions, restructuring, and mouthing.

After consulting with the transliterator about strategies that were used, Winston (1989) concluded that certain portions of the source language that were redundant in the target language were omitted. She claimed this strategy was used to achieve the transliterative goal of efficiency, to provide a pragmatic translation, even though direct lexical equivalents for transliteration purposes were available. Redundancies that were noted included repeated past tense markers, plural markers, linking verbs such as *be*, prepositions such as *of*, and previously established subject pronouns. Thus, the omission strategies outlined by Winston can be deemed "conscious strategic omissions."

The preceding discussion has clearly established that interpreters may omit information as part of a conscious linguistic coping strategy. This foundation now allows us to consider a spectrum of omission types.

Omission Taxonomy

As shown in the preceding section, previous research has established that interpreters may make conscious or unconscious omissions while they are processing information from the source into the target language, omissions that can be considered as strategies or errors, respectively. In reviewing the literature and available taxonomies, the need became apparent to develop a specific classification system for the most common types of omissions that might be identified when analyzing an interpreting task. Barik's (1975) and Wadensjö's (1998) categories were judged to be the most relevant and were adapted accordingly to reflect the theoretical perspective of this study.

Wadensjö's (1998) category of reduced renditions was combined with those of skipping, comprehension, and delay from Barik (1975) and reworded to present an omission taxonomy of complementary terminology. Thus, the adapted categorical omissions were defined as follows:

1. **Conscious strategic omissions:** Omissions made consciously by an interpreter, whereby a decision is made to omit information to enhance the effectiveness of the interpretation. The interpreter incorporates his or her linguistic and cultural knowledge to decide what information from the source language makes sense in the target language, what information is culturally relevant, and what is redundant.

2. **Conscious intentional omissions:** Omissions that contribute to a loss of meaningful information whereby the interpreter is conscious of the omission and has made it intentionally either because he or she lacks an understanding of a particular lexical item or concept or because he or she is unable to think of an appropriate equivalent in the target language.

3. **Conscious unintentional omissions:** Omissions that contribute to a loss of meaningful information whereby the interpreter is conscious of the omission but has made it unintentionally. He or she hears the lexical item (or items) and decides to "file it" before interpreting it to wait for more contextual information or depth of meaning; however, because of further source-language input and lag time, the particular lexical item (or items) is not retrieved and, therefore, omitted.

4. **Conscious receptive omissions:** Omissions that contribute to a loss of meaningful information wherein the interpreter is aware that he or she cannot properly decipher what was heard because of reported poor sound quality.

5. **Unconscious omissions:** Omissions that contribute to a loss of meaningful information wherein the interpreter is unconscious of the omission and does not recall hearing the particular lexical item (or items).

Before detailing the occurrence and types of omissions made by Auslan-English interpreters when interpreting for a university lecture, it is necessary to consider factors within the discourse environment that may have influenced the interpreters' abilities to effectively interpret the lecture and that may have affected the number and types of omissions they made.

DISCOURSE ENVIRONMENT: FACTORS TO CONSIDER

The objective of this section is to discuss linguistic and contextual issues that contribute to the changing dynamic of interpreting as a discourse process in a university lecture. Key issues to consider include the context of the situation, language variation and register, language contact, the lecture as a discourse genre, and the lexical density of university lectures.

The Context of the Situation

The functional grammar approach focuses on the purpose and use of language and examines spoken and written languages within the contexts of their usage. The relationship between words used and meanings derived is not thought of as arbitrary; therefore, language is determined as being functional whereby meaning is created through the choice of words (Gerot & Wignell, 1995). Thus, the study of functional language and, therefore, the interpretation of language cannot be separated from the situations where language use takes place (Hatim & Mason, 1990).

Many writers have discussed the relationship among language, communicative interaction, and context (e.g., Brown & Fraser, 1979; Crystal, 1984; Halliday, 1978; Halliday & Hasan, 1985; Halliday & Martin, 1993; Hymes, 1972; Ryan & Giles, 1982, Sinclair & Coulthard, 1975), propounding the notion that all languages function within contexts of situations and, therefore, are relatable to those contexts. With this idea in mind, Halliday (1978) stated that the purpose of defining the context is not to question idiosyncratic use of vocabulary, grammar, or pronunciation, rather, to identify *"which* kinds of situational factor determine *which* kinds of selection in the linguistic system" (p. 32, italics added).

Crystal and Davey (1969), Halliday (1978), and Hymes (1972) have proposed sets of concepts for describing the context of a situation, and Cokely (1992b) discussed a description of the context of situation specifically in relation to signed language interpretation. Cokely (1992b) identified components that affect communicative behavior as "interaction factors" and "message factors." The interaction factors that can influence the context of a situation and, therefore, the work of interpreters were defined within a taxonomy to include setting, purpose, and participants. The setting component takes into account a range of environmental or extralinguistic factors that can influence interactive outcomes whereas the purpose component considers the activities, participant goals, and subject matter that occur within an interaction. The participant component refers to characteristics of individuals or characteristics of actual or perceived relationships among individuals that can affect the communicative interaction. Cokely highlighted the importance for interpreters to recognize how message factors can affect an interaction. The message form and content is an obviously crucial component to consider along with the message key, its channel and language form, the interaction norms and interpretation norms, and the discourse genre.

Therefore, by defining the nature of a communicative interaction and establishing the context of the situation, one can predict what should be expected of interpreters when placed in those situations. Discussions about the context of situation have acknowledged that language use varies according to what situation a person is in and the context of any interactional participation. The language variation that arises as a consequence of contextual and situational diversity is the biggest consideration for working interpreters because they must be prepared to adapt their language use accordingly. Thus, before establishing the context of situation for this study, it is necessary to discuss the notion of situational language variation and the concept of language register.

Situational Language Variation

In discussing language variety and situations of use, Finegan, Besnier, Blair, and Collins (1992) used the term *linguistic repertoire* to describe language varieties exhibited in the speaking and writing patterns of a speech community. Others refer to *diatypic variation* when classifying language according to its use in social situations (Wray, Trott, & Bloomer, 1998).

According to Zimmer (1989), register or style variation involves differential language use that is sensitive to situational factors. Wardhaugh (1992) and Fromkin, Rodman, Collins, and Blair (1990), however, made a clear distinction between *style* and *register*. Wardhaugh (1992) described styles as different ways of speaking either formally or informally, depending on the circumstances. He defined register as "sets of vocabulary items associated with discrete occupational or social groups" (p. 49).

Fromkin et al. (1990) described styles as "situation dialects," which range between two extremes of informal and formal language use and are influenced by the speaker's attitude toward the receiver, the subject matter, or the purpose of the communication. They defined register as language variety that is determined entirely by subject matter. Fromkin et al. asserted that style or register variation includes not only changes in vocabulary but also an adaptation of grammatical rules. Different subject matters such as legal prose or cooking recipes are given as examples of different register variations: legal prose using longer sentences, more archaic words, longer adverbial elements, and explicit repetition and cooking recipes using short simple sentences, verbs in the imperative mood, and prepositional phrases.

In summarizing their concept of the linguistic repertoire of a monolingual community, Finegan et al. (1992) stated that language register is determined by a set of linguistic features combined with characteristic patterns of how the language is used in different situations, yet with all varieties of the language relying on essentially the same grammatical system. In addition, they asserted that rules governing register variations accompany nonlinguistic behavior such as standing, sitting, physical proximity, and face-to-face positioning.

Many readers will be familiar with the model of register devised by Joos (1967), which postulated five different styles of communication, ranging through different levels of formality (frozen, formal, consultative, informal, and intimate). Although these registers are presented by Joos (1967) as discrete entities, observation of language use demonstrates that overlap does occur; thus, the analysis of language needs to adopt more descriptive techniques (Halliday, 1978).

The concept of situational language variation presents a challenge for interpreters in that they need to be familiar with the norms of interaction and language use for different situations and adapt their interpretations accordingly. In searching for linguistic and cultural equivalents, interpreters need to be aware of appropriateness of language use in relation to context of situation.

The issue of variation in signed languages has been debated, and there is a general agreement within the literature that it does exist (Davis, 1989; Deuchar, 1984; Fontana, 1999; Kyle, & Woll, 1979; Llewellyn Jones, 1981; Lucas & Valli, 1989; Stokoe, 1969; Woodward, 1973; Zimmer, 1989). Some disagreement has surfaced, however, about the salient characteristics of a signed language register.

The main issues for signed language researchers has been the "continuum" of signed language varieties that can exist simultaneously within one Deaf community and whether one form of signed communication should be considered as more "formal" than another. The idea is widely accepted that signed language variation exists across age, social class, educational background, and geographical location in the form of accents and dialects (Deuchar, 1984; Kyle & Woll, 1985), but the notion of variation according to language use within particular situations gives rise to different theories.

Stokoe (1969) and Deuchar (1978) discussed notions of diglossia in signed languages and have distinguished between a "high" variety of signed language used at formal functions and a "low" variety used informally. Deuchar (1978) stated that the high variety that she observed in British Sign Language (BSL) is actually a form of Signed English[1] and that the low variety is a purer form of BSL with no English interference. In a later publication, however, Deuchar (1984) commented that the Signed English she had previously observed tended to be the variety of signed language used by hearing people involved with the Deaf community rather than that of Deaf people themselves. Woodward (1973) suggested a diglossic continuum rather than two distinct varieties.

1. Signed English is the manual representation of English word for word. Several methods for manually representing English have been used over the years. "Some use just twenty-six hand configurations to represent the letters of the alphabet, others use a combination of signs used by the deaf and fingerspelling, others use a combination of deaf signs, fingerspelling and contrived signs. They all have in common the aim of manually representing English, word for word, if

Llewellyn Jones, Kyle, and Woll (1979) accepted the notion of two varieties of signed language (that is, BSL and Signed English) but suggested that Signed English is not commonly used among members of the Deaf community, rather, is used as a form of communicating with hearing people. Thus, Llewellyn Jones et al. perceived that members of the British deaf community were not diglossic in their language use because those who used the high variety were marginal to the community or part of its elite and, therefore, had privileged access to a more formal variety of language, which was inaccessible to the majority of the community. Llewellyn Jones (1981) and Zimmer (1989) demonstrated, however, that a formal register exists in signed languages; they videotaped Deaf signed language users in different discourse environments, including formal situations, and noted linguistic features specific to formal signed language use.

Thus, it is feasible to consider signed languages as having their own form of situational language variation. Examples of situations where more formal registers of signed languages are used include academic lectures, business meetings, banquets, and church (Baker & Cokely, 1980; Lee, 1982). Another sociolinguistic phenomenon observed with the use of signed languages, which affects the issue of language variation, is that of language contact.

Language Contact and Signed Language Variation

In discussing the fact that a specific kind of signing exists as a result of contact between signed and spoken languages, Lucas and Valli (1989) stated that "one of the major sociolinguistic issues in the deaf community concerns the outcome of language contact" (p. 11). The majority of studies of language contact in the Deaf community have taken place in the United States; however, one study explored the situation in Italy (Fontana, 1999) and observed that similar phenomena are present in other Deaf communities.

Woodward (1973) claimed that this contact variety of signed language is a pidgin that results from interaction between Deaf and hearing people. Cokely (1983), Lucas and Valli (1989), and Davis (1989), however, refuted this claim. Cokely (1983) referred to criteria that are normally required as preconditions for the development of a pidgin language to

---

not morpheme by morpheme" (Johnston, 1989, p. 473).

illustrate that language contact between ASL and English has not necessarily led to the emergence of a pidgin. Instead, Cokely (1983) argued that the dynamics of "foreigner talk," judgments of proficiency, and learners' attempts to master the target language result in a continuum of language varieties within ASL.

Lucas and Valli (1989) described the characteristics of language contact between ASL and English as codeswitching and code-mixing whereby English words are mouthed on the lips or manually coded (fingerspelled) while the signer is still using linguistic features of ASL. They also noted that contact signing yields "idiosyncratic syntactic constructions . . . that fit neither the ASL nor the English grammatical system" (p. 30).

Lucas and Valli (1989) and Fontana (1999) suggested a variety of sociolinguistic factors that influence the use of codeswitching and code-mixing between a signed and a spoken language, one of which was the formality of a situation. According to Lucas and Valli, more English "interference' occurs in more formal situations when technical or specialized terms are used and, thus, are incorporated into ASL in the form of mouth patterns or fingerspelling.

Davis (1989) explored the use of these language contact phenomena in interpretations of English into ASL and found that the mouthing of English words and the use of fingerspelling was patterned. Davis's study showed that interpreters used contact varieties of signed language appropriate to the situation in which they were interpreting, which was a lecture. These findings thus agree with the conclusions of Lucas and Valli (1989), which state that the formality of a situation influences the use of language contact phenomena in signed language. Davis (1989) also stated that the signed language interpreters in his study reflected the typical language use of Deaf people in this type of situation.

The issues related to situational variance and signed language contact variety, discussed above, have explored the effect these factors have on the interpretation process. The next section will consider the specific discourse environment that was studied, that is, a university lecture.

The Lecture as a Discourse Genre

Discourse analysis can be applied to any form of communicative interaction in an attempt to identify various discourse genres. Studies of alternative discourses have included genres such as narratives (Chafe, 1980), jokes (Sacks, 1974), and conversations (Schegloff, 1972; Tannen, 1984). Discourse analysis is relevant to the study of both monologue and dialogue (Longacre, 1983); therefore, lectures, as typical monologues, can be considered as a distinct discourse genre. Cokely (1992a, 1992b) noted, however, that very few descriptive studies have focused on the particular monologic discourse of lectures. Instead, general observations have been made about the characteristics of lectures. Before discussing those characteristics, the term *lecture* must first be defined:

> A lecture is an institutionalised extended holding of the floor in which one speaker imparts his views on a subject, these thoughts comprising what can be called his "text". The style is typically serious and slightly impersonal, the controlling intent being to generate calmly considered understanding, not mere entertainment, emotional impact, or immediate action. (Goffman, 1981, p. 165)

Lakoff (1982, cited in Cokely, 1992b) defined lectures in a way similar to that of Goffman (1981), whereby one participant in the interactive discourse is in control, selects the subject matter, and decides when the discourse should start and finish. Therefore, according to these definitions, lectures can be characterized as nonreciprocal monologues, or "expository monologues" (Cokely, 1992b, p. 27).

A typical expository monologue relies on topical or logical linkage as opposed to the inherent chronological nexus often observed in narratives. The focus of expository monologues tends to be on a theme or set of related themes rather than on participants such as in narratives. In addition, more tension, that is, struggle or polarization, can be found in an expository monologue than in a narrative. Longacre (1983) noted that effective expository discourse should inherently incorporate an effort to ensure clarity of information, especially when people receiving the discourse may not have the necessary background knowledge.

In focusing on characteristics of a lecture and on the language production within this discourse genre, Goffman (1981) highlighted three different modes of speech production that establish presenters on a different "footing" with their audience. These modes are memorization, aloud reading, and fresh talk. He stated that lecturers often choose to read aloud from prepared texts, which influences the reception and responsiveness of an audience. According to Goffman, people may choose to read out printed text rather than spontaneously provide "fresh talk" because written and spoken texts have different dynamics, which implies that written language has more status. Goffman asserted that the register of language used in a lecture is important in defining the relationship between speaker and audience. Therefore, although perceptions of good writing and good speaking are systematically different, people will often choose to read aloud previously prepared texts when delivering a lecture because printed text tends to be more coherent than spontaneously produced spoken text.

This finding has implications for interpreters who are working within the context of university lectures; Halliday (1978) suggested that academics often deliver lectures using a written language structure of speech production. Halliday argued that academics are so influenced by their environment and the assumption of literate intelligence of university students, that they produce lexically dense spoken text when lecturing. Lexically dense spoken text is characterized by its conformity to typical written language structure, with a higher number of lexical (content) words than functional (grammatical) words (Crystal, 1995; Gerot & Wignell, 1995; Halliday, 1985; O'Loughlin, 1995). Richards, Platt, and Platt (1992) and Ure (1971) determined that lexical density can be used as a measure of difficulty of a piece of text by measuring the ratio of lexical and grammatical words to the total number of words in a text.

Typically, spoken text has complex sentences with simple words whereas written text has complex words in simple sentences, which Halliday (1985) suggested is because writing is static as compared with speech, which is dynamic. Consequently, spoken language tends to be less lexically dense than written language. Ure (1971) stated that, in English, the lexical density of a text is a function, first, of the medium (i.e., spoken or written) and, second, of the social function (i.e., pragmatic language use). This statement highlights how academic lecturers may be influenced when working in an environment where pragmatic language use is often based on technical research and, therefore, allows their spoken language production to be influenced by the written language medium. The lexical density of text that is often found in lecture situations would thus have implications for interpreters working in this environment.

Interpreting for Lexically Dense Text

According to Messina (1998), previously prepared texts that are read out verbatim create more problems for interpreters than spontaneous speech. He cited the "peculiarities of written texts and how they are usually delivered by speakers" as being the main factor affecting an interpreter's performance (p. 148). Balzani (1990, cited in Messina, 1998) studied interpreters' performances as they worked from a written text that was read out and found that more mistakes were made. The key issue for interpreters when dealing with lexically dense text is "higher risk of impaired understanding and interpretation as the interpreter's processing capacities reach saturation" (Messina, 1998, p. 156).

The notion of text being read out, however, is not the only difficulty for interpreters. Spoken texts that are not necessarily read out but that are prepared may also be lexically dense and, thus, provide a challenge to interpreters. Based on the measure of lexical and grammatical words to the total number of words in a text, Ure (1971) found that the typical lexical density of a spoken event is 33%, and the typical lexical density of a lecture is 39.6%; therefore, interpreters may face difficulties in interpreting for any spoken text that is more lexically dense than usual, for example, a university lecture.

SIGNED LANGUAGE INTERPRETATION OF LEXICALLY DENSE UNIVERSITY LECTURES

A university lecture that is presented in a lexically dense fashion has implications for how Deaf people will access the information. Because signed language has no conventional written orthography, a Deaf audience may have no frame of reference for what a lexically dense interpretation into Auslan should look like. This situation presents a challenge for signed language interpreters in that they have to decipher the meaning of a text and decide which lexical items are the most important to express. The task involves taking into account the following issues: (a) the language contact situation of interpreting between English and Auslan; (b) what the norms of signed language production would be for a lecture in general; (c) what cultural relevance certain lexical items may hold and, thus, what their linguistic and cultural equivalents may be; and (d) deciding what linguistic coping strategies should be adopted to ensure that a Deaf audience will come away with the same message and will have received the same information as a non-Deaf audience. The "contextual force" or "relative impact" (Isham, 1986) of the message on the receiver ultimately should be the same for both Deaf and non-Deaf audiences.

These sociolinguistic and sociocultural contexts, which require consideration throughout an interpretation, are summarized by Nida (1998) into four categories: (1) the appropriate language register to be used in the context, (2) the expectations of the target audience members as to the type of translation they expect to receive, (3) distinctive sociolinguistic features of the source text, and (4) the medium used for the translated text (i.e., written, spoken, or signed).

Signed language interpreters who are working with Deaf students in a university lecture must consider additional sociolinguistic and sociocultural factors as well as the lexical density of the text. The skills used by interpreters have to be adapted to allow for conditions specific to the university discourse environment. The interpreter needs to consider his or her role in an educational environment and the fact that Deaf people may be disadvantaged when compared to other university students (because English is their second language and they are not receiving "direct" access to the lecture content). Although all university students may attend lectures without any background knowledge of the subject and, thus, may lack familiarity with the subject-specific terminology, the interpreter is faced with the task of deciding how to provide an interpretation that is linguistically and culturally sensitive, incorporates meaningful equivalents, and still provides Deaf students with the opportunity to access specialized terminology that may be important for them to know to fully understand the subject of the lecture.

This situation presents signed language interpreters with a dilemma: whether to freely interpret the content of a lecture or whether to establish a language contact situation that occasionally relies on the fingerspelling of English words. The interpreter needs to use his or her judgment to decide what vocabulary should be interpreted conceptually and what should be interpreted literally. Thus, the interpreter also will need to judge the importance of lexical items presented in the lecture's source text and which information might be appropriate to add or omit for clarity. Through this process of decision making, interpreters inevitably will make omissions, some of which may be accidental or unconscious and some of which may be made consciously as part of the linguistic decision-making process.

THE STUDY

After evaluating various techniques of how to investigate skills of interpreters, the researcher made the decision to combine three different procedures. These procedures included (a) a "tough-case analysis," that is, analysis of a tricky interpreting situation (Moser-Mercer, 1997); (b) a task of "process tracing" whereby the subject runs through the task a second time (Moser-Mercer, 1997); and (c) a "retrospective interview" (Hoffman, 1997).

A lecture that was presented in English as part of a master's degree program for teachers of the deaf was recorded live on videotape. The lecture was selected with confidence that analysis would show it to be lexically dense because of the reputation of the lecturer and the researcher's previous experience of interpreting for this particular lecturer. At the time of presentation, the lecture was simultaneously interpreted by an accredited, professional-level Auslan-English interpreter[2] for a Deaf student, which authenticated the "interpret-ability" of the lecture. The first 30 minutes of the lecture were transcribed to analyze the text for lexical density by adopting the method proposed by Ure (1971), and that segment was found to have a density of 51%. Considering that an average lecture would contain a lexical density of 39.6% (Ure, 1971), the chosen lecture was more than suitable to use as the source material for the purposes of this study.

Ten accredited, professional-level Auslan-English interpreters with different educational backgrounds agreed to be involved in the study (see

2. Auslan interpreters are assessed by the National Authority for the Accreditation of Translators and Interpreters (NAATI), and accreditation is available at two levels: paraprofessional interpreter and professional interpreter. Paraprofessional interpreter level is defined as "a level of competence in interpreting for the purpose of general conversations, generally in the form of non-specialist dialogues . . . [whereby] interpreting in situations where specialised terminology or more sophisticated conceptual information is not required [and] . . . a depth of linguistic ability is not required" whereas professional level is defined as "the minimum level of competence for professional interpreting. . . . Interpreters are capable of interpreting across a wide range of subjects involving dialogues at specialist consultations . . . [whereby] interpreting in both language directions for a wide range of subject areas usually involving specialist consultations with other professionals . . . [and] interpreting in situations where some depth of linguistic ability in both languages is necessary (NAATI, 1999).

Appendix 4.A for a profile of each interpreter). Each interpreter was asked, first, to watch the first 10 minutes of the videotaped lecture to familiarize him- or herself with the topic and rate of delivery and, then, to interpret 20 minutes of the videotaped lecture because this length of time is the optimum period for interpreting before the qualitative output begins to suffer (CACDP, 1997). Each participant was recorded individually in a room with a television and video camera, with the only other people in the room being the researcher and a Deaf person acting as a "receiver" for the interpretation.[3] Throughout the task, the researcher referred to a transcript of the lecture and underlined any omissions that were made during the interpretation. Omissions were noted according to the following definition developed by the researcher, which was based on a review of the literature: An omission occurs when information transmitted in the source language with one or more lexical items does not appear in the target language and, therefore, potentially alters the meaning.

After completing the interpreting task, the researcher and participant reviewed the task by watching a playback of the videotaped interpreting task and pausing the video when omissions were noted in the Auslan rendition of the English lecture. The participant was asked to explain why he or she thought the omission might have occurred and whether he or she was aware of it at the time—that is, whether it was conscious or unconscious. The purpose of the review was to establish whether omissions were being made on a conscious or unconscious level. If the subject identified conscious omissions being made as a linguistic strategy, then the subject was asked to elaborate on why he or she had made the conscious decision to omit particular types of information.

Finally, a retrospective interview was carried out. Hoffman (1997) has favorably described the notion of the retrospective interview for the purposes of "knowledge elicitation." An interpreter interviewed in this way by Hoffman commented that "the process pulled out much of what

3. Interpreters often rely on feedback from their clients (in the form of facial expression, etc.) to gauge whether their interpretation is being understood and whether they need to make any adaptations (Brennan & Brown, 1997). In this study, the interpreters were able to maintain eye contact with a "real" Deaf person who "received" the information, thus making the interpretation process as authentic as possible. Interpreters were told to imagine that the Deaf receiver was a second-year university student who had some familiarity with the lecture topic. Writers (e.g., Maroney & Singer, 1996; Napier, 1998a) have commented

[I] had thought, the difficulties [I] had encountered, and the ways [I] had managed [my] interpretation process" (1997, p. 205). The ultimate goal of the retrospective interview in this study was to ask preset focus questions to elicit information from the subjects about their perceptions of the interpreting task. The focus questions asked (a) how the interpreters felt about the overall piece of interpretation; (b) whether they were particularly happy or not happy with anything; (c) what they found most easy or difficult about the piece; (d) whether they had any particular skills or knowledge that contributed to their ability to interpret for the lecture; (e) whether they thought there were any other skills or knowledge, which they did not possess, that may have helped them to interpret the lecture more effectively; and (f) what effect their educational background had on their ability to interpret for the lecture.

The researcher classified the translation styles of each interpreter to determine whether they were dominant in using a free or literal interpretation approach, which allowed for identification of any correlation between the translation style of the interpreter and the number and type of omissions made (for further information on methodology and analysis techniques, see Napier, 2001). After completing the analysis, colleagues of the researcher tested the findings and found them to be reliable.

Justification for Testing Linguistic Coping Strategies

One issue with respect to the methodology should be acknowledged and accounted for. In most circumstances, interpreters work regularly with the same client when that client attends university lectures. Quite often, an interpreter will be booked for a whole semester and, therefore, has the opportunity to get to know the client. In these situations, interpreters also have the advantage of being able to familiarize themselves

---

on the negative effect of not having a Deaf target audience when analyzing the work of interpreters; therefore, it was considered a necessary component of the data collection. It was also considered important to have the same Deaf receiver for all participants because this factor otherwise may have skewed the interpreters' notion of their target audience. Therefore, one Deaf person was hired as a research assistant for the duration of the data collection. He was present at every video-recording, and his role was simply to sit and watch the interpretation without giving any overt comments.

with the content of lectures as well as the pace and delivery style of lecturers and will develop specific ways of working with a client to suit his or her needs.

Some might argue, therefore, that the scenario for this study is unrealistic. However, an entire semester of a university course may not be interpreted by the same interpreter throughout. For example, the interpreter might become ill, and consequently, another interpreter might need to provide cover for this type of assignment without any preparation and without knowing the client. Chafin Seal (1998) often referred to last minute "substitute interpreting" in her discussion of educational interpreting case studies. In other situations, interpreters may withdraw from the assignment if they feel they cannot adequately understand the content to interpret effectively, or a Deaf student may request that the interpreter be replaced if he or she cannot follow the interpretations well enough to suit his or her needs. One Deaf person revealed to the researcher that, during one semester at university, she had 10 different interpreters for one course, for exactly these reasons. The researcher would argue, therefore, that the best way of testing interpreters' linguistic coping strategies is by testing them in a new, possibly unprepared-for situation because that scenario would seemingly be where their skills would be most challenged.

RESULTS

Hatim and Mason (1990) suggested that, when producing a written translation, translators use a process of selective reduction to decide which portions of source text should be omitted. They stated that translators "can and do take responsibility for omitting information which is deemed to be of insufficient relevance" (p. 96). The same suggestion can be made for interpreters, yet interpreters inevitably make some omissions about which they do not necessarily make strategic decisions because the nature of their work is more spontaneous and fast paced. The analysis of the interpretation output of the 10 subjects involved in the study identified and defined five key omission types (see section titled "Omission Taxonomy"), which comprised not only omissions made during a process of selective reduction but also those made inadvertently.

The 10 subjects made a total of 341 omissions across all five categories, with each subject making an average of 34.1 omissions. The highest

TABLE 4.1 *Total Omissions Made by All Subjects Across All Categories*

Omission Categories	Number of Omissions (n = 341)
Conscious strategic (CS)	87
Conscious intentional (CI)	61
Conscious unintentional (CU)	49
Conscious receptive (CR)	52
Unconscious (U)	92
Total	341

number of omissions made by one subject was 50, and the lowest number was 18. Table 4.1 provides a breakdown of the total number of omissions made by all 10 subjects in each omission category.

The figures in Table 4.1 indicate that the most commonly occurring types of omissions were unconscious, followed by conscious strategic, conscious intentional, and conscious receptive; the least occurring type of omission was conscious unintentional. Thus, in terms of strategic use of omissions, more than half of the omissions made by the subjects were at opposite ends of the spectrum.

With minor exceptions, analysis of the number and types of omissions made by individuals involved in the study shows a common thread: Unconscious and conscious strategic omissions are the most frequently occurring omission types. The figures demonstrate that interpreters do consciously rely on the use of omissions as a linguistic coping strategy and, therefore, that not all omissions should be counted as errors. The figures also demonstrate, however, that a large proportion of omissions made by interpreters are not intentional. In studying the occurrence of the discrete omission types more closely, the data show that different factors influenced the rate of particular omission occurrences.

The data show that all signed language interpreters use conscious strategic omissions as a linguistic coping strategy, regardless of their translation style, educational background, or familiarity with the topic. This researcher had hypothesized, however, that the rate at which conscious strategic omissions are used when interpreting for a university lecture would be affected by these factors. In addition, the researcher had predicted that subjects who dominantly used a free interpretation approach would tend to use more conscious strategic omissions than those who

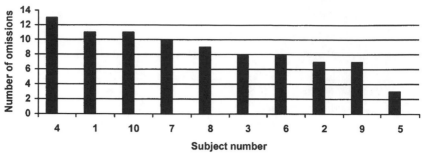

FIGURE 4.1. *Occurrence of conscious strategic omissions per subject.*

dominantly used a literal approach. The reason for this hypothesis was that the process of free interpretation necessitates the search for linguistic and cultural equivalence whereby interpreters judge what is relevant and meaningful to their target audience. Thus, interpreters using a free approach would make conscious decisions to make strategic omissions for the sake of clarity of a message. Alternatively, the researcher had hypothesized that subjects using a more literal interpretation approach would make less conscious strategic omissions because they would concentrate on the form of the message and accuracy of the interpretation rather than on meaningful equivalents.

Similarly, the researcher had predicted that interpreters who had a university qualification and were more familiar with the lecture topic would make more conscious strategic omissions when interpreting for a lexically dense university lecture than those having no qualifications or lacking knowledge of the lecture topic. This prediction was based on the assumption that interpreters with more exposure to the general academic discourse environment would feel more comfortable about making strategic linguistic and cultural decisions with respect to making omissions, especially if they had subject-specific knowledge and could thus judge the importance of terminology used.

Figure 4.1 shows that each interpreter made an average of 9.5 conscious strategic omissions, with the highest number being 13 and the lowest being 3. The majority of interpreters who made more than the average number of conscious strategic omissions dominantly used a free interpretation approach, but note also that other subjects using the same free interpretation approach made fewer than the average number of omissions. The two subjects with no university qualifications made fewer than the average number of conscious strategic omissions, yet so did other

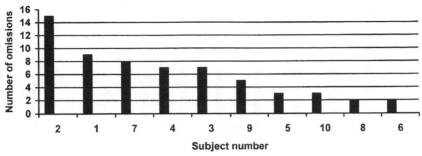

FIGURE 4.2. *Occurrence of conscious intentional omissions per subject.*

subjects with postgraduate qualifications, and paradoxically, the three subjects who made the most conscious strategic omissions were less familiar with the lecture topic. Thus, conscious strategic omissions apparently are used as a linguistic coping strategy by all interpreters, and in the particular discourse environment of a university lecture, the translation style, educational background, and topic familiarity of the interpreters did not influence the rate at which conscious strategic omissions occurred.

The other four omission categories cannot be considered as strategic, even if the interpreters were conscious of making the omissions. Therefore, the fewer number of omissions made intentionally, unintentionally, or unconsciously, the better for a meaningful and accurate interpretation of the message.

As with conscious strategic omissions, no particular pattern appears to occur with conscious intentional omissions (see Figure 4.2). On average, each subject made conscious intentional omissions 6.1 times, with the highest number at 15 and the lowest at 2. The expectation was that those who were not university educated or not acquainted with the lecture topic would make more omissions in this category because they would lack familiarity with the academic language register and subject terminology, yet this behavior was not the case. Although the subject who made the most omissions was not university educated and not acquainted with the lecture topic and the two subjects who made the least number of omissions were educated to postgraduate level and were familiar with the topic, the data did not show enough consistency to suggest that these factors influenced the outcome. Translation style seemed to have no bearing at all.

Conscious intentional omissions were made by subjects who had university qualifications and who were familiar with the subject area; there-

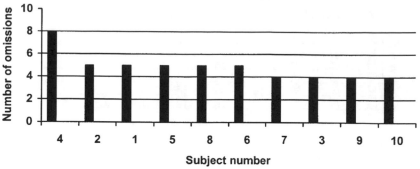

FIGURE 4.3. *Occurrence of conscious unintentional omissions per subject.*

fore, they still made omissions because they could not understand lexical items or concepts or because they did not know the meaningful equivalents in the target language.

Conscious unintentional omissions were made consistently by all subjects regardless of their translation style, educational background, or familiarity with the lecture topic. Almost all subjects made either 4 or 5 conscious unintentional omissions, except for subject number four who made 8 omissions, giving rise to an average number of 4.9 conscious unintentional omissions per subject, as shown in Figure 4.3.

This problem of unintentionally making omissions is an issue of cognitive information processing, which neither could be resolved with either better educational background or increased knowledge of the topic being interpreted nor could be dependent on translation style. All the subjects in the study agreed that they had every intention of interpreting a particular piece of information and had made a strategic decision to wait for further contextual information, but the information somehow had slipped through.

An average of 5.2 conscious receptive omissions were made by each subject, with the highest being 11 and the lowest being 1, as seen in Figure 4.4. Conscious receptive omissions occurred because of reported problems in hearing the source text, which some of the subjects attributed to the poor sound quality of the videotape used. The fact is worth considering, however, that the two interpreters who made well above the average number of conscious receptive omissions had no university qualifications and did not have any familiarity with the lecture topic.

The three subjects who made an average or slightly above average number of conscious receptive omissions were unfamiliar with the lecture

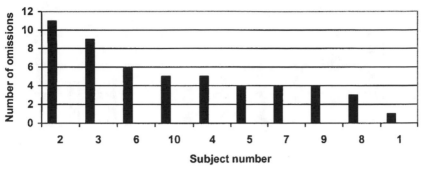

FIGURE 4.4. *Occurrence of conscious receptive omissions per subject.*

topic, but all three had a university education. All those who made fewer than the average number of conscious receptive omissions had a university education and were also familiar with the lecture content, apart from subject one who was unfamiliar with the lecture topic. No correlation was apparent between the number of receptive omissions and the translation style used.

In applying the notion of frame theory to this process, one could assume that those who were more familiar with the discourse environment and lecture topic may have been better equipped to make predictions about the information being presented and, because of their contextual knowledge, more able to "second-guess" lexical items that could not be heard properly. Even those who were not familiar with the topic but had an inherent understanding of general academic discourse may have been able to infer meaning and "fill the gaps" for what they could not hear properly. Those without the advantage of prior knowledge of the topic or familiarity with the language register, however, would have been relying solely on what they could hear, which could explain why an omission would be made if the lexical item could not be heard properly.

Finally, each subject made an average of 9.2 unconscious omissions, ranging from 3 to 16 omissions, which was a much higher figure than anticipated. Although the researcher expected that the subjects would make a number of unconscious omissions, the finding that this type was slightly more prevalent than the use of conscious strategic omissions was surprising. Figure 4.5 shows that, again, the two interpreters with no university qualifications or lecture content knowledge made the most omissions in this category. Apart from these two subjects, however, the distribution of omission occurrences was not consistent with the level of

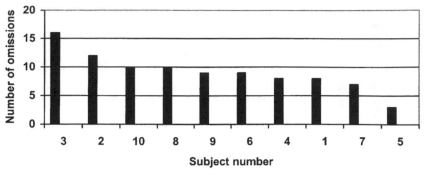

FIGURE 4.5. *Occurrence of unconscious omissions.*

qualification held or familiarity with the topic. The dominant translation style of the interpreters did not seem to affect the number of unconscious omissions made.

Interpreters and interpreter educators generally accept that interpreting every lexical item received is not necessary, but rather, the source-language message should be "chunked" into meaningful parts, and thus, equivalent intent should be sought after in the target language (Winston & Monikowski, 2000). However, the notion that interpreters are making omissions when interpreting a university lecture because they do not even hear the information in the source language, regardless of their level of qualifications or subject knowledge, has implications for interpreter training and suggests a need to raise levels of awareness as to what causes these situations.

Thus far, the evaluation of omission occurrences has demonstrated that the translation style of an interpreter does not significantly influence the rate of omissions in any omission category. On its own, the educational background of interpreters is not a major factor that affects the rate and type of omissions made, and the interpreters' previous knowledge of the lecture topic seems to have only a slight effect on the rate and type of omissions produced. When factors involving educational background and previous knowledge of the topic are combined, however, an increase in erroneous omissions is more likely, especially with conscious receptive omissions and unconscious omissions. A combination, therefore, of interpreters' familiarity with the general academic discourse environment and the subject-specific content and terminology of a lecture would appear to be the most consistent factor in affecting the rate of occurrence of omissions.

Omission Patterns and Familiarity

In analyzing the correlation between omission patterns and familiarity more closely, the data provided specific examples that demonstrated the relationship between the features of language use (which are bound both to the lecture topic and the discourse environment) and the occurrence of different omission types. Not surprisingly, a pattern emerged in which specific features of language use elicited the occurrence of particular omissions, therefore implying that interpreters used their knowledge of language use to identify the significance of the message within the context of the university lecture, which then affected the types of omissions they made.

To identify the specific language features that were involved, the researcher decided to concentrate on key parts of the text that featured a high number of omissions, regardless of the omission type, and look for identifiable relationships between the number of omissions and the text itself. The printed version of the source text produced 176 lines of text wherein only 32% of the lines produced no omissions at all from the 10 subjects. An analysis totaled the number of omissions that were made by each subject in correspondence with each line of text to find which lines of text featured the most omissions. For example, subjects 4 and 6 both made an omission on line 4 of the text, so line 4 totaled 2 omissions. On line 79 of the text, subjects 2, 4, 8, 9, and 10 each made one omission, so this line had 5 omissions. All the subjects made a total of 341 omissions, with an average of 1.95 omissions per line of text. The analysis showed that seven particular lines of text featured the highest proportion of omissions, with seven or more omissions per line. Example 4.1 shows these seven lines of text highlighted in bold in the context of the sentence or paragraph within which they were used.

EXAMPLE 4.1. Lines of text featuring highest proportion of omissions.
First Line
Line 57:   The second issue I'd like to look at is, partly by way of
Line 58: exploding a myth, is the notion of early acquisition. What some people, or we can refer to
Line 59: as precocity or precociousness in, erm, sign language acquisition. There's very much a

Line 60: sort of an idea there in people's minds that children learning a sign language, acquire sign

Line 61: language earlier than children acquiring a spoken language . . .

Second Line

Line 87: Erm, as I said, we don't have time to go into it tonight, but some of the work on early sign

Line 88: language acquisition has, erm, made some interesting points in that regard and led a lot of

Line 89: researchers to challenge the notion that that's the necessary relationship in quite the, the

Line 90: lock-step way that Piaget and others were suggesting. And the last issue that, again, we

Line 91: won't have time to go into tonight is the . . . issue of nativisation and denativisation.

Third Line

Line 103:   Where there's been a long tradition of oral education and

Line 104: very little El Salvador! El Salvador! And very little, er, use of sign language, and there's

Line 105: evidence on kids acquiring, sort of, linguistic or universal characteristics of sign language

Line 106: in the absence of good input, and then gradually as more and more exposure to a formal

Line 107: sign language occurs, denativising and moving towards that particular, erm, set of sign

Line 108: language rules and features.

Fourth and Fifth Lines

Line 114:   Erm, and a number of authors over a long period of

Line 115: time have, and Snow, that we talked about last week, Catherine Snow? Who's been so

Line 116: vocal on the issue of erm, er . . . critical period hypothesis, thank you! (*refers to student*),

Line 117: has done an enormous amount of work on this. So, over to you for a minute. What do we

Line 118: know about the characteristics of caregiver input that makes it, that seems to be a critical

Line 119: component of language acquisition?

Sixth Line

Line 137:   But the actual nature of

Line 138: the features does seem to differ slightly across certain cultural groups. (*student question*)

Line 139: It was definitely a '60s thing, I'm not suggesting you were in the '60s, but there was a '60s-

Line 140: '70s thing, a of, sort of, seeing pop psychology time, you know, making the child a genius

Line 141: type thing, which advocated a particular level of discourse with a child.

Seventh Line

Line 167:   Well you tell me, what are the features of mother-child,

Line 168: motherese baby talk? (*student comment*) Repetition . . . (*student comment*) Erm, to a certain

Line 169: extent, imitation figures more highly in mother-child, you know, "say such and such"

Line 170: (*baby talk intonation*) or "say daddy, say mummy" (*baby talk intonation*).

The types of omissions made by all subjects on each of these lines of text were noted to identify any patterns between omission categories and linguistic features of the text. Table 4.2 provides information on omission types that the subjects made on the seven lines of text.

Although a pattern can be seen with omissions being made on certain lines, not all the omissions were the same; the highest proportion of omissions were conscious strategic omissions or unconscious omissions. Line 59 had nine omissions, 22% conscious strategic and 78% conscious intentional.

The highest number of omissions occurred on lines of text with particular features of language use: (a) unfamiliar (possibly academic English) or subject-specific terms, for example, "precocity" and "precociousness" in line 59 and "critical period hypothesis" in line 116; (b) idiomatic

TABLE 4.2 *Omission Types Made by Subjects on Key Lines of Text*

Subject	Line Number						
	59	90	104	116	117	139	169
1	CS	CI	CS	U	—	U	CS
2	CI	CR	U	U	U	CS	CI
3	CI	CI	CU	CR	U	U	CS
4	CU	U	CS	U	U	CS	CS
5	CI	—	CS	U	U	—	CS
6	CS	—	U	—	—	—	CS
7	CI	U	CS	U	U	CS	CS
8	CI	—	U	—	CU	U	CR & CS
9	CI	U	U	CR	—	CR	U
10	CI	CR	U	—	U	CS	CS

English, for example, "lock-step way" in line 90; (c) names of people or places, for example, "Piaget" in line 90 and "El Salvador" in line 104; (d) repetition in English, for example, "it was definitely a '60s thing, I'm not suggesting you were in the '60s, but there was a '60s-['70s thing]" in line 139; and (e) ambiguities in English, for example, "say such and such" in line 169.

Identifiable patterns of omissions can be seen on these seven lines of text according to the linguistic feature presented. For example, in relation to unfamiliar or subject-specific terms, line 59 featured the terms *precocity* and *precociousness*, and the highest proportion of omissions on this line were in the conscious intentional category. All the subjects who made this type of omission reported either that they did not understand the use of the term in this context or that they did not know how to find an equivalent sign in Auslan. Line 116 produced mostly conscious receptive or unconscious omissions, and the most commonly omitted lexical item was the academic term *hypothesis*. Most subjects explained that, because the concept was unfamiliar to them, they either (a) had focused on the preceding two words, *critical* and *period*, which they considered to be important and did not hear the following word *hypothesis* or (b) were unfamiliar with the term *hypothesis* and could not hear it clearly enough to decipher it.

All but one of the omissions that appeared on line 117 were unconscious and occurred with the phrase "So, over to you for a minute." All the respondents remarked that they probably had not heard this phrase because they were still concentrating on the difficult interpretation of the previous sentence in line 116 and, therefore, experienced cognitive overload.

With respect to repetition in English, lines 104 and 139 both predominantly featured conscious strategic or unconscious omissions, meaning, therefore, that subjects either (a) did not hear the repetition of the words or concept or (b) heard it and chose to delete it. All subjects who had made a strategic omission reported that the repetition was redundant and, thus, that they had made a conscious decision to omit because doing so would not detract from the message.

In relation to ambiguities in English, line 169 featured the phrase "say such and such," and the majority of omissions were conscious strategic. Subjects unanimously commented that it was impossible to interpret this kind of a phrase into Auslan because it was too abstract, so they opted to omit this information in favor of the subsequent phrase "say daddy, say mummy," which presented concrete information that could be clearly interpreted into Auslan.

Finally, although line 90 did not present any consistency in the omission types that occurred, it did demonstrate a pattern when compared with the other lines of text. Several omission types occurred because of the fact that some subjects omitted the term *lock-step way* whereas others omitted the name Piaget. The conscious receptive omissions were made because (a) they were not familiar with the name Piaget and could not hear it pronounced clearly enough and (b) the term *lock-step way* either was not heard at all or was omitted consciously and intentionally because the subjects were not familiar with this idiomatic expression and were unsure how to represent it in Auslan.

The hypothesis had predicted that the type of patterning discussed thus far would also feature in other lines of text that had fewer omissions. Therefore, other lines were chosen at random from those having fewer than seven but above the average number of omissions (mean = 1.95). As anticipated, the number of omissions were higher on lines using subject-specific or unfamiliar terms such as *pronouns* (line 6), *denativising* (line 99) and *motherese* (line 143). Omissions also occurred on lines using English idioms, for example, "photocopy powers that be" (line 10) and "in a nutshell" (line 12) and in lines using names such as Reilly, McIntire, and Bellugi (lines 15 and 16) as well as Caselli and Volterra (line 66). Omissions were found on lines featuring repetition, for example, in line 166: "there's that principle in, in **mother-child**, or **caregiver-child** interaction." The same kind of omission was found with redundant repetition wherein two different words that were perceived by the interpreters to mean the same thing were used one after the other, for example, "what happens to kids when they have **incomplete** or **inadequate** input in their first language" (line 95). English words such as *saliency* (line 151) and *consumable* (line 166), which were deemed by the interpreters as being ambiguous in this context, also featured in lines with above the average number of omissions.

Therefore, one way to explain the pattern of omission occurrence in this text is in relation to interpreters' familiarity with the features of language use that are bound both to the lecture topic and the academic English used in the university discourse environment. Although their familiarity alone did not necessarily affect the number of omissions they made, it certainly seemed to affect the types of omissions that occurred in different parts of the text in relation to the linguistic features presented. In addition, lexical density, another linguistic feature of the discourse environment, was thought to have influenced the prevalence and types of omissions occurring in different parts of the text.

Omission Patterns and Lexical Density

As mentioned earlier, lexical density refers to the complexity of language (Halliday, 1985) and is a concept that can be used to measure the difficulty of a piece of text (Richards, Platt, & Platt, 1992). The researcher hypothesized that more omissions would be made on the most lexically dense parts of the text and, if this hypothesis were the case, that more omissions would therefore be made in the most complex parts of the text. To validate this assumption, it was necessary to calculate the average lexical density of a line of text and compare the number of omissions on an average line of text with the number of omissions present on those lines with higher than average lexical density. The expectation was that a correlation would be found between the number of omissions and the lexical density of a line of text.

The overall lexical density of the university lecture text was 51% (adopting the calculation method proposed by Ure, 1971). Using the same calculation method, the average lexical density of a line of text was calculated at 47.6%. This figure was reached by adding up the total number of words on the first line of each page of text, then dividing each total by the number of lexical words on that line to arrive at a percentage. Of the

TABLE 4.3 *Number of Omissions Compared With Lexical Density of Text*

Line Number	Number of Omissions	Lexical Density
117	7	21.0%
1	0	33.0%
44	1	37.5%
21	2	46.0%
67	0	47.0%
136	1	47.0%
113	1	50.0%
139	8	50.0%
159	0	56.0%
116	7	57.0%
59	10	62.5%
90	7	62.5%
104	10	71.0%
169	11	78.5%

eight lines of text selected at random, three were of average lexical density, two were above the average, and two were below the average. To test the correlation between the number of omissions and lexical density of text, the seven lines of text highlighted as those with the highest number of omissions were also calculated for lexical density. Apart from one anomaly, all the lines of text with the highest number of omissions had a lexical density higher than the average line of text. To identify whether those lines of text with a lower percentage of lexical density produced a smaller number of omissions, all the lines of text that had been analyzed for lexical density were compared for their percentage of density and the number of omissions, as seen in Table 4.3.

Apart from anomalies in lines 117 and 139, Table 4.3 shows that the lexical density of the text does seem to influence the number of omissions. The issue is not whether the lexical density of the text is higher than the average lexical density but, rather, the extent to which it is higher than the average. The lines of text with average lexical density (lines 67 and 136) or below average density (lines 1, 21, and 44) presented between 0 and 2 omissions. The correlation between omissions and density begins when the lexical density of a line of text reaches 57%, almost 10% above the average, and correspondingly shows an almost exponential increase in the number of omissions. Interestingly, those lines with the highest lexical density (104 and 169) were those that featured the highest number of conscious strategic omissions in proportion to the total number of omissions on that line (see Table 4.2).

This superficial analysis shows, therefore, that the lexical density of text does seem to influence the occurrence and type of omissions made by interpreters to some extent. If, as stated by Halliday (1978), university lectures are typically presented in lexically dense text, the results of this study illustrate that, then, signed language interpreters inevitably will make omissions, some of which will be strategic.

One can argue, however, that the lexical density alone does not influence the rate and type of omissions; rather, the lexical items themselves influence omissions, especially in connection with academic discourse and subject-specific terminology. If an interpreter is familiar with content words being used in lexically dense parts of text, then he or she is less likely to erroneously omit the meaning of those particular lexical items but might choose to strategically omit them as part of the linguistic decision-making process. As discussed earlier, however, interpreters may generally experience difficulties in interpreting lexically dense text, depending on the presentation style and whether the text is read out or spontaneous. Therefore, to establish the extent to which lexical density of text affects the rate and occurrence of omissions, one would need to analyze the omissions made by interpreters when interpreting for a lexically dense piece of prepared text that is read out. These preliminary findings do suggest, however, that the lexical density of the source text affects the occurrence of omissions.

Thus far, the analysis has established that the lexical density of source text and familiarity with the source text affects the occurrence and types of omissions made by interpreters. Findings show that the discourse environment influences the number and types of omissions made by signed language interpreters. Data have demonstrated that signed language interpreters make different types of omissions depending on their conscious monitoring of the discourse, the application of their knowledge of the discourse environment, and the linguistic and cultural expectations of the discourse participants. The interpreters' level of metalinguistic awareness during the interpreting process was instrumental in identifying the types of omissions made because, during the task review, they were able to explain exactly why they had made an omission.

During the retrospective interview, the interpreters acknowledged that they believed their educational background had an effect on their ability to interpret the lecture effectively. Some examples of the comments made by the interpreters can be seen in Example 4.2.

EXAMPLE 4.2. Subjects' comments on interpretation of lecture.

"I was hindered by my lack of higher education. . . . I haven't studied since I was 15. I found this task hard because of the academic language used in universities. I didn't have enough knowledge of the subject matter, the English language, or the terminology used."

"I am not familiar with university language and jargon, especially subject-specific words. . . . I don't have a strong educational background. . . . I didn't understand the language sufficiently enough to 'freely' interpret; I think I could have gone for the meaning more."

"I have a university education . . . so I am familiar with the language use . . . but the ideal is to have knowledge of the content. I was comfortable with the level of language because I have interpreted this type of lecture lots of times before. . . . Plus, my educational background helped me to deal with the level of language—I'm used to the university environment and the language use."

"My ability to interpret has improved dramatically since studying at H. E. level. . . . I have a greater understanding of language and how culture and language are linked. I have more familiarity with university level discourse and a better understanding of how someone can use a creative lexicon."

Omission Potential

The results of the empirical study demonstrate the importance of considering omissions within a context of omission types. The data show that interpreters do use omissions proactively, making conscious decisions as a linguistic coping strategy and as an inherent part of the interpreting process. Conscious strategic omissions can be used effectively by interpreters to manage the communication event, and therefore in this context, using omissions is something that interpreters can do well. Nevertheless, one must still recognize that interpreters also make other omissions, conscious or unconscious, intentional or unintentional. The fact that omissions can be used strategically does not negate the fact that erroneous omissions do occur, some of which interpreters are aware and

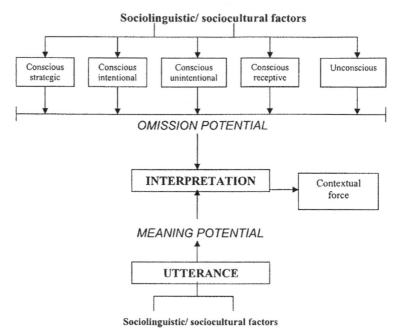

FIGURE 4.6. *Omission potential framework.*

others of which they are not. This study corroborates that, within the framework of an interpretation, erroneous omissions do occur. The key issue to note, however, is that a high percentage of the omissions made by interpreters in this study were conscious strategic omissions—the second most frequent category. When considering interpreting omissions, one should therefore recognize that, for every item of information mistakenly excluded, several more are omitted consciously and strategically to enhance the equivalence of the message.

In accounting for the occurrence of omissions within a context of omission types, the author of this study suggests that omissions should be considered within a framework of omission potential, as seen in Figure 4.6. By doing so, interpreters can recognize the sociolinguistic and sociocultural factors that may influence their production of different omission types. The framework allows for recognition of the fact that omissions can be used strategically to achieve the meaning potential of an utterance but that the potential also exists to make erroneous omissions, which may skew the contextual force of the message.

Another major issue to consider when evaluating the prevalence of interpreting omissions is the context of situation, which, in the case of this study, is the context of a lexically dense university lecture. The results showed that the highest number of omissions tended to occur on higher-than-average lexically dense lines of text (i.e., the most grammatically complex parts of the text) and on lines of text featuring subject-specific terminology or academic terms, (i.e., the most unfamiliar parts of the text). This finding is not particularly surprising; any interpreting scholar would expect interpreters to struggle when dealing with factors contributing to "cognitive overload" (Moser-Mercer, Kunzli, & Korac, 1998). What is a revelation, however, is the extent to which some interpreters in this study used conscious strategic omissions to cope linguistically with the density and complexity of information they were receiving.

Clearly, the discourse environment does have a sociolinguistic effect on the use of omissions. Thus, to make better use of omissions as a conscious linguistic strategy while interpreting for a lexically dense university lecture or, in fact, any university lecture, an interpreter needs to be familiar with academic discourse and preferably with specific subjects before interpreting in a university context. One can assume, therefore, that the more familiar interpreters are with the context of situation and with the characteristics of the discourse environment, the more they will make use of conscious strategic omissions, whether they are working in educational, legal, medical, political, or other arenas.

IMPLICATIONS OF THE STUDY: INTERPRETING IN DIFFERENT CONTEXTS

The focus of this study has been on the linguistic coping strategies of Auslan-English interpreters working in a lexically dense university lecture. However, the findings can be extrapolated to interpreters working in other languages and in other contexts. One can assume that interpreters potentially can make five types of omissions, regardless of the interpreting situation in which they are working. This study has demonstrated that the interpreters involved had high levels of metalinguistic awareness while interpreting, and there is no reason to doubt this awareness would not be the case for other interpreters who are using different signed or spoken languages in different contexts. In addition, one should recognize that sociolinguistic factors such as the context of situation, familiarity with the discourse environment, knowledge of the topic being discussed, and familiarity with the Deaf and hearing interaction participants would affect the rate and types of omission occurrences in situations other than university lectures, regardless of where the interpreting were taking place.

Implications for Signed Language Interpreter Education

The findings of this study have significant implications for the education of signed language interpreters. The results showed that signed language interpreters make different types of omissions while interpreting, one of which is used as a conscious linguistic coping strategy. In addition, the rate and type of omission occurrences were influenced by the complexity of and familiarity with the source text. This finding highlights the need for interpreters to be educated about the types of omissions they make and why they make them. In having a better understanding of various omission types as well as the sociolinguistic and sociocultural influences on their occurrence, interpreters will be able to develop skills to use certain omissions proactively as a linguistic coping strategy while having heightened awareness about the possibilities of erroneous omissions. By making students aware of the omission potential of any interpretation, interpreter educators can help students to enhance their metalinguistic awareness of the linguistic decisions made throughout the interpretation process. The implications of this study point to suggestions for further research that would expand on the ideas presented here.

Future Research

To further explore the context of situation examined in this study, researchers might consider conducting a study of signed language interpreters working in a lecture that was not lexically dense but was in a similar situation. For example, interpretation of a conference keynote presentation could be compared with the lecture interpretation in this study to highlight similarities and differences in use of translation style and omissions as linguistic coping strategies. Alternatively, researchers could conduct a comparative study of omissions made by signed language interpreters interpreting for a lecture that is read out verbatim from a prepared text, a context in which the text would be even more lexically dense than the one used in this study and, thus, more complex to interpret.

Another comparative study could involve interpretations of the same university lecture but, this time, allowing the interpreters more preparation and time to clarify terminology, academic terms, and so forth. This altered methodology would provide interesting contrastive data that would show exactly how the use of linguistic coping strategies changed and to what extent.

A valuable project would be to replicate this study in different contexts and analyze the rate and prevalence of omissions that were conscious strategic, conscious intentional, conscious unintentional, conscious receptive, and unconscious in these other interpreting scenarios. This comparison would identify the different factors that affect the use of conscious strategic omissions and the production of erroneous omissions in, for example, a medical appointment, a job interview, a conference paper, a board meeting, or a university tutorial. The research could then be taken one step further, contrasting interpreters who are working in identical situations after having received more preparation. The same replication could offer opportunities to analyze the strategic use of free and literal interpretation approaches in different contexts.

Although these suggestions for research do not represent an exhaustive list, they are offered as a way to reach the goal of discovering more about interpreters and interpreting and broadening our understanding of the various linguistic processes and factors involved. Any future research should endeavor to develop a better understanding of the relationship among interpreters, consumers, and the discourse environments in which they participate in interactive events. Additional research will allow interpreters, interpreter educators, and interpreter researchers to further explore the linguistic coping strategies of interpreters and the factors that influence the outcome of an interpreted communicative event. Research enables us to consider not whether interpreters succeed or fail but, rather, what strategies they use and what contributions they make to the outcomes of communicative events.

REFERENCES

Altman, H. J. (1989). Error analysis in the teaching of simultaneous interpretation: A pilot study. *Fremdsprachen, 33*(3), 177–183.

Baker, C., & Cokely, D. (1980). *American Sign Language: A teacher's resource text on grammar and culture.* Silver Spring, MD: T. J. Publishers.

Baker, M. (1992). *In other words: A coursebook on translation.* London: Routledge.

Barik, H. A. (1975). Simultaneous interpretation: Qualitative and linguistic data. *Language and Speech, 18,* 272–297.

Bialystok, E. (1991). Metalinguistic dimensions of bilingual proficiency. In E. Bialystok (Ed.), *Language processing in bilingual children* (pp. 113–140). Cambridge: Cambridge University Press.

Bialystok E., & Ryan, E. B. (1985a). The metacognitive framework for the development of first and second language skills. In D. L. Forrest-Pressley, G. E. Mackinnon, & T. G. Waller (Eds.), *Metacognition, cognition and human performance* (pp. 207–252). New York: Academic Press.

Bialystok, E., & Ryan, E. B. (1985b). Toward a definition of metalinguistic skill. *Merrill-Palmer Quarterly, 31,* 229–251.

Brennan, M., & Brown, R. (1997). *Equality before the law: Deaf people's access to justice.* Durham, UK: Deaf Studies Research Unit, University of Durham.

Brown, P., & Fraser, C. (1979). Speech as a marker of situation. In K. Scherer & H. Giles (Eds.), *Social markers in speech* (pp. 33–62). Cambridge: Cambridge University Press.

Chafe, W. (1980). *The pear stories: Cognitive, cultural and linguistic aspects of narrative production.* Norwood, NJ: Ablex.

Chafin Seal, B. (1998). *Best practices in educational interpreting.* Needham Heights, MA: Allyn and Bacon.

Clark, E. V. (1978). Awareness of language: Some evidence from what children say and do. In A. Sinclair, R. J. Jarvella, & W. J. M. Levelt (Eds.), *The child's conception of language* (pp. 17–44). Berlin: Springer-Verlag.

Cokely, D. (1983). When is pidgin not a pidgin? An alternate analysis on the ASL-English contact situation. *Sign Language Studies, 38,* 1–24.

Cokely, D. (1985). *Towards a sociolinguistic model of the interpreting process: Focus on ASL and English.* Unpublished doctoral dissertation, Georgetown University, Washington, DC.

Cokely, D. (1992a). Effects of lag time on interpreter errors. In D. Cokely (Ed.), *Sign language interpreters and interpreting* (pp. 39–69). Burtonsville, MD: Linstok Press.

Cokely, D. (1992b). *Interpretation: A sociolinguistic model.* Burtonsville, MD: Linstok Press.

Cokely, D. (1995, September). *When worlds collide: Reflections on interpreting differing cultural realities*. Keynote paper presented at the Issues in Interpreting 2 conference, University of Durham, Durham, UK.

Council for the Advancement of Communication with Deaf People (CACDP). (1997). *Directory 1997/98*. Durham, UK: Author.

Crystal, D. (1984). *Who cares about usage?* New York: Penguin.

Crystal, D. (1987). *The Cambridge encyclopedia of language*. Cambridge: Cambridge University Press.

Crystal, D. (1995). *The Cambridge encyclopedia of the English language*. Cambridge: Cambridge University Press.

Crystal, D., & Davey, D. (1969). *Investigating English style*. Bloomington, IN: Indiana University Press.

Darò, V., Lambert, S., & Fabbro, F. (1996). Conscious monitoring of attention during simultaneous interpretation. *Interpreting, 1*(1), 101–124.

Davis, J. (1990). Linguistic transference and interference: Interpreting between English and ASL. In C. Lucas (Ed.), *Sign language research: Theoretical issues* (pp. 308–321). Washington, DC: Gallaudet University Press.

Dean, R., & Pollard, R. Q. (2001). The application of demand-control theory to sign language interpreting: Implications for stress and interpreter training. *Journal of Deaf Studies and Deaf Education, 6*(1), 1–14.

Deuchar, M. (1979). *Diglossia in British Sign Language*. Unpublished doctoral dissertation, Stanford University, Stanford, CA.

Deuchar, M. (1984). *British Sign Language*. London: Routledge and Kegan Paul.

Enkvist, N. E. (1973). Should we count errors or measure success? In J. Svartvik (Ed.), *Errata* (pp. 16–23). Lund: CWK Gleerup.

Fenton, S. (1993). Interpreting in New Zealand: An emerging profession. *Journal of Interpretation, 6*, 155–166.

Finegan, E., Besnier, N., Blair, D., & Collins, P. (1992). *Language: Its structure and use*. Sydney, NSW: Harcourt Brace Jovanovich.

Fontana, S. (1999). Italian Sign Language and spoken Italian in contact: An analysis of interactions between Deaf parents and hearing children. In E. Winston (Ed.), *Storytelling and conversation: Discourse in Deaf communities* (pp. 149–161). Washington, DC: Gallaudet University Press.

Fox, G. (Ed.). (1988). *Collins Cobuild essential English dictionary*. Glasgow: William Collins Sons & Co.

Frishberg, N. (2000). An interpreter creates the space. In K. Emmorey & H. Lane (Eds.), *The signs of language revisited: An anthology to Ursula Bellugi and Edward Klima* (pp. 169–192). Hillsdale, NJ: Erlbaum.

Fromkin, V., Rodman, R., Collins, P., & Blair, D. (1990). *An introduction to language* (2nd Australian ed.). Sydney, NSW: Holt, Rinehart and Winston.

Garton, A., & Pratt, C. (1998). *Learning to be literate: The development of spoken and written language.* Oxford: Blackwell.

Gerot, L., & Wignell, P. (1995). *Making sense of functional grammar.* Cammeray, NSW: Antipodean Educational Enterprises.

Goffman, E. (1974). *Frame analysis.* New York: Harper and Row.

Goffman, E. (1981). *Forms of talk.* Oxford, UK: Blackwell.

Gumperz, J. (1982). *Discourse strategies.* Cambridge: Cambridge University Press.

Halliday, M. A. K. (1978). *Language as a social semiotic: The social interpretation of language and meaning.* London: Edward Arnold.

Halliday, M. A. K. (1985). *Spoken and written language.* Burwood, Victoria: Deakin University Press.

Halliday, M. A. K. (1993). *Language in a changing world.* Melbourne: Applied Linguistics Association of Australia, Deakin University.

Halliday, M. A. K., & Hasan, R. (1985). *Language, context and text: Aspects of language in a_social semiotic perspective.* Burwood, Victoria: Deakin University Press.

Hatim, B., & Mason, I. (1990). *Discourse and the translator.* London: Longman.

Hoffman, R. (1997). The cognitive psychology of expertise and the domain of interpreting. *Interpreting, 2,* 189–230.

Hymes, D. (1972). Models of the interaction of language and social life. In J. Gumperz & D. Hymes (Eds.), *Directions in sociolinguistics: The ethnography of communication* (pp. 35–71). New York: Holt, Rinehart and Winston.

Isham, W. (1986). The role of message analysis in interpretation. In M. McIntire (Ed.), *Interpreting: The art of cross cultural mediation* (pp. 111–122). Silver Spring, MD: RID Publications.

Johnston, T. (1989). *Auslan dictionary: A dictionary of the sign language of the Australian Deaf community.* Maryborough, Victoria: Deafness Resources Australia.

Joos, M. (1967). *The five clocks.* New York: Harbinger.

Karmiloff-Smith, A. (1986). From meta-processes to conscious access: Evidence from children's metalinguistic and repair data. *Cognition, 23,* 95–147.

Kopczynski, A. (1980). *Conference interpreting: Some linguistic and communicative problems.* Poznan, Poland: Adam Mickiewicz Press.

Kyle, J., & Woll, B. (1985). *Sign language: The study of deaf people and their language.* Cambridge: Cambridge University Press.

Lee, D. (1982). Are there really signs of diglossia? Re-examining the situation. *Sign Language Studies, 35,* 127–152.

Livingston, S., Singer, B., & Abramson, T. (1994). Effectiveness compared: ASL interpretation versus transliteration. *Sign Language Studies, 82,* 1–54.

Llewellyn Jones, P. (1981). *Target language styles and source language processing in conference sign language interpreting.* Paper presented at the Third International Symposium on Sign Language Interpreting, Bristol, UK.

Llewellyn Jones, P., Kyle, J., and Woll, B. (1979). *Sign language communication.* Paper presented at the International Conference on Social Psychology and Language, Bristol, UK.

Longacre, R. E. (1983). *The grammar of discourse.* New York: Plenum.

Lucas, C., & Valli, C. (1989). Language contact in the American Deaf community. In C. Lucas (Ed.), *The sociolinguistics of the Deaf community* (pp. 11–40). Washington, DC: Gallaudet University Press.

Malakoff, M., & Hakuta, K. (1991). Translation skill and metalinguistic awareness in bilinguals. In E. Bialystok (Ed.), *Language processing in bilingual children* (pp. 141–165). Cambridge: Cambridge University Press.

Maroney, E., & Singer, B. (1996). Educational interpreter assessment: The development of a tool. In D. Jones (Ed.), *Assessing our work: Assessing our worth. Proceedings of the 11th National Convention of the Conference of Interpreter Trainers, October 1996* (pp. 93–148). N.p.: Conference of Interpreter Trainers (CIT).

Messina, A. (1998). The reading aloud of English language texts in simultaneously interpreted conferences. *Interpreting, 3*(2), 147–161.

Metzger, M. (1995). *The paradox of neutrality: A comparison of interpreters goals with the reality of interactive discourse.* Unpublished doctoral dissertation, Georgetown University, Washington, DC.

Metzger, M. (1999). *Sign language interpreting: Deconstructing the myth of neutrality.* Washington, DC: Gallaudet University Press.

Moser-Mercer, B. (1997). Methodological issues in interpreting research: An introduction to the Ascona workshops. *Interpreting, 2*(1/2), 1–12.

Moser-Mercer, B., Kunzli, A., & Korac, M. (1998). Prolonged turns in interpreting: Effects on quality, physiological and psychological stress (Pilot study). *Interpreting, 3*(1), 47–64.

Napier, J. (1998a). *An analytical study of free interpretation and its use by British Sign Language interpreters.* Unpublished master's thesis, University of Durham, UK.

Napier, J. (1998b). Free your mind—The rest will follow. *Deaf Worlds, 14*(3), 15–22.

Napier, J. (2000). Free interpretation: What is it and does it translate into training? In A. Schembri, J. Napier, R. Beattie, & G. Leigh (Eds.), *Deaf studies, Sydney 1998: Selected papers from the Australasian Deaf Studies Research Symposium, Renwick College, Sydney, 22–23 August 1998*

(Renwick College Monograph No. 4, pp. 21–33). North Rocks, NSW: North Rocks Press.

Napier, J. (2001). *Linguistic coping strategies of sign language interpreters.* Unpublished doctoral dissertation, Macquarie University, Sydney, Australia.

National Accreditation Authority of Translators and Interpreters (NAATI). (1999). *Directory of accredited and recognised practitioners of interpreting and translation.* National Accreditation Authority of Translators and Interpreters. Retrieved March 24, 1999, from the World Wide Web: http://www.naati.com.au

Neumann Solow, S. (2000). *Sign language interpreting: A basic resource book* (Rev. ed.). Burtonsville, MD: Linstok Press.

Nida, E. (1998). Translators' creativity versus sociolinguistic constraints. In A. Beylard-Ozeroff, J. Králová, & B. Moser-Mercer (Eds.), *Translators' strategies and creativity* (pp. 127–136). Philadelphia: John Benjamins.

Nord, C. (2000, January). *Translating as a text-production.* Paper given as part of the on-line Innovation in Translator and Interpreter Training Symposium, January 17–25, 2000. Retrieved January 18, 2000, from the World Wide Web: www.fut.es/~apym/symp/nord.html

O'Loughlin, K. (1995). Lexical density in candidate output and semi-direct versions of an oral proficiency test. *Language Testing, 12*(2), 99–123.

Ozolins, U., & Bridge, M. (2000). Emerging needs in Auslan/English interpreting. In A. Schembri, J. Napier, R. Beattie, & G. Leigh (Eds.), *Deaf studies, Sydney 1998: Selected papers from the Australasian Deaf Studies Research Symposium, Renwick College, Sydney, 22–23 August 1998* (Renwick College Monograph No. 4, pp. 86–97). North Rocks, NSW: North Rocks Press.

Pergnier, M. (1978). Language meaning and message meaning: Towards a sociolinguistic approach to translation. In D. Gerver & H. W. Sinaiko (Eds.), *Language interpretation and communication* (pp. 199–204). New York: Plenum Press.

Peterson, R. (2000). Metacognition and recall protocols in the interpreting classroom. In C. Roy (Ed.), *Innovative practices for teaching sign language interpreters* (pp. 132–152). Washington, DC: Gallaudet University Press.

Richards, J., Platt, J., & Platt, H. (1992). *Dictionary of language teaching and applied linguistics.* Singapore: Longman.

Roy, C. (1989). *A sociolinguistic analysis of the interpreter's role in the turn exchanges of an interpreted event.* Unpublished doctoral dissertation, Georgetown University, Washington, DC.

Roy, C. (1992). A sociolinguistic analysis of the interpreter's role in simultaneous talk in a face-to-face interpreted dialogue. *Sign Language Studies, 74,* 21–61.

Roy, C. (1996). An interactional sociolinguistic analysis of turntaking in an interpreted event. *Interpreting, 1*(1), 39–68.

Roy, C. (2000a). *Interpreting as a discourse process.* Oxford: Oxford University Press.

Roy, C. (2000b). Training interpreters—Past, present and future. In C. Roy (Ed.), *Innovative practices for teaching sign language interpreters* (pp. 1–14). Washington, DC: Gallaudet University Press.

Russell, D. (2000, October). *If you'll pause a moment, I'll interpret that: Courtroom interpreting.* Paper presented to the 13th National Convention of the Conference of Interpreter Trainers, Portland, OR.

Ryan, E. B., & Giles, H. (1982). *Attitudes towards language variation: Social and applied contexts.* London: Edward Arnold.

Sacks, H. (1974). An analysis of the course of a joke's telling in conversation. In R. Bauman & J. Sherzer (Eds.), *Explorations in the ethnography of speaking* (pp. 337–353). Cambridge: Cambridge University Press.

Schank, R. C., & Abelson, R. P. (1977). *Scripts, plans, goals and understanding: An inquiry into human knowledge and structures.* Hillsdale, NJ: Erlbaum.

Schegloff, E. (1972). Sequencing in conversational openings. In J. Gumperz & D. Hymes (Eds.), *Directions in sociolinguistics: The ethnography of communication* (pp. 346–380). New York: Holt, Rinehart and Winston.

Schiffrin, D. (1993). "Speaking for another" in sociolinguistic interviews. In D. Tannen (Ed.), *Framing in discourse* (pp. 231–263). New York: Oxford University Press.

Scott Gibson, L. (1992). Sign language interpreting: An emerging profession. In S. Gregory & G. Hartley (Eds.), *Constructing deafness* (pp. 253–258). Milton Keynes, UK: Open University Press.

Sinclair, J., & Coulthard, R. (1975). *Towards an analysis of discourse: The English used by teachers and pupils.* London: Oxford University Press.

Siple, L. (1995). *The use of additions in sign language transliteration.* Unpublished doctoral dissertation. State University of New York, Rochester.

Smith, M. (2000). Enhancing self-regulation in ASL/English interpreting: Promoting excellence in interpreter education. In *CIT at 21: Celebrating excellence, celebrating partnership. Proceedings of the 13th National Convention of the Conference of Interpreter Trainers* (pp. 89–102). Silver Spring, MD: RID Publications.

Stokoe, W. (1969). Sign language diglossia. *Studies in Linguistics, 20,* 27–41.

Sunnari, M. (1995). Processing strategies in simultaneous interpreting: "Saying it all" versus synthesis. In J. Tommola (Ed.), *Topics in interpreting* (pp. 109–119). Turku, Finland: University of Turku, Centre for Translation and Interpreting.

Tannen, D. (1979). What's in a frame? Surface evidence for underlying expectations. In R. Freedle (Ed.), *New directions in discourse processing* (pp. 137–181). Norwood, NJ: Ablex.

Tannen, D. (1984). *Conversational style*. Norwood, NJ: Ablex.

Tannen, D. (1993). *Framing in discourse*. Oxford: Oxford University Press.

Tunmer, W. E., & Bowey, J. A. (1984). Metalinguistic awareness and reading acquisition. In W. E. Tunmer, C. Pratt, & M. L. Herriman (Eds.), *Metalinguistic awareness in children: Theory, research and implications*. Berlin: Springer-Verlag.

Tunmer, W. E., & Herriman, M. L. (1984). The development of metalinguistic awareness: A conceptual overview. In W. E. Tunmer, C. Pratt, & M. L. Herriman (Eds.), *Metalinguistic awareness in children: Theory, research and implications*. Berlin: Springer-Verlag.

Ure, J. (1971). Lexical density and register differentiation. In G. E. Perren & J. L. M. Trim (Eds.), *Applications of linguistics: Selected papers of the 2nd International Congress of Applied Linguistics* (pp. 443–452). Cambridge: Cambridge University Press.

Wadensjö, C. (1998). *Interpreting as interaction*. London: Longman.

Wardhaugh, R. (1992). *An introduction to sociolinguistics*. Oxford: Blackwell.

Wilcox, S., & Wilcox, P. (1985). Schema theory and language interpretation. *Journal of Interpretation, 2,* 84–93.

Winston, E. (1989). Transliteration: What's the message? In C. Lucas (Ed.), *The sociolinguistics of the Deaf community* (pp. 147–164). San Diego, CA: Academic Press.

Winston, E. A., & Monikowski, C. (2000). Discourse mapping—Developing textual coherence skills in interpreters. In C. Roy (Ed.), *Innovative practices for teaching sign language interpreters* (pp. 15–66). Washington, DC: Gallaudet University Press.

Woodward, J. (1973). Some characteristics of pidgin Sign English. *Sign Language Studies, 3,* 39–46.

Wray, A., Trott, K., & Bloomer, A. (1998). *Projects in linguistics: A practical guide to researching language*. London: Hodder Headline Group.

Zimmer, J. (1989). Toward a description of register variation in American Sign Language. In Lucas, C. (Ed.), *The sociolinguistics of the Deaf community* (pp. 253–272). New York: Academic Press.

Profile of Each Subject

Subject	Dominant Translation Style	University Qualifications	Familiarity With Lecture Topic
1	Literal	Other UG	Unfamiliar
2	Extreme literal	None	Unfamiliar
3	Extreme literal	None	Unfamiliar
4	Free	Interp PG	Unfamiliar
5	Extreme literal	Interp PG	Familiar
6	Free	Interp PG	Unfamiliar
7	Free	Interp UG	Familiar
8	Free	Interp PG	Familiar
9	Extreme free	Interp PG	Familiar
10	Extreme free	Interp UG	Unfamiliar

Note. Interp PG = Postgraduate qualification related to interpreting (e.g., Deaf studies, linguistics); Interp UG = Undergraduate qualification related to interpreting; Other PG = Postgraduate qualification not related to interpreting; Other UG – Undergraduate qualification not related to interpreting; None – No university qualifications.

Adverbials, Constructed Dialogue,

and Use of Space, Oh My!:

Nonmanual Elements Used

in Signed Language Transliteration

Bruce A. Sofinski

One widely held view in the profession is that two different disciplines are practiced within the work that signed language interpreters do: "Interpretation refers to the process of changing messages produced in one language immediately into another language" (Frishberg, 1990, p. 18) whereas transliteration refers to occasions when an interpreter translates from a signed message into spoken English and alternately also "gives the viewer English in a visually accessible form" (p. 19). Often, the voice-to-sign component is used to differentiate these two disciplines. By definition, the target language for voice-to-sign interpretation is American Sign Language (ASL). However, no comparable consensus exists with respect to the target for transliteration (Sofinski, Yesbeck, Gerhold, & Bach-Hansen, 2001).

Early descriptions of transliterating unequivocally state that the target is a form of manually coded English (MCE) (compare Frishberg, 1990; Siple, 1997; Solow, 1980). More recent descriptions posit that the product of transliteration incorporates ASL features in English order. The current consensus is that, at the very least, the target for transliterating is certainly not ASL; rather, it is English-based (Defining Interpretation ..., 1996; Frishberg, 1990; Humphrey & Alcorn, 2001; Kelly, 2001; Siple, 1997; Solow, 2001; Stewart, Schein, & Cartwright, 1998).

Stauffer and Viera (2000) sum up the current situation with respect to transliteration this way:

There is no one generally accepted, identifiable definition of transliteration in the field of interpretation today. . . . The effect on individuals who prepare to take transliteration credentialing tests is that candidates are left on their own to synthesize the various definitions and descriptions of transliteration with program training and testing expectations. (p. 75)

Although an adequate amount of linguistic research has been conducted to provide a useable description of what ASL (and by extension interpreting) is, the same obviously cannot be said of transliteration. Many questions still linger, including the question pertaining to what language features are contained within an adequate description of transliteration (Sofinski et al., 2001; Stewart, Schein, & Cartwright, 1998).

HISTORICAL DESCRIPTION OF TRANSLITERATION

Siple (1997) provides an overview of the definitions, descriptions, and research conducted on transliteration since the mid-1960s. The changes are presented with the background of the various social forces that affected the original description and subsequent modifications of transliteration. By and large, these works are necessarily anecdotal in nature because empirical evidence on signed language and the related field of signed language interpreting was generally nonexistent.

As late as 1990, texts commonly used in interpreter education defined the process of transliteration only in terms of English and MCE (Frishberg, 1990). During the last decade, the work of Winston (1989) has changed the description of transliteration to include the production of "the message in an English-based sign language while maintaining meaning" (Kelly, 2001, p. 18).

The definition of forms of manually coded English (MCE) has remained constant since the early 1970s with one exception—contact signing. Early literature establishes MCEs as a set of invented or contrived manual systems intended to represent English (Bornstein, 1973; Crystal & Craig, 1978), which does not include the naturally occurring phenomenon that Woodward (1973) called Pidgin Sign English (PSE). Lucas and Valli (1992) reanalyzed the phenomenon researched by Woodward and, instead, find a situation of language contact called "contact signing," a nonstandardized mixture of English and ASL features that varies by individual and situation. Some authors categorize contact signing as an MCE (Humphrey &

Alcorn, 2001; Kelly, 2001; Siple, 1997). Others adhere to the original definition of MCE, restricting that definition to contrived manual systems, and they place contact signing into the category of naturally occurring phenomena (Solow, 2001; Stewart, Schein, & Cartwright, 1998).

English word order and English mouth movements are commonly described as English language features that are contained in the products of transliteration (Humphrey & Alcorn, 2001; Kelly, 2001; Solow, 2001; Stewart, Schein, & Cartwright, 1998). English word order occurs in the transliteration product with "minimal changes and English is usually mouthed as spoken in the original English [source] text" (Solow, 2001, p. 14). According to Kelly (2001), "Transliterators also need to be aware of features borrowed from ASL, such as lexical choices, head and body shifting, use of location, verb modulation, and use of facial and nonmanual markers" (p. 18).

PREVIOUS RESEARCH ON TRANSLITERATION

McIntyre (1986) reported on the analysis of transliteration conducted as part of the 1984 Conference of Interpreter Trainers (CIT). The findings included different strategies that transliterators may use, including (a) omission and (b) addition, the restructuring of information or lexical items, or both.

Siple (1997) provides a historical overview of the development of the definition of transliteration. Within this work, Siple summarizes the findings of previous empirical research done with respect to transliteration. These findings include the following:

1. Winston (1989) challenged the notion that transliteration was a simple recoding of spoken English and identified five strategies used by the participant in the study—sign choice, addition, omission, restructuring, and mouthing.

2. Siple (1993) identified and described the strategy of midsentence, between-sentence, and between-topic pausing in transliteration.

3. Siple (1995) provided greater detail with respect to Winston's identification of additions as a strategy used in transliteration, further describing the strategy as being used to achieve cohesion, emphasis, clarification and modality adaptation.

Sofinski et al. (2001) identified nine core features of voice-to-sign transliteration by educational interpreters. These researchers posited that at least two different groups of transliteration—sign-driven and speech-driven—are based on these core features.

Anecdotal reports suggest that, just as the product of one competent interpreter differs in form from the product of another competent interpreter, consumer preferences also vary. In fact, the task to anticipate the signed language interpreting preferences of one individual according to those expressed by another is very difficult, if not impossible, to achieve.

Viera and Stauffer (2000) conducted a study on the preferences of consumers of signed language transliteration. The responses parallel earlier definitions of *translation* and *transliteration*. One reported preference is representative of the general consensus: "All words that appear on the mouth are exactly as spoken; no transposition of words or terms" (Viera & Stauffer, p. 94). The respondents further explained that they did not want ASL, rather, "someone who moves his/her mouth and is expressive" (p. 94).

Gonzalez (1981) wrote in support of the need for oral transliteration. In her justification, she referenced the training of signed language interpreters and how they are "taught silently to mouth what they sign" (p. 1). Gonzalez describes the problems that are associated with a consumer of oral transliteration attempting to access the English message through the mouth movements of a signed language interpreter as being part of the complex process used by a signed language interpreter:

> It is, and naturally so, very difficult to concentrate also and adequately on *saying* each word clearly. As a result, and usually without the signed language interpreter being aware of it, many words are only partially formed on the lips; others are left out altogether (especially when they are not signed). This means the person trying to speechread gets bits and pieces, rather than whole words, connected phrases, and sentences. Further, since speechreading "invisible" words and words that look alike depends heavily on the context, it is extremely important that *all* the words "be there." (Gonzalez, 1981, pp. 1–2, emphasis in the original)

METHODOLOGY

Part of the initial motivation for conducting this study was to ascertain whether or not sign language transliteration could be effective in the K–12 setting. To this end, a 10-question instrument was designed to assess each student's knowledge of the specific program information contained in the source videotape (e.g., the Technology Assistance Program [TAP] and the Virginia Relay Center [VRC]). The on-site coordinator administered this instrument to each student immediately before and then again immediately after exposure to the sign language transliteration event. The sign language transliterators were informed of this procedure before the interpreting event. However, none of the sign language transliterators were made aware of the specific items included in the pretest-posttest instrument before videotaping.

Participants

At the time of this study, the participants were either full-time employees of or full-time students enrolled in the same county public school system in Central Virginia. Each individual volunteered his or her time to take part in the study; no participant received renumeration for his or her valuable time and effort.

Signed language transliterators. The selection of the interpreters adhered to criteria determined in conjunction with the administration of the local education agency (LEA). The pool consisted of full-time educational interpreters whom the LEA uses and who satisfy the minimum criteria for signed language interpreters as established in Virginia Department of Education (VDOE) regulations (i.e., possession of a valid Virginia Quality Assurance Screening [VQAS] credential, Level III or higher). Each interpreter in this pool was then asked whether he or she would be willing to be involved in a study on the effectiveness of signed language transliteration in the K–12 setting. From those in the pool who agreed to participate, one transliterator was selected for each of the five groups of students who are deaf or hard of hearing.

At the time of the study (March 2000), four of the five full-time K–12 educational interpreters participating in this study possessed a valid VQAS Level III credential in transliteration. The fifth participant possessed a valid NAD Level IV credential.[1]

On-site coordinator. Integral to the completion of this study was the identification of the on-site coordinator at each of three schools (elementary, middle, and high school). The resource teacher for the hearing impaired students at each school was selected to perform in this capacity because of his or her ability to communicate effectively as signers in addition to being native speakers of English. Each on-site coordinator (a) identified potential participants; (b) obtained permission for the students to be involved in the study; (c) consulted with other teachers with respect to the schedule of each child to ensure participation; and (d) placed participants into groups of 3–6 students, resulting in two elementary-age groups, one middle-school-age group, and two high-school-age groups.

Deaf or hard of hearing students. Twenty-one students representing all K–12 grades except for Grades 1, 6, and 11 participated in the study. Criteria for student selection required that the students be enrolled in the county's hearing impaired program and that they have written permission provided by a parent or legal guardian to allow the student's participation in the study.

Apparatus

A 7-minute-and-45-second videotaped presentation about technology services of the Virginia Department for the Deaf and Hard of Hearing (VDDHH) was produced specifically for use as the source material for this study. (See Appendix 5.A for a transcript of the segment.) The speaker regularly presents on this topic in various settings, including the K–12 classroom. A television with a screen of at least 21 inches was connected to a regular VHS videocassette recorder in each setting. Both the television and the recorder were situated on a portable audiovisual cart. Two camcorders (one regular VHS camcorder and one Super VHS camcorder) were used to record the product of each signed language transliterator.

----

1. Within six months of the conclusion of the study, two of the participants received the RID Certificate of Transliteration [CT]; the other three study participants did not attempt the RID CT assessment. These attempts were independent of the study.

Transliterator Survey

At the end of his or her participation, each interpreter completed the survey (see Appendix 5.B), which was designed to collect specific demographic information and other information with respect to each signed language interpreter's participation in the study. This information was used to determine that the goal of the interpreter was transliteration and that the interpreter believed the goal had been achieved.

Procedure

Approximately one week before the date of exposure to the students, each transliterator was provided a copy of the source videotape in its entirety. At that time, the researcher explained that this tape would be the precise source used in the study. Each transliterator was encouraged to become familiar with the material. If any transliterator posed any questions about how to interpret the material (i.e., "What is the sign for —— — ," "How would you do ——— "), the researcher replied "I really don't want to influence your product." However, the researcher did indicate that the product should be transliteration, whatever the transliterator considered that type of product to be.

At the time when each transliterator was to produce his or her product, the transliterator entered the room and chose a location to stand. Before the students entered the classroom, two camcorders were set on tripods to face wherever the transliterator had decided to stand, which in every case was next to the television and facing the chairs that had been set up for the students. The cameras were then manipulated to capture not only the transliterator's signing space but also at least part of the television to capture references made by the transliterator to the image on the screen. The beginning of the source tape was then played to set the appropriate volume for the transliterator.

Immediately after the conclusion of the group's exposure to the videotape, the transliterator completed the transliterator survey. The researcher reminded each interpreter to record the identification number of any student who, in the interpreter's opinion, did not attend to the product.

Three variables were used to ensure that the product was signed language transliteration. First, each transliterator completed a waiver form allowing VDDHH to release to the researcher VQAS scores verifying that each transliterator satisfied the minimum requirement established

TABLE 5.1 *Total English Words Mouthed (by Segment of Source)*

Product	1	2	3	4	5	6	Total/ Percentage	Range
Spoken Source	100	116	100	107	102	116	641/100.0%	100–116
Interpreter E1	70	54	54	61	63	67	369/57.6%	54–70
Interpreter E2	82	60	81	84	80	90	477/74.4%	60–90
Interpreter M1	80	59	68	67	58	70	402/62.7%	58–80
Interpreter H1	69	64	62	62	63	61	381/59.4%	61–69
Interpreter H2	80	72	75	76	77	73	453/70.7%	72–80

by VDOE. Second, the transliterator survey was used to verify that transliteration was the goal of the interpreter. Finally, the videotaped products were rated in accordance with VQAS procedures to ensure that these specific products would not have disqualified any transliterator from potentially achieving at least a VQAS Level III in transliteration, which would satisfy the minimum requirement for K–12 educational interpreters in the Commonwealth of Virginia.[2]

After successfully completing the control process, the researcher analyzed the first half of each of the five transliteration products for nonmanual features. Those features occurring in the mouth channel were synchronized to coincide with the text of the source. Commonalities in the various products were noted. Then, the researcher analyzed in detail a 41-second, 100-word segment of this 3-minute segment to determine the use of mouth movements.

RESULTS

The researcher recorded the movements of the mouth channel of all five transliterators for the first 2 minutes and 49 seconds of the source material. During this section of the source, the presenter speaks 641 English words. The total number of English words mouthed by each of the five interpreters (see Table 5.1) during the portion of the work related to this same section of the source ranges from 369 to 477.

2. The actual achievement of a VQAS level depends on demonstrating minimal competency in three segments: voice-to-sign, sign-to-voice, and interactive (one-on-one). However, the current study addresses only the voice-to-sign component.

This nearly 3-minute section of the presentation was then divided into 44 structures of which 40 contained independent clauses (e.g., "These are two programs that we offer.") and 4 were lengthy subordinates (e.g., "and over 250 amplifiers for people all over the state."). The mouth movements of each interpreter were then recorded and compared to the actual spoken English words of the source. Although many of the mouth movements that were recorded represented English words that were the same as those words spoken in the source, on several occasions, the product incorporated English words that were not found in the source. In fact, out of these 44 structures analyzed, only one of the five products contained mouth movements representing English words in the same syntactic order, without interruption, as found in the source, and this product produced only one occurrence during this section ("Here, at VDDHH, we offer two programs.").

The researcher then more closely analyzed the data in a 41-second, 100-word segment of this section to categorize the mouth movements made by each interpreter (see Table 5.2). The findings resulted in a more precise tally of mouth movements in three categories: (a) representations of English words, (b) adverbial usage—mouth movements required in ASL to express adverbial information, and (c) omissions of English words in the source.

Representation of English Words

The mouth movements that represented English words were grouped into three categories: (a) the replication of spoken English words present in the source; (b) the substitution, on both the lexical and syntactic levels, of English words present in the source; and (c) the addition of English words not found in the source.

REPLICATION OF ENGLISH WORDS SPOKEN IN THE SOURCE

The most frequently occurring phenomenon was the replication of the mouth movements related to English words spoken in the source. The occurrence among participants, as represented by English-like mouth movements in the products, ranged from 38% to 63% of the actual source words. An example of virtually every part of speech (e.g., noun, pronoun, verb, adjective, conjunction, etc.) was replicated in the product of all interpreters.

TABLE 5.2 *Analysis of Mouth Movements in Segment 3*

Product	TOTAL (English Word) Representation	(Source Word) Replication	(English Word) Addition	(Source Word) Substitution	(Target) Adverbials	(Product) Mouth Movements	TOTAL (Source Word) Omission
E1	54	38	4	12	5	59	50
E2	81	63	4	14	5	86	23
M1	68	51	2	15	7	75	34
H1	62	47	1	14	1	63	39
H2	75	49	2	24	2	77	27

Note. (a) Representation = the total number of English words represented by mouth movements in the product; (b) Replication + Substitution + Omission = product manifestations of the 100 English words spoken in Segment 3; (c) Replication + Addition + Substitution + Adverbials = total number of mouth movement items noted in Product.

SUBSTITUTION OF ENGLISH WORDS SPOKEN IN THE SOURCE

Literal replacement (i.e., a one-for-one exchange of an English word found in the source with mouth movements representing a different English word form in the product) was the most frequently occurring substitution. For example, one section of the source reads, "This amplifier allows people who are hard of hearing to turn up the volume." One of the participants maintains the original lexical choice made by the speaker (i.e., *allows*) whereas three of the interpreters lexically replace *allows* with *let* or *lets* as evidenced by their mouth movements.[3]

This same example provides insight into the interpreting process on a nonlexical level because the fifth product syntactically restructures this structure as the following shown in Example 5.1.

(See Appendix 5.C for an explanation of all transcription formats used in this chapter.)

Examples of common (i.e., occurring in at least four of the five products) lexical replacement that were found within the 41-second segment

3. Winston (1989) identified this strategy as "conceptual sign choice."

EXAMPLE 5.1

Source: This amplifier allows people who are hard-of-hearing to turn up on the volume.

Interpreter E1:

<u>Persons hard of hearing can</u>   {MM————————————→}
PERSON HARD-OF-HEARING CAN {sh: CL-1 (moves vertically 1–2 inches)}
                                       {bh: CL-Y (stationary)—————→}
                                       {*increase volume of amplifier*   }

include the following: (a) *phone* for *telephone* , which occurred in four of the five products during the phrase "talking on the telephone"; (b) *can* for *could* (as in "Anybody in the state could apply"), which occurred in all five products; and (c) several different substitutions for *anybody* (as in, "Anybody in the state"), which included *everyone, any person* (by two participants), *any people*, and *anyone*.

ADDITION OF ENGLISH WORDS NOT FOUND IN THE SOURCE

Mouth movements found in the product that did not appear in the source were the least frequent category of mouth movements representing English words that were identified in this segment. The most common example co-occurred with a rhetorical question in the product. The source contains the question, "How do you go about getting them?" Three of the products ended with ASL rhetorical questions: (a) "How get that, how?"; (b) "How do you get {an adverbial that is mouthed in conjunction with WHAT-DO}"; and (c) How do you get them, how?"

Another example of an addition occurred in conjunction with a substitution on the syntactic level. When the source used the phrase "people who are hard of hearing" outside of referencing the four categories of individuals eligible for the Technology Assistance Program (TAP), the product of one interpreter rephrased the source as "people can't hear well." This example contains all three types of English word representation that have been identified: (a) replication (e.g., *people* used in both the source and the product); (b) substitution (i.e., lexical—*hear* for *hearing*—or phrasal—*can't hear well* for *hard of hearing*); and (c) addition (e.g., *can't, well* added to the product).

Adverbial Use

In the source, the following structure was a fertile ground for the addition of adverbials: "Any of these people, anywhere across the state, can apply to get TTYs or amplifiers." During this sentence, four participants incorporated at least one adverbial. One interpreter expressed *anywhere across* as shown in Example 5.2.

EXAMPLE 5.2

Source: Any of these people, <u>anywhere across the state</u>, can apply to get TTYs or amplifiers.

Interpreter E1:

{Puffed cheeks————————————————————→} state

{ALL-AROUND-THERE (sh moves in arc from right to left in front of chest)} STATE

Three other participants, in varied ways, used the same previously established referent (i.e., a list of categories of persons eligible for TAP who are Deaf, hard of hearing, speech disabled, or deaf-blind); they referred to this list and coproduced an adverbial wherein the index finger of the strong hand references "down the list of four categories" (see Example 5.3).

EXAMPLE 5.3

Source: <u>Any of these people,</u> anywhere across the state, can apply to get TTYs or amplifiers.

Interpreter M1:

    Any people   {Puffed cheeks ————————————————→}

sh: ANY   PEOPLE   {CL-1 (index finger pad arcs above finger pads of base hand)}

bh: {CL-"3-plus-ring-finger" (stationary)————————→}

Anyone who is deaf, hard of hearing, deaf-blind or speech disabled

Interpreter H1:

    Any (of) {(pursed lips*————————————————→}

sh: ANY   {CL-1 (index finger pad arcs above finger pads of base hand)}

bh: {CL-"3-plus-ring-finger" (stationary)————————→}

Anyone who is deaf, hard of hearing, deaf-blind or speech disabled

Interpreter H2:

{(pursed lips*————————————————→} (break) {(pursed lips——→}

sh: {CL-1 (index finger pad arcs above finger pads of base hand)}   INCLUDE

bh: {CL-4 (stationary)————————————————→}

Including people who are deaf, hard of hearing, deaf-blind or speech disabled

* Interpreters H1 and H2 may have been using "MM," but the data was not definitive.

These three products exemplify another type of syntactic substitution that combines both English mouth movements and adverbial mouth movements. In relation to the phrase "Any of these people," two products incorporated both replication of English words contained in the source and substitution of English form by an adverbial in conjunction with the reference of the established referent (see Example 5.3, products of Interpreters M1 and H1). A third participant substituted the entire English phrase with two adverbials in conjunction with manual features (see Example 5.3, product of Interpreter H2).

Omission of English Words Spoken in the Source

When the 44 structures were compared with the recorded mouth movements of each of the five products, at least one omission was identified within every structure in each product (with the exception of the one example provided above). For illustration, within the subordinate structure, "so they can hear better when they're talking on the telephone," each interpreter produced between 3 and 7 omissions of English words contained in the source:

· Interpreter E1—"hear more when talk-talk telephone"
· Interpreter E2—"hear better . . . talk on the phone . . . hear better"
· Interpreter M1—"can hear better when you talk . . . on the phone"
· Interpreter H1—"can hear better when talking on the phone"
· Interpreter H2—"They hear more clearly when they use the phone."

On a syntactic level, the above examples show that four of the five products dropped the subject (i.e., *they*) of the clause, which is a pronoun and the antecedent of "people who are hard of hearing."

Nonmanual Features Identified Outside the Mouth Channel

Numerous occurrences of nonmanual features occurred outside of the mouth channel. The products of all five participants evidenced the incorporation of three features: (a) direction of eye gaze, (b) constructed dialogue, and (c) a combination of nonmanuals (e.g., eye gaze combined with body shift, etc.) to support the use of space for comparison and contrast.

DIRECTION OF EYE GAZE

Common use of eye gaze occurred in many instances across all five products. For example, a shift of eye gaze (i.e., a change in direction of the pupils away from the audience) co-occurred during both between-sentence and between-topic pauses. Eye gaze was also commonly directed toward the location of the hands when establishing or referring to a list of categories (i.e., listing). Eye gaze and head turn directed toward the television screen also served as use of space in referencing the image of the speaker or the type of equipment being discussed.

CONSTRUCTED DIALOGUE

Numerous instances of constructed dialogue occurred in all five products. In one instance, all five participants exhibited the various roles expressed in the following passage: " You would type what [*sic*] is that you have to say. They would read it on their screen, which [*sic*] you can see the screen on here, and then they would type back to you." One example of constructed action in this passage that related to "and then they would type back to you" uses eye gaze to establish tokens and surrogates as well as body shift and body lean to identify change in speaker role (see Example 5.4).

EXAMPLE 5.4

Source: ... and then they would type back to you.

Interpreter H2:

| Then | {would type | } | {(pursed lips*)————————→} | {back | } |

THEN (point) {CL-4 (keying on TTY)} {TTY-TO (directed to surrogate)} {#BACK (directed to surrogate)}

Then they would type back to you.

* Interpreter H2 may have been using "MM," but the data was not definitive.

Similar nonmanuals supporting the use of space (i.e., in the establishment and incorporation of token and surrogates) during constructed dialogue occurred in all five products.

Constructed dialogue also occurs in the interpreter products when it is not implied in the source. For example, the source said, "So, when you go home you need to ask Mom and Dad how much they earn." During the interpretation of this passage, three participants assumed the role of the child by means of (a) eye gaze directed at the adult surrogate, (b) head movement directed in conjunction with change in eye gaze, (c) change to first person address of question, and (d) modification in body posture (i.e., like a young child addressing his or her parent). The mouth-channel movements of two of these three products are shown in Example 5.5. The third product involves no adverbial but simply expresses "ASK MOM AND DAD (role shift to child asking parents): HOW MUCH MONEY EARN?"

EXAMPLE 5.5

Source: So when you go home you need to ask Mom and Dad how much they earn?

Interpreter E1:

| {do-do} | go | home | to- | day | {you ask} | {"mom-dad" | } |

{WHAT-DO} GO-TO HOME NOW DAY {ASK-TO} {MOTHER^FATHER }(role shift to child asking parents)

| {how much | } | {"mon" | } | {MM————→} |

{HOW-MUCH} {MONEY} {EARN-MONEY }

Interpreter M1:

When	you go	home	ask		{MM———→}
#SO HAPPEN	GO-TO	HOME	REQUEST (role shift to ask Mom and Dad)		

{QUESTION-TO}

Mom and Dad,	{how much }	money (you)	{earn }
MOTHER FATHER	{HOW-MUCH}	MONEY	{EARN-MONEY}

COMBINATION OF NONMANUALS FOR
COMPARISON AND CONTRAST

The source message "So, the next program that I want to talk about, in addition to the TAP Program, here at the agency we also have the Virginia Relay" indicates a major change in topic in the source. In the corresponding portion of the product, all five products incorporated eye gaze in conjunction with head turn and other nonmanual elements (e.g., pause). Three products emphasized eye gaze in the direction of the audience during a body shift to assume a new role; one contained eye gaze and head turn following the movement of the hands as they "pushed" the TAP Program off to the right-hand side of the signing space; and the fifth product contained eye gaze and head direction after the vertical drop of the hands in producing the sign NEXT-ON-THE-AGENDA.

DISCUSSION

After considering the results of this study, one could logically question whether the data examined are examples of what is systemically called signed language transliteration or whether they are signed language interpretation. The transliterator survey (see Appendix 5.B) clearly shows that the interpreters both (a) intended to perform transliteration and (b) in their retrospective determination, reported that these products are representative of their transliteration products. Also, the raters of the VQAS agreed that these products meet the minimum requirement established for K–12 educational interpreters in Virginia for the voice-to-sign transliteration segment (i.e., VQAS Level III). Another important point to note is that, within 6 months of the study, two of the five participants were awarded an RID Certification of Transliteration (CT).[4]

The mouth movement features identified in the current study reflect the obvious English influence of the spoken English source on all five of the transliterated products. However, descriptions of mouth movements used in transliteration typically identify the goal as being the production of complete English sentences: "In transliteration, cohesive English sentences are visibly presented on the lips, either the exact words from the original text or English paraphrasing of the original text" (Kelly, 2001, p. 16).

The findings of the current study do evidence the production of English-like mouth movements. However, few of these mouth-movement patterns represent complete English sentences. Furthermore, at a point that is less than a minute into the source and immediately following the first major topic change, participants begin a marked difference in the mouth-movement patterns, which reflect less of the source's syntactic structure. Even before this change, however, the mouth movements are not complete English sentences.

For example, about 30 seconds into the source comes the sentence, "The first program, Technology Assistance Program or TAP, is a [*sic*] equipment program." Four of the five products express the following through mouth movements (an ellipsis represents a physical pause in the mouth channel of the product):

- **Interpreter E1:** "First program called TAP or Technology Assistance Program. That equipment program."
- **Interpreter E2:** "The first one . . . Technology Assistance . . . we call TAP for equipment program."
- **Interpreter M1:** "First program, Technology Assistance Program . . . equipment program . . ."
- **Interpreter H1:** "The first, Technology Assistance Program . . . equipment program . . ."

The fifth product expresses the mouth movements shown in Example 5.6.

---

4. The other three participants did not attempt the RID performance test during this time frame.

EXAMPLE 5.6

Source: The first program, Technology Assistance Program or TAP, is an equipment program.

Interpreter H2:

First   {(pursed lips*)————————————————→}, TAP ... that's

FIRST   {sh: CL-1 (contacts index finger of the wh two times} T-A-P ... THAT

         {wh: CL-2 (stationary)————————————→}

equipment   program.

E-QUIPMENT PROGRAM

The first of these two programs is called "TAP," which is an equipment program.

* Interpreter H2 may have been using "MM," but the data was not definitive.

      The influence of the spoken English source is evident in the English mouth movements on both lexical and syntactic levels. However, none of these products express a complete English sentence.

      Another example occurs after the first major topic change, which happens about 2 minutes into the source. The speaker says, "Well, through TAP, it may not cost you anything; it may be free." In conjunction with this structure, the mouth movements three of the participants are as follows:

- **Interpreter E1:** "With that program, call TAP, maybe free . . . maybe free."
- **Interpreter M1:** "When use TAP cost nothing . . . maybe free . . . none."
- **Interpreter H2:** "With TAP, maybe not cost anything . . . maybe free."

      The mouth movements of the remaining two participants are shown in Example 5.7.

EXAMPLE 5.7

Source: Well, through TAP, it may not cost you anything; it may be free.

Interpreter E2:

So	through	TAP maybe not cost you {any- thing }... maybe free ... free

TELL-YOU THROUGH #TAP   MAYBE NOT COST   {ANY THINGS}... MAYBE FREE ... F-R-E-E

(mouth open)   {(pursed lips*)}

COST   NONE

There may be no cost through TAP, it may be free ... free! No cost at all!

Interpreter H1:

TAP,	maybe	not	cost	{MM——→}. Maybe free.

#TAP ...   MAYBE   NOT   COST   NONE.   MAYBE FREE.

There may be no cost through TAP. It may be free.

* Interpreter E2 may have been using "MM," but the data was not definitive.

The products shown in Example 5.7 are typical of some of the mouth movement patterns closest to complete English sentences. One can see from this example that, although the spoken English source undeniably influences the product, the mouth movements in the product do not represent cohesive English sentences. Instead, these mouth-channel features appear to represent some type of literal, simultaneous interpretation of the material contained in the source, material that is often represented in the same syntactic order but with substantial omission and frequent restructuring. This pattern is similar to a recent description of mouth movements and other nonmanual elements in the contact signing discourse of a female deaf adult who attended 12 years of education at a residential school for the deaf before the advent of MCEs (Sofinski, 2002).

The analysis also considered a phenomenon that Winston (1989) called "conceptual sign choice" and that Kelly (2001) calls "ASL lexical choices." In the analysis discussed in this chapter, the process controlling this phenomenon appears to be a form-for-form, literal replacement of lexical items (i.e., an ASL lexical item in the target was substituted for a spoken

English word in the source). However, on several occasions, the ASL lexical item used in the target did not contain English mouth movements; in fact, some were classifier predicates or verb constructions that were co-produced with an adverbial in the mouth channel. In these cases, no English feature was identified.

There are other ASL features identified by Kelly (2001) to be included in a transliterated product. Head nod, head turn, body shift, and body lean were repeatedly noted in each product. Although these nonmanual elements occur throughout each product, they occur most consistently across products during the act of constructed dialogue. As part of this feature, the head and body shifts that are made in conjunction with eye gaze, facial expression, and body language all contributed toward the assumption of a character role. These elements were also noted during the use of space for comparison and contrast.

Evidence to Support Previous Findings of Transliteration Research

Similar to the findings reported by McIntyre (1986), the findings of this study identified occurrences involving replication of the English words of the source, omissions, additions, and restructuring. In addition, the current study identifies another type of English representation—substitution—and the use of an ASL mouth movement feature—adverbial usage.

Siple (1997) provides a detailed summary of transliteration research through the mid-1990s (Siple, 1993, 1995; Winston, 1989). The results of the present study generally support these previous findings. In particular, Winston's (1989) assertion that transliteration is not a "simple recoding" is clearly supported.

All five of the participants in the current study used pausing frequently throughout their transliterating products, and the analysis supports the findings of Siple (1993) with respect to within-sentence, between-sentence, and between-topic occurrences. Within-sentence pausing occurred frequently in all five products near dependent structures such as "These two pieces of equipment, or telephones, that are offered" Between-sentence pausing repeatedly co-occurred with eye gaze and head turn directed to the television image of the speaker. The most noticeable pause in all five products occurred during the transition between the two main topics of the speaker (i.e., the Technology Assistance Program and the

Virginia Relay Service). During this time, the speaker also takes a relatively long pause as follows: "So, you could use the telephone, all by yourself, and not have to depend on anyone else. (pause) So, the next program that I want to talk about, in addition to the TAP Program here at the agency, we also have the Virginia Relay."

The findings of Siple (1995) are also supported in the results of the current study. She detailed Winston's (1989) identified strategy of addition, identifying four categories: cohesion, emphasis, clarification, and modality adaptation. The products analyzed in this study include examples of these categories:

· Cohesion: Product of Interpreter H1 in Example 5.3 for "Any of these people, anywhere across the state."
· Emphasis: "How get that, how?"
· Clarification: Product of Interpreter E2 in Example 5.7 for "Well, through TAP, it may not cost you anything; it may be free."
· Modality adaptation: As in the interpreter points to TV screen of speaker holding up TTY.

The findings of the current study support six of the nine common features of voice-to-sign transliteration posited in Sofinski et al. (2001):

· Shadow (English mouth movements) accompanies fingerspelling.
· Nonmanual signals (NMS) include instances of topicalization.
· Lexical meaning base includes instances of prepositions.
· Space includes instances of listing.
· Lexical meaning base is ASL-semantic.
· Syntax follows form of source (with possible deletions).

However, the findings were unable to support a primarily textual or sentential mouth-movement pattern, which Sofinski et al. (2001) had identified. The final two of the common features identified by Sofinski et al. (syntax of frozen text follows form of source and lexical form includes selective initialization) were not part of the analysis of this study.

One major difference between the current study and Sofinski et al. (2001) is that the current study involved the presence of a live audience whereas the Sofinski et al. study did not. The Sofinski et al. study was conducted under the conditions of a signed language interpreter testing environment (i.e., the interpreter alone in a room with a TV-VCR and a camcorder-tripod with no live audience to provide feedback). Additional investigation is needed to determine whether and how the presence of a live audience affects the nonmanual aspects of signed language interpreting and transliteration.

A second important difference between these studies is that the participants in the current study had access to the source videotape the week before being recorded. In contrast, although most of the participants in the Sofinski et al. study had not been previously exposed to the source, those that had previous exposure did not know the nature of the source before the recording event.

Stauffer and Viera (2000) compared the needs of consumers with the preparation and practice of transliterators and concluded that "inconsistencies exist between what consumers need and/or prefer from transliterators and what transliterators actually do (the product)" (p. 75). The findings of the current study support this conclusion. The mouth-movement elements of the five products reported in the current study largely parallel the responses reported by these researchers.

The transliterators in the current study produced transliterations that included features similar to those described by Stauffer and Viera (2000). However, these transliterations do not reflect the expressed preferences of consumers. For example, the survey done by Viera and Stauffer (2000) present one consumer's feedback: "I request someone who will lip sync in English and put signs in English word order. What percentage of the time is this responded to appropriately? Never!" (p. 92). At the same time, not all of these respondents necessarily expressed a preference for a verbatim expression of the source through mouth movements; some simply wanted clear English words expressed through the product.

The demographics of the 58 respondents to the Viera and Stauffer (2000) survey are important to note: (a) respondents had an average age of 49 years, 4 months; (b) 74% of the 58 respondents reported holding a graduate degree, and all but one respondent reported having some type of college degree (i.e., associate degree or higher); and (c) a pattern was evident in which respondents self-reported a spouse or partner having normal hearing. In these respects, the respondents to the survey overrepresent one particular segment of the Deaf community.

The results of the current study also concur with the anecdotal reporting of Gonzalez (1981) that the mouth movements of signed language interpreters did not meet the need of (i.e., did not provide complete English words and sentences for) consumers or oral interpreters. Another important consideration is the context of the time during which Gonzalez used the term *interpreter* in the generic sense and not in comparison to *transliterator*. In fact, in her description, she mentions, "sign language interpreters are now taught silently to mouth what they sign" (p. 1). Clearly, this analysis shows that the earlier anecdotal descriptions of transliteration conflict with the observations of consumers, particularly those who focus primarily on mouth movements.

FURTHER RESEARCH

Winston was "unable to determine a pattern to the relationship between sign choice and mouthing" (Winston, 1989, as cited in Siple, 1997, p. 92). Although the current study did not focus on this relationship, evidence showed that each participant represented English words through mouth movements without support in the manual channel and vice versa, similar to a recent description of contact signing by a deaf adult (Sofinski, 2002). In Sofinski's (2002) single-subject study, "[s]even instances of full English mouthing without sign support were noted" (p. 39). The mouth movements that were produced without manual support in both the current study and the single-subject study included mouthing of subjects (it, that), verbs (*to* [in infinitives], was), and conjunctions (or, and).

Two texts (Humphrey & Alcorn, 2001; Solow, 2001) reference the term *Conceptually Accurate Signed English (CASE)*. With the continuing popularity and use of this term in K–12 as well as in freelance-contract situations and training, a detailed observational description of the elements that constitute a "CASE product" is needed. Humphrey and Alcorn (2001) identify CASE as the name for a system of signs, or MCE, "that has evolved primarily among interpreters" (p. 4.17). In contrast, Solow (2001) lists CASE as a subsection of language contact and describes it as a "common communication style characterized by the incorporation of traditional ASL signs, some newer signs, some contrived signs and fingerspelling, along with speech and speechreading, signed generally in English grammatical order in an effort to represent English visually" (p. 14). So, is CASE a naturally occurring phenomenon or is it contrived? If it is contrived, then where is the related literature describing its creation?

The profession of signed language interpreting, supported largely by anecdotal reports, has systemically embraced the use of the term *translit-*

eration. This usage is largely based on the notion that, in the work done by transliterators, processing from the source to the target remains in one language. However, more recent empirical investigation (Lucas & Valli, 1992; Sofinski et al., 2001; Winston, 1989) consistently report the existence of ASL features within the products of transliterators. The work and process of spoken language interpreters (Gile, 1995) is now being applied to the work of signed language interpreters (Patrie, 2001). This examination of a range of translation from "literal" to "free" (Metzger & Fleetwood, 1997) could potentially lead to a reevaluation of the concepts of a "language continuum" (Baker-Schenk & Cokely, 1980; Solow, 2001) and to the systematic separation of the work of signed language interpreters into two disciplines according to the target language.

CONCLUSION

This preliminary investigation examines the occurrence of nonmanual elements in what is commonly called signed language transliteration. During the same 3-minute section of source material, the majority of mouth movements recorded in each of five interpreter products represent English words. However, not all of the English words represented appear in the source. The replication of mouth movements representing English words contained in the source account for 38–63% of all English words spoken by the presenter. In fact, less than 1% of the 220 structures analyzed (i.e., 44 source structures compared with the relative segments of five interpreting products) are complete English sentences. These findings directly conflict with the RID definition of mouth movement patterns in transliteration: "Cohesive English sentences are visibly presented on the lips, either as exact words from the original text or as English paraphrasing of the original text" (Defining Interpretation . . ., 1996).

After replication, substitution was the next most common element found in the mouth channel. Literal replacement is the most common type of substitution on the lexical level, although this phenomenon also occurred on the phrasal level. The analysis also identified the presence of additions (i.e., mouth movements representing English words not found in the spoken English source) and adverbials in the products of all five interpreters. These findings support Winston's (1989) claim that transliteration is not just a "simple recoding" of the source.

Finally, outside of the mouth channel, the five products shared other nonmanual elements in common. Eye gaze, body shift, body lean, and head turn were frequently noted. These nonmanual elements supported constructed dialogue and the use of space for comparison and contrast. Both constructed dialogue and the use of space are commonly found in ASL discourse.

The results clearly show, then, that each of these products share phonological, morphological, and syntactic elements more in common with ASL than English. Therefore, the analysis of the products in this study support the findings of previous studies of transliteration. As is the case with previous studies, the transliteration products here are not in keeping with the common definition of transliteration (Frishberg, 1990). This finding has implications that are far reaching. With respect to interpreting practice, the transliterations produced by transliterators are not in keeping with the expressed preferences of consumers.

Further research is needed to see how consumers actually respond to the products that are being produced. Are these products tolerated or preferred? Are these products comprehended or "reinterpreted?" How do these growing findings relate to the use of transliterators in mainstream education programs that purport to expose children who are deaf and hard of hearing to English by visual means? Moreover, how do professional examinations account for the tripartite distinction among the expressed preferences of consumers of transliteration, the anecdotal descriptions by professionals with respect to transliteration, and the empirical findings of researchers of transliteration?

With respect to interpreter practice in the educational setting, how does the role of the interpreter vary at the elementary, middle school, and high school levels? Does a particular role affect the interpreter's delivery style or reinforcement of the message? Does the age of the consumer influence an interpreter's product? Is role or product variation common across competent educational interpreters working at the same educational level but housed in different school districts?

With respect to interpreting theory, to what extent is the process of transliteration similar to that of interpretation? Does the field of signed language interpretation actually comprise separate, distinct, and definable processes and products or is the issue akin to the age-old concern about free as opposed to literal translation (Metzger & Fleetwood, 1997)? With respect to interpreter education, how are students of interpretation currently being taught to transliterate? Do the skills being taught prepare these students for the professional examinations and the real world of interpreting?

Finally, this study raises questions from a sociolinguistic perspective. Where do the language choices made by interpreters and consumers converge, and how do language policy and language attitudes affect the expressed preferences of consumers and the products of interpreters?

Clearly, this study has raised numerous questions. The findings, however, make one thing extremely clear: More research with respect to the processes and products of interpretation have the potential to positively affect practicing interpreters, deaf and hearing consumers of interpreting services, professional examinations, language policy affecting deaf children, interpreter preparation curricula, our understanding of sociolinguistic issues in deaf communities, and our understanding of interpreting theory and practice.

REFERENCES

Baker-Schenk, C., & Cokely, D. (1980). *American sign language: A teacher's resource text on grammar and culture*. Silver Spring, MD: T. J. Publishers.

Bornstein, H. (1973). A description of some current sign systems designed to represent English. *American Annals of the Deaf, 188*, 454–463.

Bridges, B., & Metzger, M. (1996). *Deaf tend your: Non-manual signals in ASL*. Silver Spring, MD: Calliope Press.

Crystal, D., & Craig, E. (1978). Contrived sign language. In I. M. Schlesinger & L. Namir (Eds.), *Sign language of the Deaf: Psychological, linguistic and sociological perspectives* (pp. 141–168). New York: Academic Press.

Defining interpretation and transliteration. (1996, May). *RID Views, 13*, 9.

Gile, D. (1995). *Basic concepts and models for interpreter and translator training*. Philadelphia: John Benjamins.

Frishberg, N. (1990). *Interpreting: An introduction*. Silver Spring, MD: RID Publications.

Gonzalez, K. (1981). Why oral interpreting? In D. L. Castle (Ed.) *Oral interpreting: Selections from papers by Kirsten Gonzalez* (pp. 1–4). Washington, DC: Alexander Graham Bell Association of the Deaf.

Humphrey, J. H., & Alcorn, B. J. (2001). *So you want to be an interpreter?: An introduction to sign language interpreting* (3rd ed.). Amarillo, TX: H & H Publishers.

Kelly, J. E. (2001). *Transliterating: Show me the English*. Alexandria, VA: RID Press.

Lucas, C., & Valli, C. (1992). *Language contact in the American Deaf community*. San Diego, CA: Academic Press.

McIntyre, M. (Ed.). (1986). New dimensions in interpreter education: Task analysis, theory, and application. Silver Spring, MD: Registry of Interpreters for the Deaf.

Metzger, M., & Fleetwood, E. (1997). *What is transliteration, anyway?* Presentation to the Florida RID conference, Tampa, FL.

Patrie, C. J. (2001). *Translating from English: Teacher's guide: The Effective Interpreting Series*. San Diego, CA: DawnSignPress.

Siple, L. A. (1993). Interpreters' use of pausing in voice to sign transliteration. *Sign Language Studies, 79,* 147–180.

Siple, L. A. (1995). *The use of addition in sign language transliteration*. Unpublished doctoral dissertation, University of New York, Buffalo.

Siple, L. A. (1997). Historical development of the definition of transliteration. *Journal of Interpretation, 77–100.*

Sofinski, B. A. (2002). So, why do I call this English? In C. Lucas (Ed.), *Turn-Taking, fingerspelling, and contact in signed languages: Vol. 8. Sociolinguistics of the Deaf Community* (pp. 27–50). Washington, DC: Gallaudet University Press.

Sofinski, B. A., Yesbeck, N. A., Gerhold, S. C., & Bach-Hansen, M. C. (2001). Features of voice-to-sign transliteration by educational interpreters. *Journal of Interpretation, 47–59.*

Solow, S. N. (1980). *Sign language interpreting: A basic resource book*. Burtonsville, MD: Linstok Press.

Solow, S. N. (2001). *Sign language interpreting: A basic resource book* (Rev. ed.). Burtonsville, MD: Linstok Press.

Stauffer, L. K., & Viera, J. A. (2000). Transliteration: A comparison of consumer needs and transliterator preparation and practice. *Journal of Interpretation, 61–80.*

Stewart, D. A., Schein, J. D., & Cartwright, B. E. (1998). *Sign language interpreting: Exploring its art and science*. Boston: Allyn & Bacon.

Viera, J. A., & Stauffer, L. K. (2000). Transliteration: The consumer's perspective. *Journal of Interpretation, 83–97.*

Verbatim Script of "VDDHH Technology Programs: TAP and Virginia Relay"
Presentation by Susan Roach

Hi. My name is Susan Roach, and I work with the Virginia Department for the Deaf and Hard of Hearing. I'm here today to tell you about two programs that we offer at the agency.

Here, at VDDHH, we offer two programs. The Technology Assistance Program, known as TAP, and the Virginia Relay Service. These are two programs that we offer.

The first program, Technology Assistance Program, or TAP, is a equipment program, and what we do is provide telephones to people all across the state. There are two types of telephones that I want to talk to you about.

A TTY, which is also known as a TeleTypewriter, is one of the pieces of equipment that we offer. This phone, as you can see, has a keyboard, looks like a typewriter, but it also functions as a phone.

So, if you wanted to call someone else who had a TTY, you could call them directly. You would type what is that you have to say. They would read it on their screen, which you can see the screen on here, and then they would type back to you. So, you would take turns talking just as you do in a regular talk with your friends.

So, the TTY is one way to make telephone calls.

Another way to make telephone calls is by using an amplifier. This amplifier allows people who are hard-of-hearing to turn up the volume so that they can hear better when they're talking on the telephone.

These two pieces of equipment, or telephones, that are offered through TAP. How do you go about getting them?

Well, through the TAP Program you would need to apply. Anybody in the state could apply as long as they are deaf, hard of hearing, speech disabled, or deaf-blind. Any of these people, anywhere across the state, can apply to get TTYs or amplifiers.

So through the Technology Assistance Program, known as TAP, you can apply to get a TTY or an amplifier.

Well, as you know, when you apply or you go to buy things, sometimes it costs. Well, through TAP, it may not cost you anything; it may be free. Depends on two things, whether you can get the equipment free or not. One is how much money your parents earn. The second one is how many people are in your family.

So, when you go home, you need to ask Mom and Dad how much they earn. And then, count up the number of people in your family. There's probably you, Mom and Dad, and maybe some brothers and sisters. So when you figure out how many people are in the family, and how much money your parents earn, you'll then find out whether you would get your telephone free, or maybe have to pay part.

So, through the TAP Program you could get the TTY or an amplifier if you were deaf, hard of hearing, speech disabled, or deaf-blind.

In the course of one year, the TAP Program sends out over 250 TTYs, and over 250 amplifiers for people all over the state.

So, you can begin making phone calls directly with your TTY by calling another person who has a TTY. So, you could talk to them and talk about school or you could maybe ask them questions about (lips smack) what the homework was that you missed that day. So, you could use the telephone, all by yourself, and not have to depend on anyone else.

So, the next program that I want to talk about, in addition to the TAP Program here at the agency, we also have the Virginia Relay. So if you have a TTY, but your friend doesn't, how were you going to call them? Well that's why the Virginia Relay Service was set up.

In 1991, the Virginia Relay was set up so that people who use TTYs and people who use regular phones could talk to each other. Well how does that happen? What you do when you call on your TTY, you call to the Virginia Relay, and a communication assistant, known as a CA, answers your call. You then tell the communication assistant who it is that you want to call.

They call your friend and whatever that person says to them on the phone, they then type to you on your TTY. Anything that you want to say back, you type on the TTY and the communication assistant will tell your friend. So, it's easy to make a call.

Let's think of different uh ways or different situations that you could call a friend.

If you wanted to talk to them about a snow day and if they were sledding that day. Or, if you wanted to order a pizza and you didn't think the pizza shop had a TTY, the CA, communication assistant, could make that call for you. And hopefully, in just a short time, your pizza would arrive at the house. Or, you could call and ask somebody out on a date.

So, those are just a few examples of how you can use the Relay Service to talk to people who do not have TTYs.

So if you call someone direct or if you need to use the Relay Service, you may want to do that during the day or at night. So, you would need to call the Relay Service on your TTY you would dial 1 800 828 1120. Or if your friend wanted to call you they would call 1 800 828 1140.

And they can make these calls anytime day or night, because the Virginia Relay Service is open 24 hours a day, 7 days a week. So that you can make calls to your friends.

Remember, the CA, or communication assistant, will answer the phone, you give them the phone number, and they will place the call for you.

Right now, uh, do on an average day the Virginia Relay Service handles 4,000 calls. That's a lot of people calling their friends and ordering pizzas. On the weekends, the Relay receives about 2,000 calls a day.

If you add all that up that's over 112,000 calls in ONE MONTH! And that's a lot of calls, but that's what the Service was established for.

I want to thank you today for letting me talk to you about the Virginia Department for the Deaf and Hard of Hearing, and the two programs that we offer: Technology Assistance Program and the Virginia Relay.

I gave you a few examples of how you can use your TTY to call your friends directly or how you can use the Virginia Relay to make some calls. Can you think of some other ways that you can make calls?

APPENDIX 5.B

Transliterator Survey

LIN 781/ Guided Research Project   Bruce Sofinski/ Spring 2000
Strategies and Features of Effective Educational Interpreters

This survey will provide pertinent information to assist the researcher in qualifying the definition and effectiveness of Transliteration. Once again, your identity WILL NOT be incorporated into any reports or abstracts resulting from this study. The researcher involved in this project APPRECIATES YOUR WILLINGNESS AND EAGERNESS to continue to improve the interpreting field.

```
SUBJECT SAMPLE NUMBER:
(To be completed by researchers.)
```

BACKGROUND

Gender (please circle):   female   male

2. Current Age:

3. Years of signing experience to date FOR YOU (e.g., at least 10 hours per week):

4. Years of full-time interpreting experience (e.g., at least 20 hours per week, paid or unpaid):

5. What is the highest level of education you have completed? Please circle:

High School	9	10	11	12
College	1	2	3	4
Grad School	5	6	7	
Post-Grad				
Other				

EDUCATIONAL SETTING

6. In what educational setting do you typically interpret (i.e., elem., middle, etc.):

7. On a scale of 1–10 (1 being more ASL-like and 10 being more English-like), what number would best indicate the mode of interpreting you provide in the setting in which you typically interpret?

    [ASL-LIKE]   1   2   3   4   5   6   7   8   9   10   [ENGLISH-LIKE]

SOURCE

8. Was the knowledge gained by viewing the actual source videotape prior to your work today beneficial in your processing the information?
    YES   or   NO

9. On a scale of 1–10 (1 being of particular hindrance, 5 being of no particular consequence, and 10 being of particular benefit), how has the experience of seeing the EXACT source material affected your performance?
    [Hindrance]   1   2   3   4   5   6   7   8   9   10   [Benefit]

10. Please explain WHY you selected this number, including THE MOST RELEVANT REASON.

PERFORMANCE (The one you JUST completed)

11. When you were asked to Transliterate, what did you use as your guide? In other words, what features did you feel were important to ensure that the product was Transliteration?

12. On a scale of 1–10 (1 being completely unsuccessful and 10 being totally successful), where does the product produced TODAY fit?
[Unsuccessful]   1   2   3   4   5   6   7   8   9   10 [Successful]

13. Is the product you provided today (Transliterating) indicative of the mode of interpreting you typically provide (as referenced in question #7)?
YES   or   NO
Please explain WHY or WHY NOT?

14. Being specific, how does your product TODAY differ from what you would "normally do" in class?

15. Did each participant attend to the product? If no, please get ID number from coordinator.

16. Please list the participants for whom you have worked "regularly." (Please use ID number.)

Your participation in this study is crucial to its success. **THANK YOU** for the time you have so unselfishly given!

END

Transcription and Glossing Convention Key

1. Terms above the line represent mouth movements noted by the researcher:

    - MM = lips pressed together; used in conjunction with a verb that happens normally or regularly (Bridges & Metzger, 1996, p. 36).
    - puffed cheeks = lips closed, cheeks puffed with air; used to indicate a large amount or size (Bridges & Metzger, 1996, p. 37).
    - pursed lips = lips pressed together; used to describe the mouth movement incorporated into the product; however, data was inconclusive in determining that it was an example of MM.
    - (break) = a suspension or demarcation of prosodic features (e.g., pause in manual production, change in eye gaze, head tilt) in the product; generally indicates the end of one linguistic construction and the beginning of another.
    - Brackets { } indicate the length of the "non-manual modifier" (Bridges & Metzger, 1996).
    - ·——→ indicates continuation or perseveration

---

2. Terms below the line represent the following:

    - GLOSSES of ASL lexical items are shown in small caps.
    - E-QUIPMENT = initialization; in the example E-QUIPMENT, the handshape of the ASL base sign THINGS is modified to incorporate the hand configuration E, representing the first letter of the gloss commonly used to label the initialized sign E-QUIPMENT.
    - #SO = lexicalized fingerspelling.
    - MOTHER^FATHER = compound.
    - {Information in brackets} represents the manual portion of the classifier predicate (CL-PRED).
    - bh = base hand
    - sh = strong hand
    - CL = handshape description
    - (Terms included in parentheses) provide information about movement and location.

Marking Topic Boundaries

in Signed Interpretation

and Transliteration

Elizabeth Winston and Christine Monikowski

This chapter presents some preliminary findings from a comparison of interpreted and transliterated texts. It focuses primarily on the prosodic features used for indicating major topic segments in a spoken-English source text. For this chapter, we discuss the similarities and differences among the segment boundaries as they are produced by three interpreters.[1] These interpreters produced signed target interpretations and transliterations of the same source text, providing an opportunity to compare prosodic and linguistic features used in each type of target. The interpreters were qualified, internationally recognized experts in interpretation and transliteration. Although we have many long-term goals for this overall research, we narrowed the focus of this chapter to a very few features and strategies. This narrowing resulted from our experience as interpreter educators, from frequent questions asked by interpreting and transliterating students, and from the texts themselves.

RESEARCH GOALS: BACKGROUND AND RATIONALE

As interpreter educators, we have experienced difficulty when trying to provide students with adequate information and research-based guidance about the differences between interpreting and transliterating. Although a growing body of research about interpreting, prosody, and American Sign Language (ASL) is available to interpreting educators, only a small amount of research exists about transliteration. Some of this

1. We gratefully acknowledge the permission we received from Sign Enhancers, Inc., to include the still photos we used to illustrate our examples.

research is demographic, for example, how or where interpreting is taught, who uses it, and so forth (Stauffer & Viera, 2000). One study investigates the effectiveness of interpreting as compared with transliterating (Livingston, Singer, & Abramson, 1995). Early research focusing primarily on lexical choice, sentence structure, mouthing, and some specific strategies used in transliteration was done by Winston (1989); Siple provided more research and expanded the description of these strategies, providing more in-depth information in the area of additions (1995) and in the reflection of source-language pausing in signed transliterations (1993).

A recent study by Sofinski, Yesbeck, Gerhold, and Bach-Hansen (2001) focused on language features used by educational interpreters in transliteration. Nine features were identified as common to the transliterations in the study, including use of space for listing, mouthing, syntax choices, and lexical choices. The features were further identified as being English-based or ASL-based. McIntyre (1993) analyzed the potential and real use of space in signed transliterations.

Studies about prosody and teaching prosody are also rare. In an early study, Winston (1990) investigated the possibility of improving prosody (referred to as "gestalt" in that study) through teaching. The features of the overall signed "gestalt" were not identified, but she found that focused teaching through selective watching and shadowing (based on techniques described by Nida, 1953) could be effective in improving the gestalt of interpreting students.

Mather and Winston (1995) investigated prosodic patterns in ASL story retellings, illustrating patterns of spatial use that were prosodic in nature. Another discussion of ASL prosody by Mather (1989) also provided research about the uses of eye gaze in ASL for teaching preschool children, and Bahan and Supalla (1995) presented research demonstrating that eye gaze serves as a segment boundary marker in ASL. Winston (2000) presented a preliminary discussion of prosodic features found in ASL discourse. She listed and described several features that make up ASL prosody, including configurations of the head, eyes, face, torso, and hands within the signing space. These configurations result in patterns of intonation or prosody that are essential parts of ASL discourse.

Wilbur (1994) discussed the use of eye blink as a marker of ASL phrase structure. Brentari (1998), in her in-depth study of ASL phonology, provided information and insight into the prosodic structures of ASL at the phonological level. She detailed features such as syllable length and structure. Nespor and Sandler (1999) investigated the interaction of phonology and syntax in Israeli Sign Language, describing features such as hand dominance and phonological prosody.

In addition, studies of other ASL features are helpful to interpreters and transliterators. Some of these studies address different uses of space. For example, Locker McKee (1992) investigated the eye-gaze and body-posture cues in constructed dialogue, asides, and quotations in ASL. Winston (1995), Metzger (1995), and Metzger and Bahan (2001), have reported on performatives, constructed dialogue, and constructed action (commonly referred to as role shifting). Moreover, descriptions and papers, most especially in publications like the proceedings of the various CIT conventions, discuss ASL features found in transliteration. These provide some excellent pointers but are not clearly grounded in research. In fact, common belief is that, to be effective, transliteration requires a prerequisite knowledge of ASL and of interpreting (Colonomos, 1992). Again, these commonly accepted beliefs that are held by some in the field are not adequately substantiated by research. Unfortunately, those who do not know either ASL or interpreting find that ignoring these claims is easy because adequate research is lacking. One of our ongoing goals for this study is to investigate these commonly accepted claims.

A frequent question asked by students and working interpreters relates to the relationship of ASL to transliteration. Hence, a long-term goal of this area of research is to analyze the ASL features that are required in transliteration. In this narrowed chapter, we look specifically at pausing in both interpretations and transliterations. We compare the same person interpreting and transliterating a single spoken-English source and analyze the pausing features used at major topic boundaries.

We often hear from those who transliterate only, especially when they have learned English signs without a foundation in ASL, that they see no need for knowing ASL. A study of transliterated texts produced by skilled, qualified interpreters provides one perspective on the need for ASL as a foundation for any transliteration. The Sofinski et al. (2001) study mentioned above is another source of information on this issue. The pausing features analyzed in our preliminary study demonstrate that ASL prosodic features occur throughout the transliterations. ASL pausing and phrasing features such as use of space for sentence boundaries, lengthened final holds for signs, and head and torso shifting are essential to clear segmenting of ideas and topics within a text. No English features are used to segment these texts because the segmenting features are not English words. One could argue that pausing is a prosodic feature used by all languages. However, the nature and form of the pauses in signed and spoken languages are different. In spoken languages, pauses are defined by the length of the silence between words. In signed languages and systems, silence is irrelevant.

Both the source text as well as the interpretations and transliterations that were produced helped us to further narrow the scope of this first report. As we began analyzing the target texts, one specific type of discourse strategy quickly became our focus—the way that the major topic boundaries were marked and not marked in the targets. Other topics that were immediately salient were the ways that space was used, the strategies used to reflect the involvement strategies of constructed dialogue and action, and the cohesive use of repetition in the source. Although we do not discuss these topics in detail in this chapter, we will mention a few striking examples as they co-occur in some of our other examples. These topics will be fascinating areas of future research that will require in-depth analysis.

DEFINING OUR TERMS

For the purposes of identifying and discussing the boundary-marking strategies in this research, we first want to present some working definitions that we used. We make no claim that the definitions we use in this study are exhaustive or definitive.

Topic boundary. A topic boundary is the place in a source-language text or in a target interpretation or transliteration where the signer or speaker indicates, through the use of a variety of discourse strategies and features, that a topic is ending, changing, shifting, expanding, etc. This topic segment would usually include more than one utterance.

Utterance boundary. An utterance boundary comprises the places where a single idea unit is begun and ended.

Discourse strategy. A discourse strategy is the decision by the signer-speaker to use a set of specific linguistic, prosodic, and extralinguistic features common to a language to communicate an underlying message. This definition is based on Gumperz's (1982) discussion. For example,

PHOTO 6.1. *In this photograph, the discourse strategy is "constructed dialogue" with the features of head and eyes gazing to the right and down, torso leaning back and left, and index to right.*

pausing in a text is a strategy that enables the audience to chunk the discourse structure of a presentation and to interpret the underlying meaning of the presenter.

Features. Features are the physical productions that combine to produce a message. For example, eyebrow raise, torso shift, and head nod were considered individual features that may be combined within a discourse strategy (see Photo 6.1).

Pauses. Other studies such as that by Siple (1993) discussed the nature of pausing in transliterated texts: "[S]ign language interpreters do rely on source message pauses when creating by transliteration the target message, and tend to show a pause at the same location at which pauses are present in the source message" (p. 171). However, for the purpose of this study, we used the definitions of pauses defined in Winston (2000):

> For spoken languages, the pause may simply be the cessation of sound. But for ASL the pause can be more complex. While it is similar to spoken languages in that there is a cessation (of movement rather than sound), it is different in that the signer can continue to hold the signs in space, keeping the watcher's attention on the sign rather than in the absence of it. (p. 109)

Winston (2000) tentatively identified three types of pauses used by signers in ASL: the filled pause, the prosodic pause, and the extralinguistic pause. These are somewhat different than those of Siple. Siple's (1993) "empty" pause is our "extralinguistic" pause. Our prosodic pause includes

PHOTO 6.2. Example of a filled pause

any type of feature shift between clauses. Siple's two categories of "held" and "filled" pauses are our "filled" pause. Our preliminary types of pausing were developed from studies of ASL source texts. In our study of target texts, we have found that these kinds of pauses also occur in both the interpreted and transliterated texts.

Filled pause. A filled pause is a sign that is held in space while all other movement stops. This type of pause occurs at the end of a segment, topic, or important idea. It focuses attention on the idea or topic that has just ended and is a cue to the importance of that segment or idea in the overall meaning of the text (see Photo 6.2).

Prosodic pause. A prosodic pause is a pause that marks a boundary at the phrase or sentence level. These pauses help the watcher identify the beginnings and ends of sentences, the subject and object of a single idea, and the beginnings and ends of phrases in discourse structures such as listing and conditional clauses. In Photos 6.3a and 6.3b, the utterance in line 97 ends in Photo 6.3a, and a new utterance in line 98 begins in Photo 6.3b. The torso and head are slightly forward and to the right at the end of the utterance; as the next utterance begins in line 98, the torso and head have shifted to the center.

Extralinguistic pause. An extralinguistic pause is a pause that is used to show that the signer is thinking, regrouping, checking notes, and so forth (see Photo 6.4).

"a. 97 . . . experience fear."   "b. 98 Therefore . . ."

PHOTOS 6.3a and 6.3b. Example of utterance boundary between lines 97 and 98, marked by torso and head shift from forward right to center

PHOTO 6.4. Example of extralinguistic pause

DATA CHOICE AND APPROACH TO ANALYSIS

Interesting differences exist between the transliterations and interpretations in the types of pauses that are used to reflect segment or topic shifts and in the frequency of extralinguistic pauses in the source and target texts. However, these types of pauses occur throughout the targets and are an essential feature. Because our data suggested our primary focus in this first research—an analysis of pauses at topic boundaries—we will describe our data and approach to analysis in the following sections.

Data Choice

We chose to use a set of commercially available videotapes, *Living Fully With Interpreting Models* (Sign Enhancers, 1994a), and *Living Fully With Transliterating Models* (Sign Enhancers, 1994b). In selecting this material for our initial research, we considered several factors. First, these materials are commonly available, which means that others reading our comments, analysis, and conclusions are able to review the data and draw their own conclusions about the observations and conclusions drawn from this research. This set of videos provides a series of three nationally recognized, skilled interpreters. Each has an individual style, yet each provides (and is recognized to provide) a "dynamically equivalent" target message (Nida, 1953). In addition, this set of videos provides a rare opportunity to compare the interpretation and transliteration of the same text by the same interpreter. We believe that comparisons of this type can provide valuable information about the processes and enable the viewer to see how these skilled, accomplished interpreters produced a variety of discourse features, especially prosodic features, in two different target forms.

Another reason for selecting this material was because the source text provides a complex discourse structure. From one perspective, it is a simple exhortative text with an intent to inspire the audience to positive rather than negative perspectives. However, a mapping of discourse structures and actual presentation of the text reveals a spiraling and recurring use of prosody and linguistic features to build eloquence and inspire the audience. These features are the result of careful planning, and they can be especially difficult to manage when interpreting or transliterating. An analysis of the target interpretations and transliterations of this text should reveal a similar level of complexity.

Additionally, the source text, being a prepared presentation, tends to have a cognitive or idea load that is denser per thought unit than typical spoken text (Ochs, 1979). It includes features of both spontaneous speech and prepared, written-like materials, which are much more difficult to interpret. Yet, when interpreted effectively (i.e., when a dynamic equivalent is achieved), the interpreter uses discourse features of ASL in the interpretation and those of primarily ASL in the transliteration. Having an understanding of the quantity of ASL prosodic features that are necessary in even the most "English-like" transliteration (when dynamically equivalent) can lead interpreters and interpreter educators to a clearer understanding of the need to first be skilled and knowledgeable about ASL before rendering an effective transliteration. This research will point out whether or not all transliterators, including those working in school systems using English signing, must first know ASL and the ways to show prosody.

As with any choice of data, our data also presented some drawbacks and disadvantages. First, the source text presentation was a "constructed" presentation. It was a presentation made specifically for the production of the target texts rather than a presentation that was completely "naturally produced." This characteristic adds some sense of unreality to the source. We noted that, consequently, (a) the source contained almost no speaker repairs and (b) the rate of presentation is slower than might normally be expected in a live presentation. The presentation is much more similar to an inspirational speech at a graduation, a sermon in a religious setting, or a well-prepared and often-presented informational workshop.

The second drawback was that the interpreters had more preparation than might be expected in many situations. In many live presentations, a text is not available until the last minute or, more commonly, not at all. However, formal presentations are often written or presented; in cases such as these, the interpreter may have the opportunity to prepare. We decided that the amount of preparation for the interpreters was not unduly more than the amount for an interpreter who is working with a presenter he or she knows well and for whom he or she regularly interprets on the same topic.

Finally, the interpreters presented one target after the other. In other words, each person first produced the interpretation and then the transliteration or vice versa. Depending on whether the transliteration or the interpretation was done first, the production of the second target text might be influenced. With these benefits and limitations in mind, we began the analysis of the source text first, then proceeded to the target texts.

Approach to Analysis

Using steps from a discourse mapping process outlined in Winston and Monikowski (2000), we approached this research as a comparison of linguistic and discourse features that were used by a presenter to reflect her intended meaning. This comparison extended to the linguistic and discourse strategies and features that are subsequently used by interpreters and transliterators in their efforts to produce dynamically equivalent target texts.

ANALYSIS OF THE SOURCE TEXT

The source text is a presentation that seeks to inspire the audience to accept responsibility for the positive or negative beliefs that motivate their lives and actions. These positive and negative beliefs are caused by fear and stem from expectations; each person has the opportunity to choose the perspective that will motivate his or her future choices and decisions. The presenter uses stories to illustrate her points. A transcription of the spoken-English text is found in Appendix 6.A.

In an earlier publication, we analyzed the source text in a discussion of discourse mapping (Winston & Monikowski, 2000, p. 54). As we revisited the original map for this analysis, we added two elements. First, we added the speaker's goals and sources, and second, we added the concept of expectations to the concept of fear. The revised map is shown in Figure 6.1.

The "abstract" of the text is a simple one and indicates what we perceive to be the presenter's goal: to inspire the audience to believe her point that each person makes the difference for her- or himself. We began with this map because it provides a visual representation of the structural complexity of the source text. The external map reminds us that the goal of the presenter is inspirational rather than informational, that the topics are not presented in a chronological order, and that the presentation is formal and presented to what we perceived to be an adult audience. The internal map provides a visual representation of the major concepts and ideas that are presented.

The complexity of the presentation is indicated by the arrows that point to and from the concepts of positive and negative, to and from the reactions (either positive or negative), and to and from each story. This presentation is not a straightforward recounting of cause and effect nor of chronological events nor of a logical process. Rather, the presenter intertwines the ideas of positive and negative thoughts with their causes and with each person's approach to the thoughts and the causes. Throughout the presentation, she includes stories to expand on the interconnections

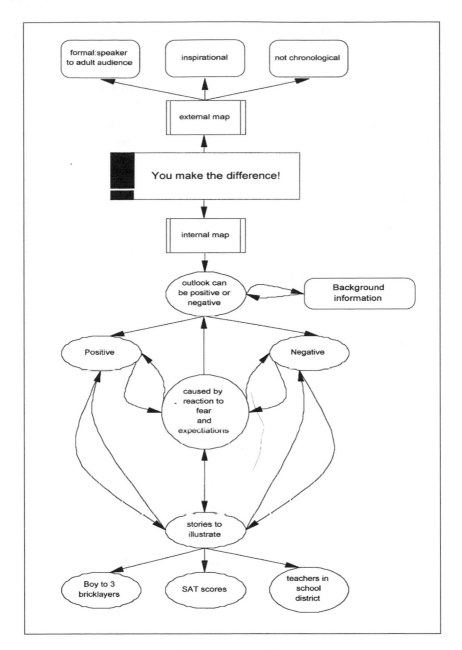

FIGURE 6.1. The source text's discourse map

of all these ideas. (One fascinating study would be to analyze the discourse strategies used by the interpreters and transliterators to reflect this interconnected weaving of ideas.)

Marking Topic Boundaries in Signed Interpretation and Transliteration : 197

From this map, we prepared a sequential map of the source text (p. 36, Steps 2 and 3) in the discourse mapping process. Then, we began a listing of the salient linguistic and prosodic strategies and features of the English in the source text.[2] This list provided some initial direction for our analysis of the target texts. For this chapter, we narrowed the analysis to the strategies and features used to indicate major topic boundaries, which are discussed in the section titled "Data Choice and Approach to Analysis" section.

ANALYSIS OF TARGET TEXTS

After completing the analysis of the source text, we identified the sections of each interpretation and transliteration that corresponded dynamically with the source; in other words, we identified where the interpreter did or did not indicate the major topic boundaries that we had identified in the source text. We analyzed for similar discourse function—not for similar discourse feature. As with any text comprehension exercise, we do not claim that the boundaries we identified are the only, or the "right," boundaries. Rather, they are boundaries that we identified as places where we understood a shift to occur in the source and where we predicted some type of boundary marking in the targets.

We noted whether each interpreter and transliterator produced major boundary markings at these predicted places and, if so, which discourse strategies and features they used. We also noted whether and where they used these same strategies in places that we had not identified. We further analyzed whether these additional strategies were used at other possible boundaries or were used for other purposes.

From this groundwork, we compared the three target interpretations for inter-interpreter similarities and differences, and we compared the three target transliterations for the same purpose. We also compared the interpretation and the transliteration of each person to see the similarities and differences that occurred. In the next section, we report the specific information from the analysis. The implications of these comparisons are presented in the final section of this chapter.

2. Prosodic features were implied in this process; we have made it a much more explicit step in this research.

FINDINGS

In this section, we describe the findings for the target texts produced by each interpreter (1, 2, and 3), first, from the interpretation produced and, then, from the transliteration produced.

Target Texts Produced by Interpreter 1: Interpretation 1 (I-1) and Transliteration 1 (T-1)

INTERPRETATION 1 (I-1)

Interpretation 1 (I-1) was, with respect to our limited analysis, more similar to Interpretation 3 than to Interpretaion 3. I-1 showed a definite pattern of the extralinguistic pause referred to as HANDCLASP at 15 of the 20 identified topic boundaries, the same amount as identified for Interpreter 3. For two other topic boundaries, Interpreter 1 held the last sign, producing a filled pause. For one topic boundary, Interpreter 1 seemed to produce the "got it?" feature (see discussion related to Figure 6.4), which is a specific type of a filled pause. For the remaining two topic boundaries, we were unable to identify either a HANDCLASP or a hold or any other boundary marker.[3] However, as stated elsewhere, we did not analyze the data for other possible representations of topic boundaries; this possibility needs to be explored more completely in future research.

A clear example of Interpreter 1's HANDCLASP strategy occurs at the end of line 45 ("that what you tell yourself is very likely to become your reality"), which we had identified as a boundary (see Figure 6.2).

One interesting finding is that I-1 also has the HANDCLASP at nine places in the text that we had not originally identified. Some of these instances were quite brief but still clearly produced. The presenter is offering specific examples of comfort zones in lines 104–109 (see Figure 6.3). The HANDCLASP after line 106 is very brief. This type of briefer HANDCLASP appears to be this interpreter's way to mark subtopics.

One interesting feature in I-1 was the "got it?" feature (this same strategy is described and used also in I-2.). This interpreting strategy functions quite clearly as a topic boundary. Lines 37–39 conclude the description of three bricklayers' mind-sets, and line 40 presents an explanation (see Figure 6.4). At the end of line 39, an identified topic boundary is marked

---

3. Boundary markers are glossed as signs because we believe they carry an important message to the audience.

45 that what you tell yourself is very likely to become your reality.

PHOTO 6.5

46 Well, if this is true,

FIGURE 6.2

104 This is known as our comfort zone.
105 We each have our very unique comfort zone
106 based on our own past experiences, our perceptions of our capabilities, and our willingness to be out in the world.

PHOTO 6.6. Example of brief extralinguistic pause, lasting 3 frames (longer pauses extend to 8 or more frames)

107 Some people are only comfortable in the confines of their own home.
108 Others venture out into the world into the workplace,
109 and others still seem to make the whole world their home.

FIGURE 6.3

37 How we experience our life's work,

38 and indeed our lives,

39 is to a great degree a function of what we tell ourselves

PHOTO 6.7a

PHOTO 6.7b

40 You see, the man laying bricks performs the very same task as the man who was building a beautiful cathedral.

FIGURE 6.4

with the "got it?" strategy. Marking the boundary is the filled pause, consisting of the sign OPEN HANDS, with eye gaze straight ahead and brows up. After this pause, the interpreter moves on to the next sign.

TRANSLITERATION I (T-I)

Transliteration I (T-I) showed a marked pattern of producing the HANDCLASP at 16 of the 20 identified topic boundaries, more than either of the other two transliterations. In addition, 26 additional HANDCLASPS occurred at places throughout the text that we had not originally identified as topic boundaries. These occurrences will require further analysis, but one hypothesis is that they mark an emphatic boundary in this transliteration. An example of this usage occurs from line 51 to line 77 (see Figure 6.5), where the presenter offers numerous examples of negative questions and then offers examples of positive questions that could replace the negative ones.

In those five lines, the interpreter produces a HANDCLASP five times. She produces a brief HANDCLASP at the end of line 50 (identified topic boundary), a slight HANDCLASP in the middle of line 51 (after "For example") and then at the end of lines 53, 54, and 55 (not identified topic boundaries).

This pattern appears again later in the text when another series of possible questions is presented. The transliterator again produces five

PHOTO 6.8. T-1: HANDCLASP at predicted boundary

51 For example, when you first wake up in the morning,

PHOTO 6.9a GIVE

PHOTO 6.9b. EXAMPLE

PHOTO 6.9c. Example of second HANDCLASP at unpredicted but potential boundary

52 do you ask yourself questions like this?
53 What do I have to do today?

FIGURE 6.5

HANDCLASP in 10 lines. This pattern definitely requires further analysis. One hypothesis is that this HANDCLASP strategy, which is very marked, is

PHOTO 6.10. T-1 after signing TODAY, with HANDCLASP at unpredicted but potential boundary

54 What problems am I gonna have ta face? (voice inflection)

PHOTO 6.11. HANDCLASP at unpredicted but potential boundary

55 What's gonna happen if I fail at the challenges facing me?

PHOTO 6.12 HANDCLASP at unpredicted but potential boundary

FIGURE 6.5 CONT.

used to mark the rhetorical emphasis created by the presenter to emphasize her point through the use of repeated "what" questions.

35 or do you always keep in the forefront of your mind (point to head) a vision of your beautiful cathedral?

PHOTO 6.13a   PHOTO 6.13b

36 Our minds are very powerful tools.

FIGURE 6.6

Target Texts Produced by Interpreter 2: Interpretation 2 (I-2) and Transliteration 2 (T-2)

INTERPRETATION 2 (I-2)

Of the 20 major topic boundaries that we identified, Interpretation 2 (I-2) shows the HANDCLASP strategy at 11 of them. In addition, at three other boundaries, the strategy that we have labeled "got it?" occurs (see the following discussion). At another three boundaries, a final longer hold occurs on the last sign. All 17 of these topic boundary markers are filled pauses. For the remaining three boundaries, we were unable to identify the HANDCLASP as an indication of the topic boundary; however, note that this initial research did not address other possibilities such as sign choices or word order, which could, indeed, represent the boundary.

One example of HANDCLASP in this interpretation occurs after the filled pause "got it?" feature between lines 35 and 36 (see Figure 6.6), where the moral of the bricklayer story is presented. This marker occurs at one of our predicted boundaries, between lines 35 and 36. The interpreter signs OPEN HANDS, with eye gaze straight ahead and brows up, and then moves to the HANDCLASP.

An example of a filled pause occurring at one of our predicted boundaries happens between lines 115 and 116 in the transcript (see Figure 6.7) where the question of what to do about fear is reintroduced. Inter-

115 and to stop us from living fully or realizing our dreams.

PHOTO 6.14

116 Well, what's the alternative?

FIGURE 6.7

preter 2 holds the last sign, OPEN HANDS, with eye gaze straight ahead.

The "got it?" feature-form of a filled pause appears at three identified topic boundaries. The last sign tends to be held (some holds are a bit longer than others), the head is tilted forward and up, and the brows are raised with eye gaze straight ahead. The interpreter's strategy appears to be one of making the implicit meaning from the speaker more explicit rather than presenting a question directly from the interpreter to the watcher. It functions as a marked topic boundary in this interpretation. The "got it?" feature also occurs in three other places in Interpreter 2's work, places where we did not anticipate topic boundaries. Although in-depth analysis of these events is beyond the scope of this chapter, these three additional productions do appear to mark other, perhaps subtopic, boundaries.

TRANSLITERATION 2 (T-2)

Of the 20 major topic boundaries we identified, only two were clearly marked by extralinguistic hand clasps. Eight boundaries were marked with a short filled pause, showing a slightly longer final hold on either the last sign or the last fingerspelled letter of the chunk. Ten identified boundaries were not marked; however, note that we did not analyze for co-occurring sign choices, word order, or numerous other possibilities for marking a boundary. Therefore, one cannot prudently assume that the boundaries were not marked. Further investigation is needed.

128 We could make progressive approximations towards expanding our comfort zone.

PHOTO 6.15. The final S is held for 12 frames.

129 You can begin by imagining the worst possible consequences.

FIGURE 6.8

Of the eight filled holds that mark our predicted boundaries, one example—this one with the last letter of a fingerspelled word held—occurs at the end of line 128 (see Figure 6.8). The presenter said, "We could make progressive approximations towards expanding our comfort zone." Transliterator 2 signed COMFORT and then fingerspelled #ZONES and clearly held the final S. The S was held for approximately 12 frames whereas the hold on Z was held for approximately 4 frames, and the holds on O, N, and E lasted for approximately 1 frame each.

Another example of a filled pause occurs at the end of line 168 (see Figure 6.9), which presents the moral of the story about the college student and his grades. Line 169 is the beginning of the story about the three teachers. A two-hand OPEN PALMS sign is used to indicate the boundary; this sign is held for 19 frames.

The "got it?" feature described above for I-2 appears in T-2 but not at our identified boundaries; it appears in four other places that, as in the interpretation, mark possible boundaries, even though we did not initially identify them as boundaries. This feature needs further investigation.

168 The only thing that had changed were his expectations.

PHOTO 6.16

169 Another example of how powerful expectations are in determining events

FIGURE 6.9

Target Texts Produced by Interpreter 3: Interpretation 3 (I-3) and Transliteration 3 (T-3)

INTERPRETATION 3 (I-3)

Interpretation 3 showed a pattern very similar to the first two interpretations. Of the 20 major topic boundaries that we identified, the extralinguistic pause referred to as HANDCLASP occurred at 15 of them. The features that Interpreter 3's strategy typically comprised included the following:

- HANDCLASP produced at chest
- Head makes a single nod down preceding the pause
- Torso returns to pause in center space
- Shoulders and torso make a single downward movement preceding the pause
- Eyes are down in "thought"

In the conclusion section, we briefly address the question of interpreters' individual styles. Each used the same HANDCLASP strategy, but for each, the specific features that made it up were slightly different.

An example of HANDCLASP occurs between lines 12 and 13 of the transcript (see Figure 6.10) where the text shifts from a listing of resources for the presentation to the telling of a story.

Marking Topic Boundaries in Signed Interpretation and Transliteration : 207

12 and finally, *Peace, Love and Feeling*, by Dr. Bernie S. Seagal.

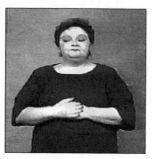

PHOTO 6.17

13 I'd like to begin by telling you a story.

FIGURE 6.10

At four of the other boundaries we identified, some other form of marking strategy (usually a filled pause) occurred. But at one boundary, only a shift in space marked the boundary; this marker is a prosodic pause. Between lines 45 and 46 (see Figure 6.11), the presenter finishes defining self-talk and begins to describe how to change one's perspective. At the end of line 45, the signing is directed to the front and center; at the beginning of line 46, the direction is shifted toward the right where the discussion of the negative self-talk is presented. Although this change of direction is not a clear shift, it becomes more salient by line 47 when the signing direction shifts to the left to present the discussion about shifting to positive self-talk. This use of space occurs in a few more places in the interpretation. It will be an interesting avenue of future research.

The third of our identified boundaries is marked by a multiple head nod that draws attention to the idea just stated in line 82 (see Figure 6.12). Depending on whether one identifies the multiple head nod as a meaningful sign or a prosodic feature, this marker would be either a filled pause or a prosodic pause. We have categorized it as a filled pause. And at the fourth boundary, a filled pause occurs with the holding of the final sign and a look at the audience. This pause is very similar to some of the filled pauses used in I-1 and I-2.

Only one of our boundaries was unmarked in I-3. Between lines 50 and 51, we had identified a boundary before the example introduced in line 51 (see Figure 6.13). Although a major boundary between these two

45 that what you tell yourself is very likely to become your reality.

PHOTO 6.18

46 Well, if this is true,

PHOTO 6.19A

PHOTO 6.19B

47 how do we turn our negative self-chatter into powerful "I can" messages?

FIGURE 6.11

lines was not indicated in the target, a marker occurs immediately following the introduction of an example. Interpreter 3 signs WAIT-HOLD-ON using her nondominant left hand, then she pauses using the HANDCLASP strategy.

This sign strategy is interesting to note because Interpreter 3 has shifted dominance, another prosodic marker in ASL (Winston, 2000). Interpreter 2 also used dominance shift as a discourse marker, emphasizing specific signs within a topic.

The HANDCLASP strategy also appeared at eight other places in the text. To determine whether this clasping was random or patterned, we also looked at where in the texts these clasps occurred. Although we had not

82 as most negative emotions are.

PHOTO 6.20

83 Fear is the biggest inhibitor of us acting upon our dreams and living our lives fully.

FIGURE 6.12

identified the places as major topic boundaries, each occurred at identifiable boundaries. What was more interesting was that not a single one occurred at a nonboundary such as in the middle of an utterance or the middle of a topic.

TRANSLITERATION 3 (T-3)

In the transliteration of this text, the extralinguistic HANDCLASP strategy occurred at 10 of our identified major boundaries. At eight of the other boundaries, other boundary marking strategies occurred, for example, filled and prosodic pauses. These strategies were described above in the description of Interpreter 3's interpretation. Two of the boundaries we had identified were not marked with pausing or any other major strategy. The HANDCLASP also occurred nine times at places we had not predicted; however, as in the interpretation, each occurred only at identifiable boundaries, and none occurred in the middle of utterances or idea segments.

The major difference between the hand clasps in the transliteration and the interpretation was that they tended to be held for a shorter period in the transliteration. For example, the clasp between lines 12 and 13 in the interpretation lasted for approximately 16 frames (see Chart 6.1). But the hand clasp that Interpreter 3 used at this same boundary in the transliteration continued only for approximately 4 frames.

50 you have a head start on seeing the world in a positive way.

PHOTO 6.21

51 For example,

PHOTO 6.22

when you first wake up in the morning,

FIGURE 6.13

Similarly, the main difference at other boundaries was the length of time that many of the behaviors lasted. For example, at the boundary between lines 82 and 83, Interpreter 3 used a final hold in both versions. However, the length of the pause in the final hold was shorter in the transliteration than in the interpretation. The hold in the interpretation lasted for 32 frames whereas, at the same boundary in the transliteration, it was held for 3 frames. This length is illustrated in the two photos in Chart 6.2. The length of boundary markers and their internal structures is one more area that will provide interesting research opportunities.

CHART 6.1

Frames	2	4	6	8	10	12	14	16
Interpretation								

PHOTO 6.23A

Frames	2	4						
Transliteration								

PHOTO 6.23B

Discussion

PAUSING IN THE SOURCE TEXT

The presenter, in chunking her utterances and topics, generally relied less on pausing and more on intonation and lengthening of final syllables for stress and chunking. The source text contained no extralinguistic pauses because it had a formal and rehearsed nature.

PAUSING IN THE TARGET TEXTS

The data show a significant difference in the pausing that occurs in the interpreted texts and the transliterated texts. This study makes no claims about the appropriateness of these differences. Because these texts were produced by qualified interpreters and transliterators, we make the assumption that these differences are common for interpreters and

CHART 6.2

Frames	4	8	12	16	20	24	28	32
Interpretation								

PHOTO 6.24A

Frames	3–4							
Transliteration								

PHOTO 6.24B

transliterators. Future research must include the study of consumers' perspectives as well as studies of many more interpreters and transliterators. This research is only a preliminary study in which we have found some interesting tendencies that bear further investigation.

PAUSES IN THE TARGET INTERPRETATIONS

We investigated in detail one striking type of pause that occurred frequently and regularly in all three interpretations—the extralinguistic pause. Although no extralinguistic pauses occurred in the source, each of the three interpretations had clear patterns of extralinguistic pausing. Each interpreter used a form of hand clasping at the chest or abdomen area, with a stopping of movement, some type of head nod preceding the pause, and often, a type of eye gaze that we have labeled "thinking."

These pauses occurred at many major segment or topic boundaries throughout the target texts. They less frequently occurred elsewhere, but with one possible exception: They never occurred at nonboundaries. In other words, the interpreters were reliably and regularly recognizing that these units were segments of meaning, or chunks. They appear to be using these boundaries to think or to process the incoming message.[4] Thus, they are using extralinguistic pausing to show where the presenter is changing or shifting topic.

Extralinguistic pausing is a very clear and effective means of indicating chunks. The watcher (receiver of the message) receives information that should allow him or her to understand that one idea or topic is closing and that another is opening. These pauses seem to be long enough to notice without intense concentration, thus making them more easily accessible to the watcher. These extralinguistic pauses are an interesting intrusion of the interpreting process. They are not part of the presenter's source strategy for marking topic boundaries; rather, they seem to reflect the thinking of the interpreter. Nevertheless, they provide a visual break that occurs only at topic boundaries, providing the watcher with a road map of the topics throughout the text. Our emphasis here is that the extralinguistic pauses are additions to the message; however, these additions occur in, and only in, places where major topic boundaries occur in the source text.

One important note is that we did not look for nor did we expect any type of utterance-by-utterance representation of the source. Rather, we looked at the ideas and topics in each chunk and noted when, where, and how the source text shifted as well as when, where, and how the texts reflected these shifts. Our focus, the extralinguistic pause, was not the definitive and only kind of boundary marking shift; we hypothesized that a large majority of our identified boundaries would be reflected in the targets in some way. We also expected some variation, depending on the person's own chunking styles.

PAUSES IN THE TRANSLITERATED TEXTS

The major difference in pausing behaviors between the interpreted and transliterated texts was the type of pauses that were used. At the

---

4. Prosodic and filled pauses also occurred throughout all three interpretations. We have not yet analyzed these pauses in detail, but they appear to be the expected ASL pausings that occur within and between utterances.

major topic boundaries was where this major difference occurred. Where the interpretations uniformly show extralinguistic pausing at most major boundaries, the transliterations show noticeably fewer extralinguistic pauses. And in contrast to the interpretations, the extralinguistic pauses that did occur in the transliterations were not as uniform. The differences ranged from adequate and expected patterns of pausing and pausing features within and between utterances (by two of the three) to almost none (by one of the three).

The major boundaries were generally reflected with less marked pausing; instead of the frequent use of the extralinguistic pause (HANDCLASP), the boundaries were frequently marked by less noticeable strategies such as filled pauses that took the form of holds on final signs in the segment, prosodic pauses that took the form of torso or head shifting in space, and head nodding. The length of the stop between segments was perceptibly shorter in the transliterations and, at times, was almost imperceptible.

One question to investigate is whether this lack of a major visual break as well as the similarity of the filled pausing and prosodic pausing between boundaries and within utterances is salient enough to help watchers follow the larger text structures in transliterated texts. In other words, do all the pauses seem so similar that the watcher cannot tell when a major boundary occurs? Of course, other strategies are used that we have not yet investigated, linguistic choice being one example. For example, if the source text presents a series of facts, then the transliterator may add a sign indicating LIST at the beginning, number each item, and then sign FINISH at the end of the series. This production would indicate to the watcher that the topic or list segment were completed, and there would be no need for the addition of a major pause. But the question still to be answered is, How many chunking and prosodic features are needed in a target to make it easily perceptible rather than subtle and more easily missed? Another is, How does "ease of understanding" compare where source and targets are compared?

SIGNING STYLES

Signing styles appear to spread across interpretations and transliterations. In those places where the HANDCLASP pause did occur in both interpreted and transliterated forms for each interpreter, those HANDCLASPS were similar. For example, the CLASP STANCE of Interpreter 3 in both the interpretation and transliteration showed the same torso, head, and hand

PHOTO 6.25A   PHOTO 6.25B   PHOTO 6.25C

positions. This consistency was true of each of the three interpreters. Yet each person was slightly different from the others. Photos 6.25a, b, and c show how this stance varied among the three interpreters.

This observation begins to touch on the question of signer style, which is another topic about which many interpreting students ask. The ability to identify specific features incorporated in a "style" could lead students to an understanding of their own style and, therefore, to an understanding of what may be missing. Each of the signers frequently used the extralinguistic pause as a discourse strategy, and each included several of the same features in the production of that kind of pause. But each configuration is slightly different. For example, in the photos above, the eye gaze direction, the height of the clasped hands, and the tilt of the torso and head are all unique to each signer.

DIRECTIONS FOR FUTURE RESEARCH

Although the primary focus of this initial research was on the pausing at major segment boundaries, we also noted some interesting patterns in other areas. Again, these are observations of patterns that have provided us with an even longer list of new research questions. Our comments are not intended to present any final description of these patterns. Additional areas of interest include the following: openings and closings of topics; utterance boundary markings; repetition and reiteration; and involvement strategies such as use of space for comparisons, constructed dialogue, and action. We will briefly describe some of our initial observations in two areas: uses of space and lexical choice for repetition.

PHOTO 6.26

Uses of Space

We have discussed the prosodic use of space as it occurred in the pausing behaviors above. But another use of space that occurred was linguistic.
The data showed patterns of both performatives (constructed action and
constructed dialogue) and of comparisons in all of the targets, both interpretations and transliterations.

The story of the bricklayers in the source text generated the use of
performatives in both the interpreted and transliterated texts. All used
constructed action to represent the boy approaching the brick masons
and the interactions that occurred. All used constructed dialogue to show
some part of the boy's questions and the brick masons' responses. This
same strategy was used when presenting the story of the college student
and the dean. Constructed action was used to represent the meeting between the student and the dean to discuss the student's poor grades.

One interesting use of constructed dialogue was in I-2. The presenter
talks about how everyone experiences fear in his or her life and offers
some positive strategies to control that fear. Interpreter 2 actually places
"fear" to his right and interacts with it, as if this abstract concept were an
interlocutor in a conversation. For example, the presenter says, "If we
could shift our perspective and see fear instead as an ally that is telling us,
proceed with caution, but proceed" (line 117–118). Interpreter 2, having
previously established FEAR down and to his right, now interacts, if you
will, with this established entity (see Photo 6.26). This strategy is a fascinating approach to an abstract concept. Is this strategy a matter of style on
the part of the interpreter, or is it a common practice in ASL? If the latter,
how can this strategy be analyzed so students can master the skill?

Repetition

This source text provides an unusual opportunity to study the use of formulaic repetition. The presenter uses a formal, repetitive style that emphasizes her points in various sections. Unfortunately, many interpreting students report that they have been taught to avoid repetition, to use it as a "resting spot" or a thinking time, and therefore, they do not produce a dynamically equivalent target. In the six texts that we are studying, each target demonstrates the inclusion of the repetition and provides an excellent opportunity to analyze how this rhetorical discourse strategy can be dynamically reflected in both interpretations and transliterations.

One example of this formulaic repetition is the presenter's repeated use of rhetorical questions as she discusses negative and positive self-talk. Another is in the story about the three bricklayers where she represents the boy's question to each bricklayer using exactly the same words. This use of repetition is a rhetorical strategy that involves the listener in the story itself (Mather & Winston, 1995; Metzger, 1995; Roy, 1989; Tannen, 1989).

This repetition also appears in the interpretations. One example can be seen in I-3; it also can be seen in T-3. Although the number of signs, the sign choice, and so forth for the boy's question are different overall, each iteration of the question in the interpretation is WHAT'S-UP, #DO? in the form of constructed dialogue. Additional repetition is in the form of the space used: Each question from the boy is directed in the same direction, and each answer is directed back toward the boy. This use of space in repeated utterances reflects the rhetorical repetitions of the source.

Interpreter 2 used this same strategy. In the interpretation, he established the boy and the bricklayers in the same location and repeated the same question every time: WHAT (open hands), ASK-TO, #DO-DO 2h. In addition, when the source message finished that brief story and addressed the audience in lines 29–31 ("Now, if this little boy approached you and asked you, 'What are you doing?' How would you respond?"), Interpreter 2, shifting from right to center, signed WHAT (open hands), ASK-TO, #DO-DO 2h. In T-2, the sign choices more closely represent English, as we would expect, but the symmetry and the repetition remain.

SUMMARY

The analysis presented above represents a beginning look at ASL prosody in interpreted and transliterated texts. Prosody has been viewed as an elusive skill, one that is hard to explain and difficult to teach to second-language learners (in ASL-English interpreter education programs). We hope that others will see the benefit in this analysis and continue to examine these complex features. Perhaps one day, interpreter educators can help our students better understand prosody and teach them to produce dynamically equivalent texts that "look like" the ASL of the Deaf community. In this initial report, we have narrowed the focus to a very specific pausing strategy. We have observed significant similarities and differences within and across interpretations and transliterations as well as within the productions of the same person performing those two different tasks.

These observations have just begun to address the questions we asked at the start: How do we teach this? And how do we explain to students what the differences between interpreting and transliterating actually are? We look forward to future research that uses these initial findings to take us where no one has gone before.

REFERENCES

Bahan, B. J., & Supalla, S. J. (1995). Line segmentation and narrative structure. In K. Emmorey & J. Reilly (Eds.), *Language, gesture, and space.* Hillsdale, NJ: Erlbaum.

Brentari, D. (1998). *A prosodic model of sign language phonology.* Cambridge, MA: The MIT Press.

Colonomos, B. (1992). *Processes in interpreting and transliterating: Making them work for you.* Videotape. Westminster, CO: Front Range Community College.

Gumperz, J. J. (1982). *Discourse strategies.* Cambridge: Cambridge University Press.

Livingston, S., Singer, B., & Abramson, T. (1995). A study to determine the effectiveness of two different kinds of interpreting. In E. Winston (Ed.), *Mapping our course: A collaborative venture. Proceedings of the tenth national convention of CIT* (pp. 175–204). N.p.: Conference of Interpreter Trainers.

Locker McKee, R. (1992). *Footing shifts in American Sign Language lectures.* Unpublished doctoral dissertation, University of California, Los Angeles.

Mather, S. A. (1989). Visually oriented teaching strategies with deaf preschool children. In C. Lucas (Ed.), *Sociolinguistics of the Deaf community* (pp. 165–190). San Diego: Academic Press.

Mather, S., & Winston, E. A. (1995). Spatial mapping and involvement in ASL story-telling. In C. Lucas (Ed.), *Pinky extension and eye gaze* (pp. 183–210). Washington, DC: Gallaudet University Press.

McIntire, M. L. (1993). Getting out of line (and into space): A perspective on strategies for student interpreters. In E. Winston (Ed.), *Student competencies: Defining, teaching, and evaluating* (Proceedings of the Ninth National Convention of CIT, pp. 61–74). N.p.: Conference of Interpreter Trainers.

Metzger, M. (1995). Constructed dialogue and constructed action in American Sign Language. In C. Lucas (Ed.), *Sociolinguistics in Deaf communities* (pp. 255–271). Sociolinguistics in Deaf Communities series, vol. 1. Washington, DC: Gallaudet University Press.

Metzger, M. and B. Bahan. (2001). Discourse analysis. In C. Lucas (Ed.). *The Sociolinguistics of sign languages* (pp. 112–144). Cambridge: Cambridge University Press.

Nespor, M., & Sandler, W. (1999). Prosody in Israeli Sign Language (Parts 2 and 3). *Language and Speech, 42,* 143–176.

Nida, E. A. (1953). Selective listening. *Language Learning, 4*(3), 92–101.

Ochs, E. (1979). Planned and unplanned discourse. In T. Givon (Ed.), *Syntax and semantics: Vol. 12. Discourse and syntax* (pp. 51–80). New York: Academic Press.

Roy, C. (1989). Features of discourse in an American Sign Language lecture. In C. Lucas (Ed.), *Sociolinguistics of the Deaf community* (pp. 231–252). San Diego, CA: Academic Press.

Sign Enhancers. (1994a). *Living Fully: With Interpreting Models.* [Videotape, #INT-LF]. Salem, OR: Author.

Sign Enhancers. (1994b). *Living Fully: With Transliterating Models.* [Videotape, #TR-LF]. Salem, OR: Author.

Siple, L. (1993). Interpreters' use of pausing in voice to sign transliteration. *Sign Language Studies, 79,* 147–180.

Siple, L. (1995). *The use of addition in sign language transliteration.* Unpublished doctoral dissertation, University of New York, Buffalo, NY.

Sofinski, B., Yesbeck, N., Gerhold, S., & Bach-Hansen, M. (2001). Features of voice-to-sign transliteration by educational interpreters. *Journal of Interpretation,* 47–68.

Stauffer, L. K., & Viera, J. (2000). Transliteration: A comparison of consumer needs and transliterator preparation and practice. *Journal of Interpretation,* 61–82.

Tannen, D. (1989). *Talking voices: Repetition, dialogue, and imagery in conversational discourse. Studies in interactional sociolinguistics: Vol. 6.* New York: Cambridge University Press.

Wilbur, R. (1994). Eyeblinks and ASL phrase structure. *Sign Language Studies, 84,* 221–240.

Winston, E. A. (1989). Transliteration: What's the message? In C. Lucas (Ed.), *Sociolinguistics of the Deaf community* (pp. 147–164). San Diego, CA: Academic Press.

Winston, E. A. (1990). Techniques for improving accent in sign language interpreters. In A. L. Wilson (Ed.), *Looking ahead: Proceedings of the 31st Conference of the American Translators Association* (pp. 47–58). Medford, NJ: Learned Information.

Winston, E. A. (1995). Spatial mapping in comparative discourse frames. In K. Emmorey & J. Reilly (Eds.), *Language, gesture, and space* (pp. 87–114). Hillsdale, NJ: Erlbaum.

Winston, E. A. (2000). It just doesn't look like ASL! Defining, recognizing, and teaching prosody in ASL. In *CIT at 21: Celebrating excellence, celebrating partnership. Proceedings of the 13th National Convention of CIT* (pp. 103–116). Silver Spring, MD: RID Publications.

Winston, E. A., & Monikowski, C. (2000). Discourse mapping: Developing textual coherence skills in interpreters. In C. Roy (Ed.), *Innovative practices for teaching sign language interpreters* (pp. 15–66). Washington, DC: Gallaudet University Press.

APPENDIX 6.A

Transcription—*Living Fully*

1 Welcome, to what I hope will be an opportunity for personal growth to all who join me today.

2 My name is Jenna Cassell,

3 and in my life, I've assumed several different titles and numerous roles,

4 but, today, I simply wish to share with you some exciting ideas in order to help us all to grow.

5 For when we open ourselves to growth at a personal level, we enhance our ability to more fully experience our lives.

6 These ideas come from many rich sources;

7 however, the main resources used to formulate this presentation,

8 which I highly recommend,

9 include an audio program entitled, *Freedom from Fear,* by Reverend Mary Boggs of the Living Enrichment Institute,

10 A book entitled, *Feel the Fear and Do It Anyway,* by Susan Jeffers,

11 *Life is an Attitude,* by Elwood N. Chapman.

12 and finally, Peace, *Love and Feeling,* by Dr. Bernie S. Seagal.

13 I'd like to begin by telling you a story.

14 There once were three brick masons working together on a building.

15 A little boy happened by

16 and asked the first brick mason, "What are you doing?"

17 Without even looking up, he responded,

18 "I'm laying bricks!"

19 The little boy approached the second (index front right) brick mason,

20 and asked him,

21 "What are you doing?"

22 The second brick mason looked kindly at the boy, and said,

23 "I'm building a wall."

24 The little boy approached the third brick mason

25 and asked the same question.

26 "What are you doing?"

27 The brick mason faced him squarely and replied with enthusiasm, (body shifting during role play) and obvious pride,

28 "I am building a beautiful cathedral."

29 Now, if this little boy approached you and asked you,

30 "What are you doing?"

31 How would you respond?

32 Do you feel as though you simply lay bricks

33 or do you retain the original joy and enthusiasm of your life choices?

34 Do you simply go through your routine in an unconscious manner

35 or do you always keep in the forefront of your mind (point to head) a vision of your beautiful cathedral?

36 Our minds are very powerful tools.

37 How we experience our life's work,

38 and indeed our lives,

39 is to a great degree a function of what we tell ourselves.

40 You see, the man laying bricks performs the very same task as the man who was building a beautiful cathedral,

41 but his inner experience was quite different.

42 We do have the power to affect our own perspective

43 and, therefore, our internal experience of external events.

44 We've all heard about positive self-talk,

45 that what you tell yourself is very likely to become your reality.

46 Well, if this is true,

47 how do we turn our negative self-chatter into powerful "I can" messages?

48 Well, one thing to understand is that the brain tries to find answers to the questions posed to it.

49 So, if you could ask yourself questions that will elicit a positive response,

50 you have a head start on seeing the world in a positive way.

51 For example, when you first wake up in the morning,

52 do you ask yourself questions like this?

53 What do I have to do today?

54 What problems am I gonna hafta face? (voice inflection)

55 What's gonna happen if I fail at the challenges facing me?

56 Or try some of these questions instead.

57 What am I excited about today?

58 What challenges can I look forward to learning from today?

59 What new opportunities can I create today?

60 When facing a new challenge,

61 or what some people call a problem,

62 what kind of questions do you ask yourself?

63 Do you ask,

64 What could I lose if I try and fail?

65 Or, how about this?

66 What could I lose if I don't try?

67 What could I gain by trying, whether I succeed or not?

68 Often, we're stuck in negativity or negative emotions

69 such as anger, depression, anxiety, to name a few.

70 It's important to recognize that these negative emotions that we're experiencing

71 are actually based in fear—

72 fear of failure,

73 fear of being hurt,

74 fear of being humiliated,

75 fear of not having enough money,

76 fear of being alone.

77 I'm sure you could add to the list.

78 For example, if you get angry because someone cuts you off when you're driving,

79 the first thing that actually occurred was that

80 you experienced a fear of having a collision.

81 The anger was actually based in fear,

82 as most negative emotions are.

83 Fear is the biggest inhibitor of us acting upon our dreams and living our lives fully.

84 We hold back from participating in life fully

85   because we are afraid.

86   We're afraid to speak our truth,

87   we're afraid to show up in the world as we are,

88   and we're holding back in some way because of our fears.

89   Well, sad to say, it's not possible to do away with fear completely.

90   Every person on this planet experiences fear.

91   We all have fear in our lives.

92   Think about it.

93   Where is fear controlling you right now?

94   We all have fear in our lives.

95   Even the people who are very successful and self-confident,

96   who are out there making their dreams a reality,

97   experience fear.

98   Therefore, fear is not the problem.

99   What we do with the fear is what determines how we live our lives.

100   Although we can't eliminate fear,

101   we can view it differently

102   and deal with it in healthy and productive ways.

103   You see, we each have places, events, situations with which we're comfortable.

104   This is known as our comfort zone.

105   We each have our very unique comfort zone

106   based on our own past experiences, our perceptions of our capabilities, and our willingness to be out in the world.

107   Some people are only comfortable in the confines of their own home.

108   Others venture out into the world into the workplace,

109   and others still seem to make the whole world their home.

110   But when a challenge is presented that is outside our personal comfort zone,

111   fear appears.

112   Sometimes, our fear induces enough self-doubt

113   that it actually prevents us from moving ahead.

114   We allow the fear to immobilize us

115   and to stop us from living fully or realizing our dreams.

116   Well, what's the alternative?

117   If we could shift our perspective and see fear instead as an ally that is telling us,

118   proceed with caution, but proceed.

119   A warning, if you will,

120   that says clearly and boldly,

121   "Growth opportunity ahead."

122 So, when you felt the fear, you would know that you are actually
      moving in the right direction

123 towards growth, towards expanding your comfort zone, towards living
      fully.

124 If we can face our fears squarely and imagine in the safety of our
      minds,

125 which after all is where fear exists,

126 how we might deal with the challenge,

127 we could take steps towards experiencing the fear and moving forward.

128 We could make progressive approximations towards expanding our
      comfort zone.

129 You can begin by imagining the worst possible consequences.

130 What if the worst happened?

131 And imagine yourself handling it.

132 Every experience we've had began in thought and was projected into
      the world of being.

133 Thoughts with feeling become reality.

134 We must create what we do in this world twice—

135 once in our minds

136 and then again out in the world to make it so.

137 So facing the fear and imagining,

138 "How would you handle that situation?" (overlap of constructed
      dialogue and indirect)

139 makes it easier to proceed with optimism.

140 And, as Oscar Wilde said,

141 the basis of optimism is sheer terror.

142 But how can we get past our fears?

143 As Susan Jeffers says in her book of the same title,

144 feel the fear and do it anyway.

145 Each time we venture beyond the confines of our comfort zone,

146 we discover new ways of being.

147 We discover inner strength and abilities.

148 We learn to expect bigger and better things from ourselves.

149 Expectation is another very powerful determiner of events.

150 I'd like to share a story with you about a young man who took the
      scholastic aptitude test,

151 the SAT,

152 as part of the college entrance procedures.

153 When he received his test scores back, he saw the number 98 on the paper.

154 Well, he was quite distressed and concerned about his ability to succeed
      in college with an IQ as low as 98.

155 But he did go to college.

156 His first term he received Ds and Fs.

157 His second term was no better,

158 and the dean called him in for a conference.

159 The dean warned him that, if his performance continued at this poor level,

160 he would be asked to leave the school.

161 "Well, whaddo you expect?" replied the young man.

162 "I only have an IQ of 98."

163 The dean took out the file and explained to the young man,

164 "You don't have an IQ of 98.

165 You scored in the 98th percentile.

166 That means that your score was equal to or better than 98% of the students in all of North America."

167 Well, the next term, that student pulled a 4.0 grade point average.

168 The only thing that had changed were his expectations.

169 Another example of how powerful expectations are in determining events

170 was shown in a research project conducted in San Francisco.

171 Three teachers had been brought into the principal's office and told,

172 "You three teachers are the best teachers in this whole school.

173 We have decided to reward your performance by giving you each thirty of the best students."

174 These teachers were asked,

175 "Don't tell any of the students or the parents about this."

176 At the end of the year, it was found that these students tested significantly higher than all of the students,

177 not only in the school

178 but in the entire district.

179 The teachers were brought in again.

180 They were informed that this had been an experiment

181 and that the students had actually been selected at random.

182 Well, the teachers were amazed,

183 and they could explain the high scores only by the fact that, they were, after all, the best teachers.

184 Well, then the researchers informed them,

185 "Actually, we put all the teachers names in a hat

186 and yours were the three that were pulled.

187 This was a double blind study

188 with the only factor not being controlled for being expectation.

189 In summary, if we learn to live with fear as an ally,

190   which navigates our path in the direction of growth,
191   use our minds and strength of spirit to expand our personal comfort
         zone,
192   and learn to expect bigger and better things of ourselves,
193   we will enhance our ability to live more fully with a constant focus on
         our beautiful cathedrals.
194   I'd like to leave you with a poem that says,
195   "Come to the edge, he said,
196   No, they replied, we will fall.
197   Come to the edge, he said.
198   No, we will fall.
199   Come to the edge.
200   They went to the edge.
201   He pushed them, and they . . . flew.
202   I wish you all a good flight.
203   Thank you.

Note. Transcription was made from the spoken text recorded on *Living Fully: With Interpreting Models,* 1994, Salem, OR: Sign Enhancers, Inc. Copyright 1994 by Sign Enhancers, Inc. Used with permission.

Contributors

Claudia Angelelli
San Diego State University
San Diego, California

Christine Monikowski
National Technical Institute of the Deaf
Rochester Institute of Technology
Rochester, New York

Jemina Napier
Macquarie University
New South Wales, Australia

Mary Ann Richey
Garden Ridge, Texas

Laura M. Sanheim
West Allis, Wisconsin

Bruce A. Sofinski
University of Virginia
Charlottesville, Virginia

Elizabeth Winston
Educational Linguistics Center
Loveland, Colorado

Index

Italic page numbers indicate photographs.

representation of words, 162–64
substitution of, 163–64
Enkvist, N. E., 109
equivalence
dynamic equivalence, 86
as goal of interpreter, 80–81, 90
interpreter of ASL sermon and, 85,
88
errors and omissions, 107–9
extralinguistic pause, 191–92, *193,*
200, 213–16. *See also* HAND-
CLASP strategy
eye gaze
as boundary marker, 188, 189
as nonmanual element in sign
language transliteration, 167,
177
turn taking and, 29–30

features defined, 191
filled pause, 192, *192,* 209, 215
filtering by interpreters, 13, 24, 35–36
Finegan, E., 114, 115
fingerspelling
used to ask for local sign for term,
67–68
used when appropriate to situation, 118
Fisher, S., 32–33, 52
Fontana, S., 118
frame theory, 102–6
application to interpreting process,
104–6, 131
free interpretation approach, 105, 128
Fromkin, V., 115
future research needs
discourse strategies of interpreters
and transliterators, 197
interpreter's role, 5
nonmanual elements in sign language transliteration, 174,
176–77
omissions in sign language interpretation of university lectures,
144–45

pastor's use of questions to congregation, 89
question-answer use in formal ASL
lectures, 90
topic boundaries in signed interpretation and transliteration, 190,
197, 199, 205, 206, 211, 213,
216–18
turn exchange, 51–52

Garcia, A., 10
Garton, A., & Pratt, C., 106
gender differences and topic transi-
tions by physicians, 34–35
Gibson, S., 101
Goffman, E., 5, 57–58, 119–20
Gonzalez, K., 157, 175
Gumperz, J. J., 190

Halliday, M. A. K., 113–14, 120
HANDCLASP strategy, 199–205, 207–
12, 215–16
Hatim, B., & Mason, I., 103, 104,
126
head movements, 30
held pauses, 191
Hornberger, J., 10
Humphrey, J. H., & Alcorn, B. J.,
176
Hymes, D., 114

initiation, 30
interpreter education, 144, 178
interpreting
community interpreting, 4–5
coping strategies for, 99–100
in courtroom, 4, 7
different contexts, 143–45
doctor-patient encounters, 3–26.
See also doctor-patient encounters
dual membership status of interpreter, 51
emergency medical situations, 6–
7

interpreters involved in, 123–24, 153

justification for testing linguistic coping strategies, 125–26

results, 126–32

types of omissions

conscious receptive omissions, 127, 130–31

conscious strategic omissions, 110–11, 127–29, 142

conscious unintentional omissions, 127, 130

future research needs, 145

interpreting omissions, 107

omissions as errors, 107–9

study results, 127

taxonomy to refer to, 112–13

unconscious omissions, 127, 131–32

Parvin, D. W., 62

pastor-congregation interaction. *See* sermon in ASL using question-answer adjacency pairs

patient. *See* doctor-patient encounters

pausing

defined, 191–92

empty, 191

extralinguistic pause, 191–92, *193, 200, 213–16*

filled pause, 192, *192*, 199, 209, 215

in interpretation, 204–5

in transliteration, 205–6

HANDCLASP strategy, 199–205, 207–12, 215–16

held, 191, 211

in interpretations, 213–14

prosodic pause, 191–92, *193*, 208, 209, 215

signing styles and, 215–16, *216*

in source text, 212

in spoken languages, 190, 191

in target texts, 212–213

in transliteration, 173–74, 214–15

types of, 191–92

Pentecostal churches, 60–62

persuasional strategies, 33

pidgin, 117

Pidgin Sign English (PSE), 155

police stations, interpreting at, 4–5

preaching, 59–62. *See also* sermon in ASL using question-answer adjacency pairs

presentational strategies, 33

Prince, C., 6

professor-student conference, use of ASL-English interpreter, 5, 31

prosodic pause, 192–93, *193*, 208, 209, 215

prosody, 188–90

Protestant religious service. *See* sermon in ASL using question-answer adjacency pairs

Quebedeaux, R., 61

questions and answers

doctors' use of information-seeking questions, 6, 33

formal ASL lectures using, area for future research, 90

sermon using question-answer session, 55–96. *See also* sermon in ASL using question-answer adjacency pairs

WH questions, 65, 69, 73, 80, 87

yes-no questions, 65, 68–71, 82–83, 86, 87

redundancies. *See* repetition

regional variation. *See* local sign usage

regulation of turns, 29–30

Reid, C., 59

religious interpretation. *See* sermon in ASL using question-answer adjacency pairs

repetition, 111, 137, 218

revival service, 59–62. *See also* sermon in ASL using question-answer adjacency pairs